FRANK O'CONNOR

Frank O'Connor

A Life

JIM MCKEON

EDINBURGH AND LONDON

Copyright © Jim McKeon, 1998
All rights reserved
The moral right of the author has been asserted

First published in Great Britain in 1998 by
MAINSTREAM PUBLISHING CO (EDINBURGH) LTD
7 Albany Street
Edinburgh EH1 3UG

ISBN 1 84018 082 X

No part of this book may be reproduced or transmitted
in any form or by any means without written permission
from the publisher, except by a reviewer who wishes to
quote brief passages in connection with a review written
for insertion in a newspaper, magazine or broadcast

A CIP catalogue record for this book is available from
the British Library

Typeset in Garamond
Printed in Great Britain by Butler & Tanner Ltd

CONTENTS

Introduction	7
1. In the Beginning	9
2. Into the Revolution	24
3. Rebel in Love	53
4. The Pembroke Librarian	71
5. Theatre of Dreams	100
6. The War Years	126
7. The New World	150
The Works of Frank O'Connor	180
Index	190

*To Nancy McCarthy
who is scattering sunshine now
and dancing with the angels*

INTRODUCTION

FRANK O'CONNOR WAS THE PSEUDONYM OF MICHAEL O'DONOVAN. He was such a ubiquitous individual that it is difficult to know where to start when dealing with his achievements. He thought of himself first and foremost as a poet, and his love, enthusiasm and knowledge of poetry knew no bounds; yet he was also a novelist, lecturer, linguist and critic, the managing director of the Abbey Theatre, a librarian fifty years before his time, a playwright, broadcaster, brilliant translator and short-story writer. But none of this meant anything to me when I was a child of eight years of age and first read one of his short stories. I was immediately hooked. He didn't just capture my imagination; he grabbed it and hasn't let go since. Hence this book. I was the frightened boy in *First Confession* and the brave child looking after his sick mother in *Man of the House*; and how I empathised with the nervous youngster in *Old Fellows* who bought a toy dog to protect him on his long, late walk home.

Frank O'Connor is best remembered for his short stories. It has been said that Anton Chekhov and Guy de Maupassant were the masters of this difficult discipline but maybe they suffer in translation. To me, O'Connor was the greatest ever exponent of the art of the short story. Superbly structured and filled with beautiful sensitivity and warm intimacy, their heroes always seemed to be lonely boys like myself, fighting dragons in their imaginations, or some poor orphan standing up to some terrible injustice. Even today, the man still fascinates me. As a child I thought he was writing just for me. I have spoken of him to people from as far apart as California and Copenhagen and they have confided that they too thought O'Connor was writing just for them. His pen was truly universal. No other writer could get inside a child's mind and really understand it quite like he did. He attended national school for only four years, yet with this minimal formal education he taught himself to speak Irish, French and German, and he could read Russian. Against insurmountable odds he rose like a phoenix from the ashes of terrible poverty and deprivation to become one of the world's literary greats.

Every effort has been made to contact and thank everyone who has helped me in the writing of this book. If I have failed to acknowledge any individual, I humbly apologise. I would like to thank the following: Macmillan Publishers for the use of lines from *The Green Helmet* by W.B. Yeats; Maurice Fridberg, publisher, for an extract from O'Connor's translation of Brian Merriman's *The Midnight Court*; Cuala Press for the use of the lines from Frank O'Connor's *The Wild Bird's Nest – The Lament for Art O'Leary*, *The Old Woman of Beare Regrets Lost Youth* and *Kilcash*; Longmans Green, publisher, for lines from *An Irish Journey* by Seán O'Faoláin. My deepest appreciation goes to the staff of the following: St Patrick's School; North Monastery; Munster Literature Centre, especially Pauline Jackson and Aisling Meade; Archive Centre, South George's St; Research Library, Pearse St; the National Library, Dublin; Boole Library, UCC; St Mary's Rd library, especially Ann Riordan and Ger Desmond; Grand Parade library, especially Tom McCarthy, Mary Fitzgerald and the omniscient Ciaran Burke; Tim Cadogan, County Cork library; Stella Cherry, Cork Museum; *Irish Times*; *Irish Independent*; *Cork Examiner*, especially Jim Desmond and Martin Cloyne; BBC Radio; RTE Radio; Cork Arts Council; Cork Corporation; city manager Jack Higgins; assistant manager James O'Donovan; Brian and Bernard, Digilog Computers. I would also like to thank Barry Keating, photographer; the good people of Douglas St, Blarney St and Dillon's Cross, especially Joe Collins and Mossie Lordan; May O'Flynn, Seán French, Mary Ahearne, Dermot Foley, Denis McGarry, Desmond O'Grady, Noel Walsh, Dennis O'Mahoney, Liam O'Murchú, Ann Quain, Tom Donnelly, Noel O'Donovan, Pat Egan, Liadain O'Donovan Cook and the charming May O'Donovan and her daughter Frances; Richard T. Cooke, photographer, for his help and encouragement; Kevin Power, UCC, for his time, guidance, patience and academic wisdom; and the inimitable Nancy McCarthy for her kindness, her endless chat and for just being herself. Finally, I wish to express my eternal gratitude to Frank O'Connor's widow, Harriet. She has a heart as big as Texas. Without her co-operation and generosity, this book could not have been written.

Jim McKeon, Cork, 1998

1. IN THE BEGINNING

MOST PEOPLE ASSOCIATE FRANK O'CONNOR WITH THE NORTHSIDE of Cork City, especially the Blarney Street and Dillon's Cross areas, but, in fact, he hails from the southside. He was born in a flat over his Uncle Tim's cobbler's shop at 84 Douglas Street on a dull, windy Thursday, 17 September 1903. Over the years the brown, two-storey house near the corner of Rutland Street has changed little. The ground-floor shop window and the upstairs room where the child was born are still the same. At the turn of the century Douglas Street was a thriving little community, full of pubs and small shops, mainly because the railway terminus was situated near by. The train which ran from the busy West Cork town of Macroom was usually thronged with affluent farmers.

Ellen Connell was the midwife. Ironically, she couldn't read or write and signed the birth certificate of the future writer with an X. The South Chapel, Cork's oldest Catholic church, was just around the corner. On the following Sunday the child was christened here by Father Mark Leonard. He was named Michael John O'Donovan, after both grandfathers.

The city was still buzzing and the papers were still full of stories about the King and Queen of England, Edward VII and Alexandra. The royal couple had just visited the city to open the Great International Exhibition. On the day Michael John was born there was a huge advertisement on the front page of the *Examiner* telling the whole world that the King and Queen had luncheon in the Tivoli Restaurant in Patrick Street. Beside it, in bold print, the Catholic Presentation Brothers stated that windows were for hire at their premises in the Mardyke to view the passing parade. Each window cost two and six (12½p). It was an early case of Christian enterprise.

The royal barge docked at Victoria Quay; boats packed with people came right up to Patrick's Bridge in the city centre, and one of the first items on the itinerary was a gala extravaganza in honour of the royal guests. A plethora of bands thundered out 'God Save the King' as the royal carriage, splendidly drawn by four horses brought specially down from Dublin for the occasion, made its way up the cobblestoned quay to the City Hall. Etiquette insisted that the Lord Mayor, Edward Fitzgerald, walk dutifully alongside the carriage. But the committee in charge of the concert were in a terrible state. Trying to make a few extra pounds, they had increased the admission fee. But it backfired, and people, including indignant season-ticket-holders, wouldn't pay the additional sixpence and refused to attend. The committee made an instant decision and threw open the doors. Word about the free concert spread quickly and the hall was packed in no time. Cork's face was saved.

Later, the royal carriage, with its exalted occupants, trotted up the Mardyke in a colourful procession with the unfortunate Lord Mayor still hanging on for dear life. After a hasty meal in the Shrubberies, now the museum, the Great International Exhibition was officially declared open. The King and Queen returned home by yacht and a few days later the Lord Mayor, for his troubles, was made a baron, and the exhibition ground was turned into a recreation garden and named Fitzgerald's Park for posterity.

This was the Cork of Michael's childhood; a city of 80,000 people, at the head of one of the finest natural harbours in the world. It was the spawning ground of his imagination; his land of make-believe, from the shawled women of the open-air markets in the Coal Quay with their sing-song voices, to the lordly mansions of Montenotte. Saucer-shaped and loquacious, Cork was a great place for walkers and talkers who boasted about their sporting heroes from beagles to bowl-players. Unique and individual, it reeked of black pudding, crubeens, tripe and drisheen. With conversation as natural as Guinness, Cork was as parochial as any village; yet in other ways, with its centre situated between the two channels of the River Lee, it was as cultured as Paris. In the winter, when the rains came, it was more like Venice. This was where the shy youngster roamed the streets, experiencing the bustle and the colour, and listening to the contrasting noises, each sound vying for attention: the army bands, the non-stop ululating of the convent bells, each chirping forth with its own personal message, the sirens from the nearby docks, the half-drunken choruses of the come-all-ye's wafting through the windows of the innumerable pubs, and the huffing and puffing of the clitter-clatter trams as they went on their merry way. Above all this, towering high over the rooftops of the narrow lanes of the northside, where the people wore their badge of poverty with pride, stood Shandon Steeple, stiff and erect, like a mother hen keeping its beady eye on the whole scene below.

Eventually, Michael would leave Cork but, as he said himself, Cork never really left him.

There is a common misconception that writers are born with a special gift which owes nothing to family or social background; this misconception perceives the writer as a person who just sits down and, with little or no effort, uses his imagination to create characters and stories on a blank page. In actual fact, the writer is the product, victim and conqueror of his society and environment. Imagination plays its part in a writer's work, of course, but the real secret of the gifted writer lies in his capacity to reflect on his experiences with adults in his own childhood and, as a writer, to ponder on what had made these adults into the people they had become. Frank O'Connor's background is a classic example of this. A brief study of the O'Donovan family tree reveals nothing which suggests that a great writer would emerge from such mundane stock.

Let us look back at the ancestry of the child, Michael O'Donovan, who became the adult writer, Frank O'Connor. In the middle of the 1860s, his grandfather, also Michael O'Donovan, a labourer from Caherlagh, courted Mary Kelly, a peasant woman from Aghada. They married and went to live in Douglas on the outskirts of Cork. On 1 April 1869 their first child, also named Michael, was born. Shortly after, they moved into the city and settled down in the Barrack Stream, just a stone's throw from the British Army's Victoria Barracks at the top of a hill on the northside of the city. Only a few years previously, Queen Victoria had honoured this working-class area with a visit. Officers lived in the big houses around the barracks and, even today, you can still see the British military influence in the local street-names: Waterloo Place, Windsor Terrace, Trafalgar Hill, York Terrace, Victoria Street, Grosvenor Place, Belgrave Avenue, Balmoral Place, Wellesley Terrace and Wellington Road.

For the O'Donovans, Lady Poverty was never very far away and she seldom lowered her ugly head. Like their neighbours, they scratched and struggled to keep above the breadline and barely survived on occasional part-time work and odd jobs in the docks. There was no money and even less education; yet for the young Michael growing up, it was an exciting place full of army activity, gun carriages and never-ending bugle calls. He could pick out the various regiments by their different colours and he loved to march in step behind the army bands with a stick or a hurley held stiffly across his shoulder, mimicking the bandsmen and the soldiers. With no real schooling and no prospects, he eventually enlisted in the Munster Fusiliers in 1888 at the age of nineteen; at least there was a uniform and three meals a day. His height and military bearing may have helped him. He stood six foot four in his stocking feet.

His best friend and drinking comrade was a fellow soldier named Tim O'Connor. They were both stationed at Charlesfort near Kinsale for a while and they also served overseas together. Tim had an older sister, Minnie, who would eventually marry Michael O'Donovan. She was born at 148 Blarney Street on 18 July 1865 and christened the next day at the North Cathedral by Father Joseph Shinkwin. (It is interesting to note the social statement in the fact that Minnie, Tim and their two sisters, Margaret and Hanorah Ellen, were each born in a different house just a few yards apart at the top of Blarney Street. It seems that at that time it wasn't unusual for a woman, when she was due, to move temporarily to a neighbour's house and give birth to the baby. Hence, all the children in the family had different places of birth.)

Minnie's father, John, a local man who worked in Arnott's Brewery near the South Gate Bridge, died after an accident at work. A powerfully built man, he was a champion bowler, and Minnie had hazy memories of visiting him in the Mercy Hospital just before he died. Her mother, Julia Corcoran, from a well-off family in Donoughmore, couldn't cope with widowhood and poverty, and was evicted from her home. She managed to hold on to Minnie, the eldest, and Margaret, but Tim and Hanorah Ellen were taken in by friends and neighbours. The latter was never seen again. As her poor mother sat outside her former house in Blarney Street, hopeless, homeless and penniless, the young Minnie, who was only seven, begged her to go home. Her reply,

'But, *astore*,* I have no home, now,' remained with Minnie for the rest of her life. The nuns in the Good Shepherd Orphanage took Minnie and Margaret into their care. Julia was simply unable to cope and entered Our Lady's Mental Home. Later, she got a job as a maid but ended up in the workhouse where she died shortly after. Minnie and Margaret were given a good education by the nuns. Minnie was taught bookbinding. She was a willing pupil and loved reading and music. The habits of convent life were a big influence on the child and she was to remain a religious, neat, fastidious woman all her life.

Margaret, who became very ill and ended up crippled, had a completely different personality. Of all the members of the family, Michael was perhaps most like his Aunt Margaret. She held strong, stubborn opinions on most subjects and wasn't slow to express them. Furthermore, she could read and retain practically anything and had an amazing capacity to memorise poetry. Again, like Michael, she despised injustice of any kind. Sadly, she was only a young teenager when she died.

When Minnie was fourteen she took up a series of domestic jobs, each one more disastrous than the last. Normally, the nuns vetted these houses before the inexperienced orphan girls commenced work; but Minnie turned out to have one misfortune after another. In one house she was nearly starved to death. In another, through jealousy, all her hair was cut off and in yet another it was only her innocence of all things sexual which prevented her from being molested in her own bed by a lodger. She had a dreadful youth and, on one occasion, even contemplated suicide. Fortunately, the nuns got word of her plight and came to her assistance. They were shocked at her condition: thin, dirty and bedraggled, her hair infested with lice. They insisted that she return immediately to the convent. At first she was ashamed and refused but later changed her mind.

When she recuperated she took one or two short-term positions before she started working in a house owned by a man called Ned Barry in Lower Janemount, a well-to-do area in Sunday's Well. It was quite near the convent. Ned lived with his unmarried sister, Alice, who was almost the same age as Minnie. Minnie loved the big house with its beautiful orchard and this was where she spent what were probably the happiest eight years of her life. She grew very close to Ned, and she and Alice were practically inseparable; but when Alice eventually married,

---

*Term of endearment for a child

the nuns worried about the good name of an unchaperoned girl living under the same roof as a single man and insisted that she return to the safety of the Good Shepherd Orphanage. So, on the day after her twenty-fifth birthday, after much contemplation and many prayers, she reluctantly resumed life in the convent.

It is idle to speculate on the possibility of what might have happened if Minnie had married Ned Barry and borne him a son. Would that son have become a writer? Probably not, though he most certainly would have been comfortable and well-off. The first twenty-one years of Michael John O'Donovan's life were a struggle against terrible poverty and uncertainty. This difficult childhood was a rich source of material; but when he became Frank O'Connor, being angry, indignant or frustrated by people or situations seemed to stimulate his creativity.

Minnie O'Connor was nearly thirty-one when she left the Good Sheperd Convent for the final time. She worked for a short while as a maid for Mrs Riordan of Parkview at the top of Wellington Road. She didn't stay long and went from job to job and place to place, including England and Limerick, before she settled down with a family in Cobh. By this time she had met Mick O'Donovan, the army friend of her brother Tim. Mick was a big handsome man who was kind enough when sober, but Tim warned her that he was a devil for the drink. He once boasted that he drank forty pints in one day and he often brought home twelve bottles of stout and a half-pint of whiskey just for an early-morning 'cure'.

Mick played the big drum in both the Munster Fusiliers and the Quarry Lane Band. He was very fond of marches and he took great pride in his ability on the drum. The Quarry Lane Band were regular participants, in more ways than one, in the numerous political rallies of that time. These passionate gatherings invariably started in unruly disarray, continued with reciprocal insults, before careering downhill into a free-for-all fistfight and ending up in chaotic mayhem.

Still, Minnie must have felt some sense of security with Big Mick because she finally married him in the South Chapel. Father Tom Barrett performed the wedding ceremony on Tuesday, 8 October 1901. She was thirty-six years old. With practically no money, the newly-weds went to live with their in-laws, who had even less. Minnie, used to the cleanliness of convent life, was never at ease with the roughness of the O'Donovans, who lived in Maryville Cottages near Victoria Barracks. They, in turn, thought that she was a snob. She put up with it for a year but, when her husband sailed from Cobh aboard the *Sundra* on 18 December 1902 to fight in the South African War, she immediately moved back across the city to her old flat above Tim's cobbler's shop and it was here, while her husband was away, that she gave birth to her only child, Michael John O'Donovan, whom the world would later know as Frank O'Connor.

There is some confusion about the writer's birthplace. He states in his autobiography that he was born while the family lived over Wall's shop in Douglas Street. There is no record of this to be found anywhere, however, and his birth certificate clearly states that he was born at 84 Douglas Street. The owner of the house, elderly neighbours and close relatives have all confirmed this. Before Minnie got married she lived here and it was shown as her address on her marriage certificate. It was also the address of Annie O'Connell before and after she married Tim O'Connor on 11 September 1892. Annie was Minnie's bridesmaid and godmother to the young Michael. In the five years between leaving the convent and getting married, when Minnie was between jobs, she lived in a flat at number 84. In 1994 the city fathers in Cork erected a plaque over number 31, where Wall's shop was, stating that this was O'Connor's birthplace. This is incorrect and locals derive great amusement from it. Minnie was in her eighties when she started to tell her son about her own childhood. There are some other minor inaccuracies in his first volume of autobiography, *An Only Child*. For instance, he says that Hanorah Ellen, the baby, was younger than her brother Tim when, in fact, she was four years older. Considering Minnie O'Donovan's great age, it was only natural that these distant recollections were not always accurate.

The question that has to be asked is why Minnie ever married Big Mick O'Donovan. There was an obvious difference in their respective heights, he being tall and well built, she small and fragile, but there was an even greater disparity in their backgrounds. Although she was quite an attractive woman, she may have felt that, at thirty-six, this was her last chance of marriage. But, even though she had a great capacity for love, it is doubtful she ever loved Big Mick the way she loved Ned Barry. She and Mick were together for forty-one years although it could not be described as a 'good' marriage. Had she lived today, she would probably have left him, but in those days, if anything went wrong in a marriage, it was generally deemed to be the woman's fault. She must also have been afraid that if she left her husband her only child would be taken from her and placed in an orphanage – and she was well aware of the anguish and sadness of the orphan child.

It is somewhat surprising that Minnie had only one child. She longed for a daughter. It could be that her husband, for one reason or another, was away from home quite a lot. But it may have been the age factor: she was thirty-eight when her son was born. In those days, this would have been considered almost too old for child-bearing. It is more than likely that the baby was conceived the night before Big Mick left for Africa, on 17 December 1902, exactly nine months before the birth. This would have been only natural. It is generally said that Mick went off to fight in the Boer War but this is not the case, as that particular war had ended six months before he left. It is possible that the Munster Fusiliers went on a relief mission or mopping-up operation, and it was several months after his son's birth before Mick eventually arrived back in Cork again. Travel in those days, of course, was painfully slow.

Even today, although it's becoming less prevalent, there is still a feeling of resentment towards Michael O'Donovan in the Dillon's Cross area of Cork. The fact that he changed his name to O'Connor did not go down too well and it has been pointed out that he 'lost his faith'. After the Civil War he was refused Mass and the sacraments because of his Republicanism. In those turbulent times most Republicans, including Michael, were excommunicated. Furthermore, O'Donovans didn't take too kindly to the way Big Mick, one of their own, was portrayed in *An Only Child*. Nor did they like the treatment Michael's grandparents received in the short story, *First Confession*. Later on, the writer's opposition to the Church and his controversial lifestyle (plus the fact that he was married twice in a registry office) didn't help. His 'terrible' books were banned by Ireland's draconian censorship board. The young O'Donovans, in fact, were forbidden by their parents to read their cousin Frank O'Connor's books.

There were several instances over the years of Michael being snubbed in Cork on family occasions. When he travelled down from Dublin in

1949 to attend his cousin Jimmy's funeral in St Patrick's church, for example, he was completely ignored and isolated. He stood by the morgue, like nobody's child, with a wreath in his hand, as most of the O'Donovans moved away and turned their backs on him. The dead man's widow, May, was always very fond of Michael and he also had great time for her. May took Minnie into her home and looked after her for a year just before she died. Minnie referred to May as 'the daughter I always wanted'.

Michael also had a lot of affection for his Uncle Lar but in 1961 he was given the same cold-shoulder treatment when he attended Lar's funeral. Michael stood at the back of the church, trying to remain as inconspicuous as possible. This was very difficult because he was a tall, handsome man with a mane of white hair. As the coffin was carried slowly from the altar and down the aisle, the priest walked solemnly behind it, ceremoniously spraying holy water as he went. Just near the exit the priest noticed Michael out of the corner of his eye, took a few steps in his direction, and nearly drowned him with holy water . . .

Some of the O'Donovans resented Minnie's frequent trips up to Dublin to help her son recuperate from one illness or another. He was a grown man at this stage and she often stayed with him and nursed him for months on end. They felt her place was with her husband in Cork. When she died it was intimated that the family grave in Caherlag was full and she really 'wasn't an O'Donovan at all'; very few of the family attended her funeral.

Nancy McCarthy was a close, lifelong friend of Michael. I once put it to her that I thought he was maybe a little hard on his father in *An Only Child*. She strongly disagreed and felt that he wrote it as he had seen it – through the eyes of a child. She stressed that the young Michael was a nervous, impressionable boy. For instance, his Uncle Lar had a scar on his face and when the inquisitive children around the Dillon's Cross district asked him about it they were told that the scar was the result of a bayonet fight in the First World War. In reality, that scar was caused by his brother, Big Mick, when he struck him with a poker over some disagreement. The young Michael witnessed this incident and it must have been a traumatic experience.

At the end of 1903 Big Mick eventually returned from South Africa and the family moved across the city to number 251 at the top of

Blarney Street. It was little more than a cabin with a tiny candle-lit attic. The Clogheen Harrier Club was next door and number 148, where Minnie had been born, was directly opposite. Blarney Street, a long, lazy street, spider-webbed by narrow lanes, went from the countryside just above Sunday's Well right down in a bottleneck to Shandon Street. Colloquially called 'Spy Lane', it was a hotbed of fervent nationalism. Whispered stories of gunfights and heroism were told and retold in the local pubs. Many a Black and Tan got his come-uppance there; executions were commonplace and, even today, the walls are still riddled with bullet holes.

Michael was to live here for nearly seven years and all his earliest memories are of this area. It was an important influence, the background material of his literary future. The people, the endless characters he encountered in the pubs when he was with his father, all surfaced, one way or another, in his books.

When Big Mick went for a walk or went off playing with the band, Minnie often sent her reluctant young son with him, hoping he might act as a watchdog or a brake on his drinking activities. This ploy rarely worked.

Two of Michael's best short stories originated in this area. One was the classic *My Oedipus Complex*, where the lonely boy, Larry, longed for a little brother but was told by his mother that it cost seventeen and six for a new baby and she just couldn't afford it. But Larry had his suspicions; Mrs Geaney up the road got a new baby and the whole street knew that they had no money. Eventually, Larry's mother did 'buy' a new addition to the family, Sonny, but Larry became very jealous of the child. The story ends with Larry's father being turned out of his own bed and forced to sleep with the indignant Larry.

That beautiful story, *The Drunkard*, is also set in Blarney Street. It was a terrible shock to everyone when Mr Dooley died suddenly and Larry's father, Mick Delaney, was anxious to attend the funeral at the Curraghkipane Cemetery even though he had been on the dry for months. (Larry is again the boy hero and brother Sonny also makes a brief appearance.) Larry's mother was against this as there were too many danger signals: a long abstinence, a hot, dusty day, and Peter Crowley, an old drinking comrade who only went to funerals for free drink. Larry was sent as a deterrent to his father, just as the young Michael was in real life. When Mr Dooley was duly seen off on his final journey, Mick Delaney and Peter, as expected, ended up in the pub. Mick ordered his pint and placed it on the counter but talk-wise he had a lot of catching up to do. Larry was bored, curious and thirsty and he managed to drink his father's pint behind his back. In turn he got sick, fell and banged his head, was thrown out of the pub and finished up staggering and singing all the way down Blarney Street, much to the amusement of the nosey neighbours. Poor Mick Delaney got a terrible tongue-lashing from his wife and was accused of being a drunkard although he hadn't touched a drop. How could he have, when his son had drunk it all! The story ends with Mrs Delaney hugging her unfortunate son and thanking him, and God, for successfully keeping her husband off the drink. That story was based on events that really happened to Big Mick and his child in a local pub after a funeral.

Soon after the O'Donovans had settled down in Blarney Street, Minnie opened a grocery shop. It was a disaster. Firstly, with her orphan background, she couldn't refuse anyone anything and in no time she was owed money all over the place; secondly, she caught her husband with his hand in the till once too often. Still, the top of Blarney Street, her childhood playground, held many memories for her: she had been born just across the street, Ned Barry's house wasn't far away and the Good Shepherd Convent where she was brought up was just around the corner. She used to call there regularly to visit her old friends and show off her new-born baby. Next door to the convent was the Women's Prison which was later to play such an important part in her son's life. He was incarcerated here during the Civil War and he also used it as a rehearsal venue for his plays with the Cork Drama League. The prison, a big, grey, imposing building, was opened in 1824.

For years after it was built, there was a lot of leftover stone lying about. It was decided to build a Protestant church from the surplus stone as most of the prison staff were Protestant and their nearest place of worship was Shandon. But a Catholic priest, Father McCarthy, stepped in and was instrumental in building Strawberry Hill, Cork's first national school. Strawberry Hill opened in 1835 and was Michael's first school. The old records indicate that he missed classes quite a lot. As a youngster and as an adult he was frequently ill. The records also incorrectly show his name as Donovan, the same as his birth certificate, although in his baptismal lines it is O'Donovan. At that time registrars were very careless and slapdash. The records show that some of Michael's classmates were only three years old. By the time Michael started school, Big Mick had finished his army service. In 1909 he had completed his twenty-one years and was now a labourer with an army pension. He was still a sturdy, robust man. Every morning in the back yard, whatever the weather – hail, rain or snow – he washed himself under the freezing cold tap water, stripped to the waist. The sight of his sensitive, frail son huddled indoors by the fire, clinging to his overprotective mother and his little kittens, must have sickened him.

Sadly, 251 Blarney Street was demolished in 1977; even today, tourists still flock to the top of Blarney Street looking for the house. All that is left is a small, insignificant flagstone on the pavement stating that Frank O'Connor once lived here.

In the summer of 1910 a house became available in Harrington Square and Big Mick, like a salmon at sea, slowly but surely made his way back across the city to his beloved Barrack Stream. When the O'Donovans left Blarney Street, everything they possessed was stacked on a donkey and cart, a clear indication of their poverty. Minnie and her husband walked alongside the cart while their son sat aboard, carefully guarding his cardboard box of kittens.

Big Mick was back where he belonged, his homeland, O'Donovan country. It was the place of his youth, near his parents, his cousins and Victoria Barracks. Now he could meet his comrades every day and talk about old battles in the good old days in the war.

For the next fourteen years the Barrack Stream was to have a huge bearing on Michael's life: the colourful neighbours, the rich talk, the idiosyncratic characters, the bustle and noise and the optimistic determination of the people as they struggled to get on with their lives all left an everlasting impression on him and was an endless source of material for his future writing.

Harrington Square, a rough, slanted patch of land between the Old Youghal Road and Ballyhooly Road, was usually criss-crossed by clothes lines of army uniforms hung out to dry. Several women made a few badly needed extra pennies by washing officers' clothes and they each had their own individual line.

Minnie and her son never really got on with the O'Donovans except for Jimmy, his wife May, and Uncle Lar. The main character in many of Michael's stories was often called Lar (he wrote thirteen Larry Delaney stories) and may have been a tribute to his uncle. Big Mick's parents lived next door and when the grandfather, who was Michael's godfather, died, the grandmother moved in to live with them. Her rough, country ways nearly drove the youngster to distraction. With her in the house he couldn't bring his friends home. She later appeared in what is probably his best known short story, *First Confession*, as the barefoot peasant woman who took snuff and porter and ate her dinner with her bare hands. The young boy in the story, Jackie, innocently confessed that he planned to murder his overbearing grannie (surely Michael's own sentiments), chop her up with a hatchet and then take the body away in a wheelbarrow and bury it. The tale is said to have been based on a real event in Belfast. However, the story ends happily for Jackie.

For young Michael John, the one redeeming factor in his grandmother's stay was that she was a native Irish speaker and was the first to introduce him to the language. He wrote about her again in *The Long Road to Umera*. This is the poignant tale of an old woman who, on her deathbed, longed to be brought back to the place of her birth.

The youngster did eventually settle down in the Barrack Stream. His room was a little attic with a skylight and he used to climb out through this window, scamper along the roof and sit on the chimney. He could see right down over the rooftops to the sprawling docks below, while far away to his left were the vast hills of Mayfield. Behind his home there was a quarry and he loved to climb out onto a high rock; for hours he would sit there, secretly observing the comings and goings away down below: the passing drunk, the rough boys playing football and the girls with skipping ropes keeping time to the sing-song of their nursery rhymes. He felt safe from the bullies who taunted him and called him names. He spent ages perched up there like a bird, often hungry and lonely, lost in his own dream world until, at last, the tram bringing his mother stopped at St Luke's Cross and he ran down to help her bring the shopping home.

Big Mick, now a part-time docker in his forties, was inescapably trapped in the environment of that time. Surrounded by relatives and friends, he was an erect, old-fashioned man who dressed well. He sported a waistcoat and wore trousers with a knife-edge crease, and his boots were highly polished. He carried a walking stick and ceremoniously tipped his black bowler hat to passing women as he strolled like a peacock the long way around Summerhill to Mass. On returning home, the Mass clothes were removed and replaced by his fatigues. He was the arch-enemy of the ball-playing youths in the area. It was a daily, ongoing feud. He usually sent them scattering across the square where, in safety, they repetitiously scourged him with 'Big Mick, Big Mick, the long-arsed drummer'; but Mick got sweet revenge, whenever the opportunity arose, by grabbing their precious ball and puncturing it with a knife. At that time a macho culture was very prevalent. He was to be the man the sensitive young Michael was to fear, hate, misunderstand and love till the day he died. Both father and son spent their entire lives as jealous rivals for Minnie's affection.

There were a lot of good times, too, however, especially when Big Mick wasn't drinking. Michael's parents both loved music and they often sang together for him. Minnie was very fond of Thomas Moore's melodies;* her favourite song was 'How Dear to Me the Hour When Daylight Dies'. When her husband was in a good mood he liked nothing better than to give a melancholic rendition of 'The Burial of Sir John Moore'. He considered himself an expert on brass bands and marches. His special favourite was 'The Flowers of the Forest'. Most nights he read the *Evening Echo* out loud, from cover to cover, adding his own personal opinion on every story. Like any child, Michael loved those happy days when his father's behaviour was not influenced by drink. At those times, Minnie got a cup of tea in bed first thing every morning and there was peace and tranquillity in number 8, Harrington Square.

During these good times Big Mick felt that he was the perfect husband. It gave him immense pleasure to point out his long list of money-saving devices to anyone who cared to listen. His favourite was his old army hair-cutting machine; like himself, it had survived several wars. This was his most precious possession. It was lovingly cleaned and meticulously oiled every day. He frowned on anyone who wasted their hard-earned money in the barbershop and insisted on personally cutting their hair. He charged nothing for this neighbourly service but graciously accepted any few pennies they left him. He often practised on his reluctant son, usually leaving the boy looking like an escaped convict.

All the money saved and scrupulously stored in a biscuit-tin in the

---

* Irish composer of drawing-room songs

attic would vanish when, at last, the dreaded rainy day arrived. The good intentions and the hair-clippers were wrapped up and put away, and the contents of the biscuit-tin quickly disappeared. Then a familiar ritual would begin; Big Mick would fail to turn up for work and lose his job; then his good suit would be brought to the pawn, followed at short intervals by his wife's clothes, the kitchen clock and, finally, Minnie's wedding ring. This was the bottom of the barrel. With no suit, Mick couldn't go to Mass and he paced around the house like a caged animal. Eventually, he would get a few days' work in a different job; he was too proud to return to his previous one. Then, one by one, in reverse order, the pawned items were redeemed and he began to attend church again.

When Michael got his first real job he bought a gas stove so that his mother could grill food, thereby saving him from the indigestion caused by fried food. He also purchased a second-hand gramophone and when Mozart or Schubert were playing Big Mick occasionally liked to show off by accompanying Mozart on his big drum, much to the disapproval of the long-suffering neighbours.

2. INTO THE REVOLUTION

WHEN MICHAEL O'DONOVAN WAS TEN HE SUFFERED FROM SEVERE headaches which often caused him to miss school. At first his father thought he was shamming but, in time, it was discovered that the headaches were brought on by his poor eyesight, probably because he was by now an avid reader. He spent hours in his dim little attic reading anything he could get his hands on, whether it was Latin, Russian, German, Greek or Shakespeare. His fertile imagination ran wild when reading about the heroes in his favourite comics of that time, the *Marvel*, the *Magnet*, the *Gem* and *Our Boys*. Just a few years later his own writing was first published in *Our Boys*.

He was now attending St Patrick's School which was just around the corner, facing Gardiner's Hill. To this timid mother's boy, it seemed a hell where some of the teachers looked for any excuse to flog their poor, unfortunate pupils. He hated school so much that he often clung to the leg of the big kitchen table while his mother practically dragged him and the table out through the front door.

But in 1912, after two years, a new teacher appeared in St Patrick's. He was different: gentle, sympathetic and approachable, he really cared about his pupils. Ireland was under British rule at the time and the Irish language was frowned on. But this new, exciting teacher, Daniel Corkery, encouraged the use of Irish. His first day in class he defiantly wrote on the blackboard '*Muischail do mhishneac a banba*'. Turning to his wide-eyed students, he announced: 'Waken your courage, Ireland.' Corkery set the first seeds of learning in Michael's soul and became his first real hero and father figure. Michael was to have many more such figures after Corkery including Richard Hayes, George Russell and William Butler Yeats. But certainly Corkery was extremely influential in Michael's young life and he helped to guide his protégé in the right direction.

At first, Michael was overawed to find that not only was Corkery a lover of Irish and a dedicated nationalist, but that he was also a poet, a painter and a novelist. They continued to meet regularly, even when Michael was an adult, but eventually drifted apart when the pupil finally outgrew the master. They spent only twelve months together in St Patrick's, as the youngster left a year after Corkery arrived. The old school records again show that he missed school frequently, mostly because of his headaches and poor eyesight. His classmates unkindly called him 'Specky four-eyes' and 'Winkers' because of his thick spectacles. In 1912 he was kept back in third class for twelve months. This usually happened to slow pupils with a poor attendance record, yet he later won prizes for English and Irish composition. Once, a schoolfriend won a book as a prize for English and Michael won a *sliothar** as a prize for Irish. He had a long persuasive chat with his friend; the result was that they swapped prizes and both boys went home happy.

In 1913 he didn't attend St Patrick's for five months, and when he did resume school, it was to the North Monastery that he went. Minnie had high hopes and ambitions for her son. She dreamed that one day he would have a nice job in a nice office where everyone would call him 'sir'. She approached the Brothers in the school and pleaded with them to accept her son. She was influenced by a neighbour's child, a 'Mon' boy, who had passed exams and was attending college and had had his photograph in the newspaper.

The North Monastery was a famous old school, run by the Christian Brothers, renowned for its strict discipline and proud of its record of annually churning out 'college' material. At that time, the leaving-certificate results were displayed publicly in Dublin and there was fierce rivalry between the best schools in Ireland. Invariably, the North Monastery came out on top. Its list of prominent ex-pupils was endless. There was also a high level of sporting expectation and active participation in Gaelic football and hurling was strongly encouraged. Michael, though, was never a lover of the rough and tumble of Ireland's national games. He much preferred the more genteel game of cricket, like the English boys in his weekly comics. He liked the noble art of boxing as well, and shadow-boxed at home, diligently practising his straight left in front of the mirror. Once, at school, he made use of all this practice. He was now nicknamed 'Moll' and, with his pronounced glasses and

---

* Leather ball used in the Irish national game of hurling

thin, gangling figure, was generally left alone. One day, however, an over-aggressive boy attacked him but Michael gave as good as he got and, with a few neat straight lefts, sent the bully on his way with a bloodied nose.

Initially, he was happy enough in his new school but gradually the monks made up their minds that he was not likely to pass exams and he would never have his picture in the paper. Firstly, he was an eternal dreamer, his mind was always miles away and, secondly, he was always late. The North Monastery was a long trek across the hills of the northside. It didn't help that he came down Old Youghal Road by the top of Patrick's Hill. The astonishing view fascinated and delayed him. He could look out over the vast valley, to St Finbar's Cathedral on his left, and across the whole southside. Right in front and below him, between the twin towers of the North Cathedral and Shandon, was a sprawling maze of narrow lanes. Even today, this same view fascinates me as much as it did Michael.

The boy's attendance record was very poor and by now the North Monastery had decided that, in their opinion, he was not university material so he was transferred to the technical school with a view to learning a trade. This was a crushing disappointment to both himself and his mother. His thirst for education had kept him going; it was his goal, his dream of escape from the stigma of poverty. It didn't take him long to discover that he was not cut out to be a tradesman. Like his father, he was all thumbs. As a potential electrician he was a disaster, and in woodwork classes he was a danger to himself. Once, in a science class, he succeeded in blowing the eyebrows off a nearby classmate. The Christian Brothers had had enough. In their infallible wisdom they 'invited' Michael to leave, so in 1916 he gave up school at just twelve years of age.

By now, the First World War had broken out and Big Mick, a born soldier, was recalled, along with his big drum, to the Munster Fusiliers. While the war raged in Europe, peace and tranquillity reigned at number 8, Harrington Square. Minnie had a regular income and not only had her son weekly pocket-money but he also had his mother all to himself. Back in uniform where he belonged, Big Mick was one of the few soldiers who actually enjoyed the war. He was not sent overseas because of his age – he was now almost fifty – but instead was assigned to garrison duties in the Irish midlands for nearly five years. His brother Lar, another ex-soldier, also rejoined; he was in the Leinster Fusiliers. There was a simmering rivalry between them. Lar was granted a second pension because of a bad chest (which later was to be the cause of his death). Big Mick, a lover of pensions, was a little envious of Lar's success but, when the war finally ended, he, too, was given a disability pension. Some of the old soldiers at that time engineered and nurtured a chest complaint: just before visiting the doctor for the compulsory medical check-up, they would drink a bottle of whiskey and then run up Patrick's Hill. Naturally, they failed the examination with flying colours.

Michael was now finished with school and when Minnie wasn't working she often brought her son to the Opera House or into the Coal Quay and Cornmarket Street to help her with the shopping. Sometimes he accompanied her to work in the big houses in Tivoli or Montenotte, but mostly he either stayed at home and spent the day observing from his 'nest' high above St Luke's or he passed the time in his little attic, lost in Shakespeare and his comics. With his weekly allowance he was able to buy his favourite comics which he stacked neatly against the wall by his bed. This was his own personal, miniature library and his only education at this time. Caught between the rougher boys from the top of the square and the more refined ones from the bottom, on Ballyhooly Road, he was a loner and was treated as an outsider by both groups. He was unusually tall and skinny for his age and, with his heavy glasses and the way he sometimes used the big words of the middle-class English schoolboys in his comics, he was considered a bit of a freak. He was also looked on as a cissy because he read so much and was constantly with his mother.

Throughout his life he wrote approximately two hundred short stories and a large percentage of them are based in the Barrack Stream. If I had to choose my own favourite it would have to be *The Genius*. The very first sentence is: 'Some kids are cissies by nature but I was a cissie by conviction.' It is an extremely funny yet sensitive account of young Larry (again) and his innocent and unrequited love. The thorny question of the birds and the bees looms large on the horizon. Larry explains the mystery of the facts of life to his even-more-naïve girlfriend by telling her that a new baby can be easily made by daddy starting the engine in mummy's tummy with his starting handle. It is a hilarious yet beautifully poignant story. Michael's own favourite was *The Luceys*. He rewrote it over and over again for thirty years and he still wasn't happy with it. He must have been one of the greatest rewriters of all time. Forever striving for perfection, there is hardly a single O'Connor story left in its original form. It is interesting to compare the same story as it appears in different books. It is usually full of word substitutes and paraphrasing. For instance, in *First Confession* published in 1946, the opening sentence is: 'It was Saturday afternoon in early spring.' In the *First Confession* published in 1963, it begins: 'All the trouble began when my grandfather died and my grandmother, my father's mother, came to live with us.' It was the same story but told differently.

Minnie was aware that her son had quickly outgrown his weekly comics, so she decided to broaden his horizons and enrol him in the children's section of the Carnegie Library, an old red-brick building adjoining the City Hall. The youngster loved it and spent every spare moment there immersed in books. Daniel Corkery tried to teach him to paint but he never really grasped it. His impatience and poor eyesight didn't help. Corkery even arranged a scholarship in London in the hope that the boy might become an art teacher but Michael was more interested in learning to teach Irish so that he might earn some badly needed money.

In the middle of the First World War, when the British armed forces were severely stretched in Europe, the leaders of the volunteer movement sensed that it was an opportune time to strike for Irish freedom. Nationalist feeling was growing and more and more people enlisted in the volunteers and many, especially young boys like Michael, were proud of their new-found identity. The two leading figures in Cork were Tomás MacCurtain, the volunteers' commandant, and his second-in-command, Terence MacSwiney. Both were constantly hounded and arrested by the British Army. There were regular meetings in the Volunteer Hall in Sheares Street to discuss tactics, and well-known national personalities were often invited to lecture. James Connolly, who had been in the British Army for seven years before deserting at the age of twenty-one, was one but, strangely, he was not particularly popular. When he arrived to speak on guerrilla warfare and street fighting, hardly any of the rank-and-file members showed up. It seemed that they didn't like either his strong northern accent or his even stronger socialist opinions.

In April 1916, everyone associated with the nationalist movement in Munster was prepared, willing and ready for action. Over one thousand men were assembled in County Cork, bogged down in atrocious weather conditions, endlessly waiting for the word to march on Dublin. James Connolly gave Patrick Pearse* the signal for Cork at five o'clock on Easter Monday morning but, through a series of unfortunate accidents and the bad weather, the uprising had already started when MacCurtain received the message. To confound matters further, the validity of the note was questionable because it had the unusual signature, PHP. MacCurtain was uncertain what to do. For a while he contemplated attacking the city barracks but eventually dismissed the men and returned home bitterly disappointed at not being involved in the rising and frustrated at not being able to help his comrades in Dublin. To make it worse, all kinds of stories of bravery and heroism in Dublin were filtering back to Cork.

At noon on Easter Monday strategic points in the city of Dublin, especially the GPO, were taken over. Although brave and courageous and well timed, it was badly planned and the Alamo-like situation was doomed from the start. In less than a week the uprising was defeated by the might of the British artillery. A youthful Michael Collins was one of the men under fire in the GPO but he didn't like the idea of being pinned down like a sitting-duck and would have preferred to use the more successful hit-and-run tactics. Some of the thirstier rebels had brought along a large supply of Guinness. Collins showed his singlemindedness by destroying the drink. He was determined that this rising wouldn't fail because of alcohol. On the following Saturday, at half past three in the afternoon, it was all over and the tricolour was symbolically hauled down from the GPO. Sixty-four Republicans and one hundred and three British soldiers had been killed.

The British media accused the Irish of being traitors and branded the rebels a bunch of misguided poets and dreamers. As Michael was a confirmed dreamer, and harboured schoolboy aspirations to be a poet, he immediately took notice. Initially, the public were hostile towards the revolutionaries but when the British shot the fifteen leaders (with one, James Connolly, propped up in a chair), it was a shock and the

---

* Teacher, writer, IRA leader and signatory of the Republican Proclamation

mood of the nation quickly changed and was united in anger towards Britain. Roger Casement* was executed later for his part in the rising.

It will never be known what influence, if any, visionaries like Pearse and Connolly would have had on the future of a fledgling nation struggling to find its feet. They could have lived right up into the 1950s. It is similiarly a matter of conjecture, and an even more tragic one, with Michael Collins who was killed in 1922 at only thirty-one years of age. He could very well have lived into the 1970s. Would he have been as effective a politician as he was a soldier? We will never know.

When Michael discovered that the rebel leader, Patrick Pearse, on the night before his execution, had written a poem to his mother in Irish, he was captivated. It triggered off his desire for learning again. He now practically lived in the Carnegie Library. It has been said that he quickly went through the entire children's section and then borrowed his mother's ticket and started on the adults' department. As inquisitive as ever, he brought home books on Greek art and had a particular interest in books on Irish mythology. He often spent hours meticulously copying down long sections of poetry and learnt them off by heart. He realised that if he was to achieve his goal of getting a decent education he had to find a job to get money so that he could buy books. First thing, every morning, he went to the library where the newspapers were available and painstakingly read through the Situations Vacant column, applying for every job. He then made his way to Patrick Street and carefully studied the advertisement board outside the *Examiner* office and did likewise. Minnie prayed for the day when, complete with white collar, her son would hand up his weekly wages. The jobs that always caught his eye started WANTED: SMART BOY. He had no success until one day, after confession in St Joseph's church, a priest, at long last, got him a job. It was in Dwyer's, a large drapery shop in the city centre. All he did, the whole day long, was fold shirts as if he was laying out a dead body. He was also required to drop everything immediately, no matter what he was doing, and jump to attention whenever his name was called. The old daydreaming habit proved to be an insurmountable problem, however, and he lasted only two weeks. His next job, as a messenger boy in Allen's chemist in St Luke's Cross, didn't last very long either, his inability to ride the delivery bicycle being a major disadvantage. He then got a job in a

---

* Sir Roger Casement was considered a traitor for supporting the 1916 rising

printer's. With his love of words, this should have suited him, but his stay there was even briefer: just one day. His boss enquired about his spelling ability. Michael proudly told him, as a boy from Eton or Harrow would, that spelling was his forte. But the boss derived great pleasure from spreading this story around the office and the ever-sensitive Michael was never seen again.

Eventually, he landed a job in the railway station on Lower Glanmire Road. Even though the hours were long – eleven hours a day from eight in the morning till seven at night, six days a week – the money wasn't bad: one pound a week. With money like that he felt he could purchase plenty of books and get a good education. He worked in the goods department and his job, along with many other lads his own age, was to trace missing parcels. The other boys, usually sons or relatives of the older railway employees, found the work very easy but it didn't take the nervous young Michael very long to find out that he was not cut out to be a tracer of missing goods. Firstly, most of the goods were simply misplaced in one carriage or another or in the wrong warehouse or else they were just stuck in a remote corner covered by other parcels. Perishable goods, like fish or meat, took priority. While Michael struggled, the other boys seemed to sniff out these parcels quite easily. He was envious of the way they went merrily about their work, laughing and swapping witty banter with the men. The goods department phraseology and the codeword system were another hurdle and he never really got to grips with them. The dreaded telephone was an even bigger obstacle. He hated answering it and, in his nervousness, usually took down the wrong message.

From very early on, he was picked out as a soft target and was continually the butt of pranks, pawed and victimised by many of the older men. On his very first day in the job he was sent over to the stationmaster's office for the key to open the tunnel to let the trains in (it is about ninety by twenty feet). Another day they unkindly made up a docket for him to trace one bale of missing foreskins and for weeks, much to their delight, he searched high and low innocently asking everyone if, by any chance, they had come across a bale of foreskins on their travels. When asked if he could describe this missing bale, he told them that it probably was the same as any other bale of foreskins. They nicknamed him 'The Native' because of his ability to speak Irish. Then, one day, out of the blue, he was fired. With his poor eyesight, he often injured himself by tripping over parcels and hand trucks. The railway decided to let him go; they were afraid of a claim for personal-injury compensation.

While he was working in the railway, he had led a strange double life. Sometimes, the only thing that softened his despair and kept him going was the thought of his hard-earned weekly wage. He was one person by day, enduring the sniggering insults and the foul-mouthed jibes of some of his superiors, but when he walked home up Summerhill at seven in the evening he became a different person, his head immersed ecstatically in a poetry book. In his fantasy world of education and literature he read Goethe, Heine and Turgenev and endeavoured to translate Spanish and French poems into Irish. He also memorised and quoted lines from several obscure Latin and Greek poems. There was a brief success with one translation, from German to Irish, which was critically acclaimed in the *Sunday Independent*. Daniel Corkery invited him along to the weekly literary gatherings in his home in Gardiner's Hill. With his love of Irish he never missed the lectures in the Gaelic League Hall on Saturday nights, and on Sunday, usually with a book tucked under his arm, he hung around the street corners on the fringes of the older men and tried to participate in the heated discussions on war, women, literature and Ireland. Then, on Monday morning, the books were put away and he became another person when he crossed the road by St Patrick's church and entered the gates of the goods department on the quay to face the drudgery of the railway.

On the night he was fired, as he walked slowly up the steep hill to the Barrack Stream, he dreaded going home to face his mother and father. Big Mick had now returned from his army adventure. Harrington Square was a small intimate community with very few secrets and the word would soon be out that Big Mick's son had lost another job. The boy had gone through it all before: the hushed whispers, the knowing glances, the cruel jibes and the fingers pointing behind his back. Once again penniless and unemployed, he knew he would be branded as a good-for-nothing, with his head in the clouds, who couldn't keep a job. It was yet another hiccup in his quest for knowledge. Aware that there was no turning back, he recalled with rueful irony how, when his childhood gang came to an orchard wall which seemed too high to climb, they all took off their caps and, in an act of bravado, threw them over the wall. They then had no choice but to follow them wherever they had fallen. Years later, when Michael had reached middle age, he was a great admirer of Pope John XXIII and President John F. Kennedy. The latter gave his last public speech at Brooks Air Force Base in San Antonio, Texas. At the time, he had received some harsh criticism of his space programme and, in his defence, he quoted Frank O'Connor's story of tossing his cap over the orchard wall as a child. Kennedy, who was proud of his Irish ancestry, compared that incident to the need for the USA to be brave and metaphorically to daringly throw its cap over the wall of space. When informed of the tragic death of the president, Michael was overcome with grief. Two days later he wrote a tribute to the late president in the *Sunday Independent* and for years tried, unsuccessfully, to persuade the Irish Government to have the Rock of Cashel in Tipperary designated as a monument to the memory of John F. Kennedy.

Out of work and with plenty of time on his hands, Michael spent his days either berthed in the Carnegie Library or roaming aimlessly around the streets of Cork looking for inspiration. One night, through Daniel Corkery, he met Seán O'Faoláin, an arts student at the local university, at An Grianáin* in Queen Street. To Corkery, they were his two fledgling writers, steeped in poetry, determined to rewrite all the great books and solve all the world's problems. Both, especially Michael, were great walkers but their personalities were poles apart. There was also a considerable difference in their backgrounds – O'Faoláin, whose father held the lofty position of an RIC constable, considered himself slightly higher on the social ladder. He once boasted to a friend that when Michael was broke he was penniless but when he himself was broke he was tuppenceless. O'Faoláin, three years older, was born over Alaska Jack's pub opposite the stage door of the Opera House in Half Moon Street. Alaska Jack's was run by a famous character who proudly displayed a gold nugget on the shelf behind the bar. When business was poor he pawned the nugget for money but once he got back on his feet the nugget was redeemed and reinstated in its rightful place. This practice went on for years.

In Cork at that time there were hundreds of pubs but very few theatres. Daniel Corkery had his own small theatre across the street

---

* The hall where the Gaelic League held their meetings

from An Grianáin where he put on his own plays. Thrown together, these two aspiring young writers were a perfect foil for each other. With no money, they walked endlessly, argued and agreed to disagree about practically everything. Michael was a nervous nonstop talker, blowing hot and cold with equal ferocity and spouting literary flame. O'Faoláin was cool, disciplined and sophisticated, with a look of ecclesiastical royalty about him. For different reasons they couldn't go home; there was generally no coal in Michael's fireplace and you just couldn't get near O'Faoláin's fire since it was usually surrounded by their theatrical lodgers from the nearby Opera House.

O'Faoláin's girlfriend, Eileen Gould, sometimes accompanied them on their walks. One day she noticed the terrible condition of Michael's footwear, took pity on him and bought him a new pair of boots. O'Faoláin was soon to go on to college and Corkery confided in Michael, that in his opinion, O'Faoláin was a born writer. This only succeeded in making Michael madly jealous; yet, years later, Eileen, then married to O'Faoláin, said that Michael was the first real genius she ever met.

Ireland was now burning with patriotic frenzy. Cork, the rebel county and the garrison town, was a cauldron of political passion. People everywhere were bursting with nationalist pride and everyone was united in supporting the 'cause'. Many changed their names to the Irish version: John Whelan became Seán O'Faoláin and all Michael's early letters to the newspapers were signed Mícheál O Donnabháin. The Gaelic League, trying to promote Irish culture, held concerts which were usually attacked and broken up by armed police. When Michael was fourteen he attended one of these concerts. He was asked to sing and he obliged by giving a fervent rendition of 'Lament for the Woodlands' in Irish. But, as self-conscious as ever, he broke down halfway through the song.

Most young men joined the Irish Volunteers and were constantly involved in minor skirmishes with the RIC. They secretly drilled out in the fields of Upper Glanmire, chopped down trees and blocked roads, dug trenches, delivered dispatches, quietly spied on the enemy and generally played at being soldiers anxiously waiting for a war. Big Mick strongly resented his son's politics but, luckily, was completely unaware of Minnie's involvement in the revolution. She often did odd jobs herself like carrying messages and, sometimes, guns in her shopping bag. Michael once took a chance by limping along the length of Ballyhooly Road with a useless old rifle stuck down his trouser-leg. If caught, he would have been sent to jail.

By this time every spare moment he got was spent with Corkery, often walking miles into the quietness of the countryside to watch him paint. Michael once said that he was only there to hold the cow's tail. Corkery lived with his elderly mother and sister in a small house at the top of Gardiner's Hill and Michael loved to visit, listen to Mozart and passionately discuss literature. An enthusiastic pupil, he rarely left without a book or two under his arm. Accompanied by O'Faoláin and Seán (or Jack) Hendrick, an insurance clerk whom he had met at a Gaelic League meeting, he often stayed late and regularly found himself locked out by his belligerent father. Minnie, shushing and shishing, usually let him in.

With each confrontation with the British Army, tension grew in every town in Ireland. People had grown tired of turning the other cheek. It all reached boiling point in Cork during the spring of 1920. On 30 January, after a dramatic council meeting, Tomás MacCurtain had been elected Cork's first Republican lord mayor but, sadly, his term in office was to last only seven weeks. At 1.15 a.m. on Saturday, 20 March, his thirty-sixth birthday, he was murdered in his home by Crown Forces. Members of the RIC, with blackened faces and socks pulled over their boots to muffle the sound, hammered on his front door and got his wife, Lizzie, out of bed. While two held her, their comrades ran up the stairs and shot MacCurtain in front of his young children. His assassins ran quickly off into the night and left him mortally wounded on the bedroom floor. His last words, in the arms of local priest, Father Burts, were 'Into thy hands, oh Lord, I commend my spirit.' Word of the murder spread like wildfire. Rumour followed counter-rumour. People were confused and frightened and locked their doors not just in the immediate Blackpool area but all over the stunned northside.

That weekend Cork was a city of mourning. It was revealed that two days before his death the late Lord Mayor had received a threatening letter saying, 'Prepare for death. You are doomed'; it is interesting to note that the message was written on official Dáil Eireann notepaper, which suggests that British military intelligence had found ways and means of acquiring nationalist stationery. Typically, MacCurtain only laughed at this threat.

MacCurtain's death affected Michael; accompanied by MacSwiney, the lord mayor had regularly called to the Gaelic League and An Grianáin and conversed in Irish with him.

The funeral on the following Monday was a sad affair. The cortège slowly wound its way from the North Cathedral through the city streets to St Finbar's Cemetery. Cork came to a standstill; the docks were shut, factories and shops were closed and there were no trams or newspapers. Volunteers now wore uniforms openly. There wasn't a policeman or a British soldier to be seen. Terence MacSwiney spoke briefly over the grave, the Last Post was played, and three volleys of gunfire were defiantly fired to the heavens. There was a mounting anger in the city but the MacCurtain family appealed for no retaliation. MacCurtain's killers were instantly identified by local IRA men. They demanded revenge but the perpetrators had fled to different parts of the country. Divisional Inspector Swanzy of the RIC, who was allegedly one of the murderers, was transferred up north. He was tracked down to an RIC barracks in Lisburn. A First Cork Brigade man was given the job and, on 22 August, as Swanzy left church, he died in a hail of bullets from MacCurtain's own personal revolver.

Although still only sixteen, Michael was now a fully fledged volunteer. He was impatient for action but was allowed to linger on the fringes of rebel activity. His superiors only gave him safe jobs like reconnoitring the enemy and carrying messages. Through the Gaelic League, he had been working as a teacher. Wearing tweed knickerbockers, woollen socks knitted by his mother and black boots, he regularly cycled out to the country villages to teach Irish in the evenings. Once again, he lost his job but this time it was not his fault. After MacCurtain's death a strict curfew was enforced on the city, which meant Michael could no longer go out at night. Anyone caught breaking the curfew was shot. Ominously, five days after the Lord Mayor's death, the Black and Tans were sent to Ireland. People thought the RIC or the Auxiliaries were bad – and they were; the Auxiliaries were former British officers who were generally drunken, reckless, illdisciplined bullies, but they were like boy scouts compared to the Black and Tans (so called because their uniforms had the same colouring as the famous Limerick hunt, Scarteen Black and Tans). Because of the shortage of uniforms they wore the khaki trousers of the regular soldiers and the RIC's black tunic. They were almost totally made up of vicious, brutal ex-convicts and down-and-outs. They carried bullwhips and frequently lashed, terrorised and robbed innocent people. They were sent to several specific trouble-spots to keep the natives down. Cork was one such place. My own father used to hide his wages in his cap but he was often stopped, searched and had his money stolen on his way home from work on Friday nights. He once witnessed a priest being forced down on his hands and knees and made to eat horse manure. The Black and Tans were despised and were a law unto themselves. Anyone who stood up to them was quickly and violently dealt with.*

At noon on Tuesday, 30 March, Terence MacSwiney was unanimously elected Lord Mayor. He was seconded by the famous volunteer leader, Tom Barry. Not alone did MacSwiney follow MacCurtain as commandant of the IRA, but he also stepped into his shoes as the city's first citizen. His first act in office was to give £250 of his £500 salary to a memorial fund for MacCurtain's widow.

The City Hall was packed on that Tuesday when he stood up before a hushed and expectant audience. They weren't disappointed. He gave a long emotional speech. He began by eloquently stating: 'I come here more as a soldier stepping into the breach than an administrator,' and he made the point that MacCurtain's murder was an attempt to terrify the country, and stressed that the Irish people should show themselves completely and utterly unterrified. He finished with the immortal and often misused quotation: 'It is not they who can inflict the most but they who can suffer the most will conquer.' The tense gallery erupted in thunderous applause.

Terence MacSwiney realised only too well that his life was in danger. His friends wanted an armed guard with him day and night but he wouldn't hear of it. He felt he wouldn't be able to get his work done. Still, he hardly ever stayed in his own home. He and his friends came to an arrangement that he slept in a different house every night.

The Black and Tans weren't slow in making their presence felt. All through that summer of 1920 they terrorised the country. There began mass resignations of members of the RIC who, up to this point, were mainly Irish. Also, magistrates resigned by the dozen and there was

---

* Interestingly, my own father often confided in me that 'our own were worse'. He never qualified this statement.

hardly a day went by when a village or a creamery wasn't burned down. The Black and Tans had first-class transport and plenty of guns but the IRA had the complete support of the people. Every house was a safe house. The nation was united in its contempt and its fear of the Black and Tans.

When he wasn't playing the young rebel or living in the Carnegie Library, Michael devoted all his time and energy to a new debating society which grandly called itself the Twenty Club. Corkery invited him to join. They met every Sunday and vigorously dissected all the relevant issues of the day, such as Tolstoy, art and the importance of French literature. They later brought out a Republican periodical called *An Long* which lasted only three months. Michael's contribution to the first issue was two poems, 'Mozart' and 'Invictus'.

On the night of Thursday, 12 August 1920, the City Hall was surrounded and Terence MacSwiney, who often worked late in his office, was arrested. It was Daniel Corkery who broke the news to Muriel MacSwiney of her husband's arrest. The mayor was taken to Victoria Barracks near Michael's home where he was court-martialled and found guilty on trumped-up charges and given two years in London's Brixton Prison. In protest, he immediately went on hunger-strike. For the next ten weeks the world watched while MacSwiney stubbornly refused to eat and, despite pleas from all sections of the community, he suffered a slow, painful death. The situation turned out to be a huge propaganda victory for the IRA. On one day alone, forty thousand people in Cork said the Rosary by the National Monument and, another day, thirty thousand English workers demanded his release. But it was not to be. On Monday, 25 October, after seventy-four days' fasting, he passed away.

When MacCurtain died it affected the young O'Donovan, but he had hero-worshipped MacSwiney and the tragic circumstances of his death left their mark. MacSwiney was a man of culture, music and poetry. Michael empathised with him and was drawn to him and felt MacSwiney was all the things he himself longed to be; he was handsome and intelligent with a degree in mental and moral science. He was a published poet, using the pen-name An Cuireadír. He was also a novelist; *Principles of Freedom* was his best-known book. He had written several critically acclaimed plays; one was in the Cork Opera House for a week; and, just like Michael, he had also worked in

Dwyer's Shop for some time.

When MacSwiney's body was eventually returned to Ireland from Brixton it was laid out in Cork's City Hall. Thousands filed by, including Minnie and her son who were shocked by the gaunt, hollow-cheeked features of the late Lord Mayor. Michael was appalled at the change in his face since he had last seen him just a few months previously.

MacSwiney's death brought a dramatic escalation of the tit-for-tat violence. The Black and Tans went berserk. In one week twenty-four towns were badly damaged, looted and burned, including Trim, Balbrigan, Ennistymon, Fermoy, Lahinch, Mallow and Milltown Malbay. On 21 November they fired recklessly into the crowd at a football match in Croke Park, killing twelve people including one player. A few days later, the First Cork Brigade, led by Tom Barry, spectacularly ambushed a convoy at Kilmichael and killed sixteen members of the British Army. But every time the Black and Tans were hit, they retaliated with a vengeance. On Saturday night, 10 December, near Michael's home in Harrington Square, six IRA men attacked a lorry-load of Auxiliaries, killing one before making their escape. The whole area reeked with the fear of reprisals. Everyone knew it was going to happen. Behind locked doors, Big Mick, Minnie and their son heard the whole thing, the noise of the ricocheting bullets, the confusion, the shouting, the sound of running men as the events outside dramatically unfolded in their mind's eye. The reaction and retaliation of the army was instant and savage. People all around the square were dragged out of their beds, robbed and viciously beaten. Their homes were set on fire and when they tried to save their possessions they were shot at. Luckily, the O'Donovans' house was left in peace. The Black and Tans then swept into the city centre and, with drums of petrol, systematically burned building after building. Catholic shops took priority and the way certain premises were picked out and destroyed by different groups strongly suggests the attack was very organised and prearranged. A tram was set on fire near Patrick's Bridge and the looting went on all through the night. The fire brigade were called but weren't allowed to do anything.* The ambulance carrying an injured fireman to hospital was spattered with bullets.

---

* My grandfather, a retired soldier and very pro-British man, lived in town and was hauled from his bed and sent scampering half-dressed down a side lane. He witnessed the cutting of hoses with bayonets and the shooting at the fire brigade.

The O'Donovans spent the night, huddled together in fear, listening to the non-stop gunfire, the crackling flames and watching the sky aglow with red. No one slept. The stench of smoke was everywhere.

Although the alcohol was slowing them down as the night went on, the Black and Tans never let up; they continued to smash and loot pubs, shoe shops and jeweller's as they made their way to the City Hall, the symbol of Republicanism. There had been several unsuccessful attempts to burn the building down and the lower windows were covered with corrugated-iron shutters. This didn't stop them. With the aid of sledgehammers, they quickly broke down the doors. Tins of petrol, bombs and incendiary devices were swiftly ferried from the nearby Union Quay Barracks by their comrades. The bombs were strategically placed all over the building and soaked with petrol. The raiders ran to safety, the all-clear was given, and within minutes a series of loud explosions was heard and fire rapidly consumed the building. Then the adjoining Carnegie Library was given the same treatment until both buildings roared in an uncontrollable inferno. Symbolically, as the clock high up in the City Hall struck 6 a.m., the entire dome gave way and crashed down, sending a spray of sparks into the dark night.

At first, the British blamed the IRA. Then they accused the people of burning their own city. The media stated that the City Hall caught fire and flames from this accidently set Patrick Street ablaze. As the City Hall was across a river about four hundred yards away, it seems unlikely. To back up this theory, one English newspaper printed a diagram of Cork with the City Hall conveniently relocated in Patrick Street.

In that night of madness, many were shot and injured. One Auxiliary was killed in the IRA ambush at Dillon's Cross earlier in the night. At two in the morning the worst atrocity occurred when a lorry-load of British soldiers called to a house in Dublin Hill not far from MacCurtain's home. Wearing handkerchiefs over their faces, they ordered two young brothers, the Delaneys, from their beds and shot them dead.

The next morning Michael made a tour of the still-smouldering rubble. Everywhere people gathered and just looked on in silent disbelief. When he arrived at the ravaged Carnegie Library, he was distraught. What was once his beautiful, old, red-brick building was now a grotesque skeleton; a desolate, black shell with only one wall remaining. What had practically been his second home for years was gone forever and he realised that life for him would never be the same again.

Although the cleaning-up and rebuilding were to take a long time, life in the city went on pretty much as usual. With the strict curfew, the social scene in Cork was very dull; dances, get-togethers and musical events were held in hotels on Sunday afternoons. They generally finished at four o'clock so as to give the patrons enough time to get home before the dreaded five o'clock deadline. Courting was a dangerous pastime. A young man had to see his girl home and then be fairly lively in getting home himself by curfew – or he was simply shot. O'Faoláin, who was now in his third year in college, once facetiously remarked that, at that time, you did not *commit* sin; you *achieved* it. The ever-vigilant Black and Tans nabbed him one afternoon near curfew time and forced him to sing 'God Save the King' at gunpoint before dispatching him with a flurry of bullets. This was quite a common practice and many young men were forced to learn the words of the English national anthem in case the necessity arose.

Sometimes if the Black and Tans didn't like the look of an unfortunate individual he would be tied onto the roof of their armoured car as a shield for the night. The IRA had a habit of occasionally dropping hand-grenades on the roof of these vehicles. The Black and Tans found it difficult to cope with the hit-and-run tactics of the IRA but any time they were attacked it was the innocent civilians who suffered most from their retaliation.

The West Cork Brigade were a small daring group of volunteers who darted here and there, striking at the enemy, hiding in cowsheds and safe houses, before resuming their normal civilian lives again. They were up against 12,500 British troops in Cork alone. Their commander was Tom Barry. Like many Irish leaders before him, he had been trained by the British Army. In March 1921, led by Barry, the West Cork Brigade savagely ambushed a convoy at Crossbarry. Although they were outnumbered ten to one, they killed 39 British soldiers. Barry was a ruthless, fearless man and he particularly hated Major Percival and his Essex Regiment who were based in Cork. This regiment had a reputation for cruelty and torture. The enmity proved lasting: in 1942, when Percival, as commander-in-chief of the impregnable Singapore base, surrendered to the Japanese without a fight, Tom Barry made a point of sending him a tongue-in-cheek telegram congratulating him on his bravery.

The vicious fighting continued until, out of the blue, a cessation of violence was dramatically announced in July 1921. Michael was still only seventeen when the truce came. Ireland sighed with relief. The guns were put away and a tremendous feeling of euphoria enveloped the nation. Boys and girls could, once again, stroll in peace and freedom through the city streets. People cycled out to the countryside for picnics. Roadblocks disappeared and the fear of searches and beatings was gone. Most bridges were also gone – bombed or burnt down – and young people had great fun wading across the narrowest part of the river to get to the other side. People could stay out all night if they so wished. The Black and Tans were still around and unpleasant but at least there were no shootings.

This idyllic situation wasn't to last very long, however. Michael was now getting more and more involved with the volunteers. The nationalist movement was completely split. Throughout that autumn the rift between the Republicans (who demanded a complete nation under Irish rule) and the pro-treaty element (who were content to accept 26 counties as a temporary solution) was widening. In December a delegation led by a reluctant Michael Collins and Arthur Griffith went to London for talks. Churchill lurked menacingly in the background with the threat of the navy in one fist and the army in the other. After much bargaining, they were outflanked by Lloyd George and signed the treaty. The following month, after a dramatic debate, the Dáil voted 64 to 57 in favour of accepting the treaty.

For the next six months the country held its breath while a bitter war of words unfolded before them. By this time Michael was a Republican delegate and even went to Dublin as a representative. On 22 May he witnessed something he never thought he'd see: the British Army leaving Cork. They streamed quietly out through the front gate of Victoria Barracks as the Irish Army marched in through the back gate. An officer solemnly hauled down the Union Jack and in a final act of British defiance cut down the massive flagpole so that there was no place to hoist the Tricolour. A young Michael watched in silence as the British Army, complete with flagpole on a horse and cart, filed past the Barrack Stream. Centuries of British occupation were over.

But all over Ireland tension was growing; the Republicans could not swallow two bitter pills – neither the oath of allegiance to the British crown nor that a partitioned Ireland was to become part of the British Empire. The heroics and expectations of the 1916 rising and the dream of a thirty-two-county Republic were well and truly buried. Slowly but surely the guns reappeared. In frustration, the Dublin Brigade of the IRA took over the Four Courts as their headquarters. Assassination and counter-assassination followed. In the end of June, under pressure from Downing Street, Michael Collins bombarded the Four Courts with guns borrowed, ironically, from the British Army. The Civil War had effectively begun. According to his own account, Michael took the Republican side simply because it was Corkery's side.

The Civil War was fought with bitterness, filled with retaliation and atrocity, and was one of the blackest periods in Irish history. One incident above all others indicates the hatred which prevailed then. At Ballyseedy Cross in Kerry a group of Free Staters tied nine Republicans to a landmine and set it off. Eight were blown to bits and it was said that for days afterwards the birds were eating flesh off the branches of the trees. And these were boys who only a short time before had stood shoulder to shoulder against the might of the British Army. Now the British had stepped back and left the Irish to tear each other apart. Lord Birkenhead summed up their attitude when he said, 'War by the Irish on the Irish is the kind of political development which I observe with great pleasure.' The Free Staters were better equipped and more organised and in the following months they edged successfully bit by bit, battle by battle, further and further south, towards the Republican stronghold.

Michael and his friend Seán Hendrick acted as censors to the *Examiner* and then as writers for the Munster edition of *An Phoblacht*. Erskine Childers, a small, efficient ex-British army officer who was helping in the Irish troubles, was their immediate superior. It was a vicious and tragic war. Many people switched allegiance and sometimes, on Sundays, they stopped fighting to go to Mass. Michael was frustrated with his safe position as a newspaper censor and it didn't help matters when he once spotted O'Faoláin, grasping a rifle, flash by in an army lorry. On one occasion, he and some friends lay in wait to ambush a Free State lorry at Dillon's Cross. When the lorry finally passed by, they threw a rusty old bomb in its general direction and beat a hasty retreat. But the whole thing was a damp squib and nothing really happened. A year later he wrote a poem about the incident.

AMBUSH
We crouch in the darkness,
In the wet grass,
In the falling rain,
Whelan and Sean and I

Vincent carries a bomb.
Whelan wears yellow gloves,
I see them hanging dead from his left hand.
In his right he carries
A dark revolver.
No one has passed beneath the lamp,
Darkness, dreariness, only
The broad bright window
Of the public house opposite
Has life. There they are singing but
We do not speak a word.
Dreariness. The wet cloth hugs my knees.
Suddenly a low hum;
Nerves tauten.
Closer, closer,
Louder, as if the general judgement
Drove in a Lancia car,
To our undoing,
Churning the mud.

Something blots the bright window;
The revolver leaps in my hand,
Like a thing gone wild;
Something cracks close to me.
Then, after an age,

The bomb peals;
A dark figure runs beside me breathing heavily.

The singing has ceased,
The broad bright window is shattered,
The lovers in the lane disturbed are hurrying homeward
And to the four young men hurrying homeward
An old woman speaks,
'Pardon me, gentlemen, but has something happened?'
And Vincent, doffing his hat, says mildly,
'No, madam,
It is merely the old lady in the corner shop
Who, being deaf,
Amuses herself by blowing paper bags.'

Eventually, Michael did get to see some real action but it nearly ended in disaster. General Deasy sent him to North Cork to deliver some dispatches one Sunday morning. The place was unusually quiet; neither friend nor foe was to be seen for miles around; even the road-blocks were left unattended. Everyone was at Mass. Suddenly Free State troops appeared from behind a bush with rifles pointed menacingly in his direction. He managed to tear up the dispatches before he was ignominiously grabbed and hauled off to a nearby farmhouse. He was embarrassed at being captured on his very first day at war.

A few hours later, Republican soldiers turned up after Mass and attacked the farmhouse with a barrage of bullets and hand-grenades. There were several casualties before the Free State troops surrendered and pushed Michael, the young rebel, out through the front door waving a white handkerchief. Initially, he had a problem trying to convince his new captors that he was really on their side. On that sunny Sunday afternoon he was forcibly reminded of the futility of war when he looked down at the bodies of the young men as they lay dead in the yard.

To all intents and purposes the Civil War ended when the Free State Army invaded Cork by sea and the demoralised Republicans were sent fleeing in the direction of West Cork. Michael, still under the command of Childers, hopped from hayshed to cowshed, sleeping rough, with the victorious enemy in hot pursuit. Disillusioned, he sometimes lay awake at night counting the stars, forever composing poetry in his head, and longed for a quiet walk down the Marina or a stroll up the Mardyke.

In August, Michael Collins was shot in an ambush at Béal na mBláth. Erskine Childers was public enemy number one and was now being blamed for everything, even Collins's death. Some of his own avoided him for fear of being shot on sight. Eventually, he was captured in Wicklow and this inoffensive Englishman was executed because he was carrying a tiny, toy-like pistol pinned to his braces – given to him, ironically, by Michael Collins. The Free State government, in trying to end the war quickly, adopted a get-tough policy. IRA prisoners were executed by the score.

Dan Corkery heard gossip about Michael carrying on and drinking while hiding out in West Cork. These stories were untrue – he was never really a drinking man; he had seen enough evidence of what it had done to his father. Corkery sent word and ordered him back home. He did return to the city but rarely stayed at home. His great friend, Seán Hendrick, was caught and interned in Newbridge. Michael was an inveterate letter-writer and had an impish humour and an irreverent, caustic wit. In January he wrote to his friend:

> 8 Harrington Sq.
> Dear Seán,
>   I have been moved to pity of your case by hearing that you are incarcerated in company with Bottles [a mutual friend]. If I were your greatest enemy I would have wished you no worse fate.
>   I am at present convalescent but still rather weak and as usual reading new literature while confined indoors.
>   I received a letter from Chester Allan.* He is at present in Florence and leading an idyllic existence according to himself writing his book in the morning, seeing the beauties of the city in the afternoon and attending the opera at night. Reminds me of Shelley's life in Italy. He says Dan's [Corkery] books created a great sensation among his continental friends. By the way have you seen the *Ireland's Eye* cartoon on *The Threshold of Quiet*? It represents the usual henpecked husband supporting two

---

* American writer of westerns

screaming babes on his knees. Dan has got his gramophone with some beautiful records including the 'Moonlight', Fifth Symphony and other classics. We shall have a great night when you come out. Cis* wishes to be remembered to you.

    Let me know if you want any books or papers.

    Best of love

    Miceál

Now a marked and wanted man, and not well, he kept on the move and stayed in safe-houses. One of his favourites was Seán French's place up in Wellington Road. Seán, who was to be the future Lord Mayor of Cork for twelve years, was at this time in jail and Michael loved the musical gatherings surrounded by pretty young ladies who supplied him with cups of tea, cigarettes and sympathy for the Republican cause. He was treated as a hero home from the war and enjoyed the relaxed atmosphere and the female company. Seán's wife, Ethel, was an accomplished pianist and, with a bit of cajoling, Michael's rich baritone voice often finished the night off with a few songs; his favourite was that melodramatic German love song, '*Ich grolle nicht*', by Schumann.

This song was taught to him by Seán Neeson who lived directly across the road in Mount Verdon Villa, a beautiful, sleepy old house overlooking the city. Seán and Geraldine Neeson were a fascinating couple. Seán, a Belfast Republican who was jailed several times, was the head of Radio Eireann in Cork. He was also a theatrical producer and a singing teacher. When Michael MacLiammoir and Hilton Edwards, the well-known acting partners based in Dublin, first came to Cork in the early days they were practically penniless and Edwards, who had a wonderful voice, approached Seán Neeson for a job singing on Radio Eireann. They became great friends and Seán often put them up in his home and fed them. He once lent Hilton a shirt when he was going for an important interview.

Geraldine Neeson, a sister-in-law of Nancy McCarthy, was for many years a respected journalist and critic for the *Examiner*. She was also a fine pianist and, through music, became very close to Terence MacSwiney's wife, Muriel. MacSwiney wore his volunteer uniform, which was banned, when he got married in England. It was Geraldine who smuggled the uniform over from Cork in her suitcase and she was

---

* A mutual friend

bridesmaid at the wedding. As a young woman she sometimes acted as a courier for the old IRA. She was said to be ideal for the job because she was so petite and innocent-looking. Once, when she was carrying a suitcase of money in London to the rebels, she got lost in the fog. She innocently asked a policeman for directions and he kindly carried the suitcase and took her personally to the address.

The French home was a well-known Republican house and, unknown to Michael, it was under constant surveillance. In the first week of February 1923 he had just thanked Ethel and said goodbye when he was spotted and arrested by Free State soldiers. He was immediately searched. In his inside pocket was a half-read copy of Dostoevsky's *The Idiot*. Had he been carrying a gun he would have been executed. He was hauled at gunpoint to a military court where he was promptly sentenced to jail. That afternoon his captors marched him up to the Women's Prison in Sunday's Well, a place he was so familiar with as a child. He and three others were locked up in a tiny cell which was condemned as unsuitable for one. It had a damp, earthen floor and was filthy and crawling with rats. There was barely room for them to lie down and sleep. The large barred glassless window ensured that they were wide open to the vagaries of the weather. Every meal was served up cold.

Even to men on the run, used to sleeping rough, the conditions were dreadful in this hundred-year-old prison. Worse was the feeling of uncertainty, of not knowing if they were to live or die, if they were next to be dragged out and shot. There were daily executions and the inmates could hear the abuse, the screams, the crash of bullets, followed by the long deadly silence. Irishmen being shot by Irishmen. Some could not bear it and committed suicide by throwing themselves from the high, steel balcony. Nets were put up in an attempt to halt this practice.

Michael did not mix much with the other prisoners. He preferred to read alone. Corkery smuggled in some books, tobacco and cigarette papers. He felt that Michael, now a heavy smoker, might learn from the discipline of rolling his own. Like literary saboteurs, they also exchanged coded letters. There was a touch of theatrical cloak-and-dagger in the way Corkery paid his weekly visits disguised as Martin Cloyne, the main character in his own book, *The Threshhold of Quiet*.

Ironically, when Michael looked through the cell bars all he could see were the pregnant girls waving up at his barely visible face as they worked in the side field of the Good Shepherd Convent adjoining the prison – the very place where his mother was reared and educated. Although the prison is now a renovated heritage centre, the old cell walls remain. Michael scraped a line of poetry on his wall with a nail and other walls are scarred with sad messages signed by young boys, teenagers from County Kerry and Limerick about to be taken out and shot. Even today, the smell of death, lost souls and hopelessness surrounds these cells. They are a grim monument; a reminder of terrible times.

Eight weeks later, very early in the morning, Michael and dozens of other prisoners were herded onto a lorry and taken to Glanmire Railway Station where he had spent such unhappy times at the age of fourteen. The inmates began a long, slow journey; several tracks and bridges had been blown up. They were given only tinned fish to eat; Michael couldn't touch his and gave it away. It was night by the time the train eventually pulled into a little station, near the sea, an hour north of Dublin. The tired men could barely make out the rows of flat buildings and wooden huts surrounded by high barbed wire. A distant searchlight swept menacingly across the fields and lit up the sky. They had arrived at Gormanstown Internment Camp, a former First World War American aerodrome. It was almost dawn before they struggled through the front gate. Michael was in the camp only a few hours when he collapsed from the stomach trouble which was to plague him for the next forty years. He couldn't believe it when he woke up in a real bed, his first for a long time, to the smell of the sea air and the warmth of the spring sunshine. He settled down very quickly and came to enjoy and accept the organisation and pattern of the camp. Decisions were made for him and he had daily showers, three meals a day, and plenty of exercise and fresh air.

All his life it annoyed him that he never had a college education, but surely Gormanstown was his university. Every day he worked hard on his French and he himself taught German and Irish. Although he had some training as a teacher he didn't realise how poor his grammar was until he started seriously to consult his textbooks on Irish. This drove him to non-stop study of the subject and he wasn't happy until he had achieved a complete mastery of every aspect of Irish. Books were readily available and there were classes, concerts, lectures and debates on every conceivable subject. He mixed with intelligent, educated men of the world: doctors, teachers, journalists; men who read Swift and quoted Thackeray and listened to Bach and Beethoven; his kind of people. Among his fellow internees were Fred Cogley who taught Spanish; Frank Gallagher, later editor of the *Irish Press*; Seán McEntee, who was to be minister for finance and father-in-law of Conor Cruise O'Brien; Seán T.O'Kelly, future President of Ireland.

His mother, Minnie, sent him regular parcels of cigarettes and food which were most welcome but he was well aware of the sacrifices she must have made to be able to do this. In all probability she starved herself. Once, he wrote and told her how sorry he was for all the trouble he had caused her; but she wouldn't hear of it and, in a soft, maternal rebuke, reassured him that if there were no wild boys, there would be no great men.

But all was not calm in the camp; De Valera had ordered a ceasefire, though under no circumstances would he recognise the Free State Government. Republicans were still being executed. As news of these killings seeped into the camp, the feeling of helplessness, anger and resentment grew more bitter among the internees. Michael tried to keep busy; when he wasn't teaching or reading he wrote poetry, an essay in Irish on Turgenev and letters to Seán Hendrick and his mother. He had been in the camp two months when he had a poem published in the *Catholic Bulletin*:

THE ROSARY
When byre and house with sleep are dim,
And all their fields are drained of light
They say the Rosary for him
Who walks the darkening hills tonight

From voice to voice the rich prayers swell,
Seeds of such strange and splendid fruit,
Oh Rosary of pain you tell
Of hearts Life trampled underfoot

With 'pray for us' and 'full of grace'
The links of sacrifice are bound
In chains of prayer that hold this race
From battle-ground to battle-ground.

Above the altar and the priest,
Above the organ-chant of faith
The human heart climbs up, released
In ecstasy that mocks at Death

Here Faith that is not Faith but more,
And Hope more holy and more wise,
And Charity all blend and soar
In temples freed of human eyes

He also wrote a lovely little poem, 'For The End', which was never published:

FOR THE END *(Gormanstown, 1923)*
Hush lips and breath!
For the great play of Death
Is ended: the lights fade
And silent, shade on shade,
Back to bare streets and grey
Each takes his way.

Hush! heart be wise,
For a dream is in your eyes
Of men you have seen live;
Their earnestness may give
Joy yet, and trust,
And spirit in the dust.

Hush heart your cries!
When the swift light dies
Does the play end?
Nor voice, nor laughter send
An echo, nor their names
Who died bring answering flames?

Life seems such common stuff
When plume and sword are off
But here, O heart

Motley and grey no more have part
This play was Life, this hour
Of light and power

The Civil War dragged tediously on. The death toll had reached almost seven hundred and over twelve thousand Republicans were in jail. One of Corkery's letters, dated November 1923, stated that Michael had been interned for nine months and he was very ill with bronchitis.

In many ways, Michael went into Gormanstown a child and came out a man. There were constant personality clashes between different men from different backgrounds and counties. Once, in a vote about what punishment should be meted out to a fellow internee, Michael alone voted against the entire camp; one nineteen-year-old boy against a thousand men. With his stubborn streak he was never afraid to make an unpopular decision and it wasn't to be the first time he stood up against something he felt was wrong.

Another time, in an angry gesture of defiance, the men decided to give up food as a protest. A mood of martyrdom prevailed but the frustrated Michael argued that the men's decision was insane and he was one of the few who wouldn't go on hunger-strike because he felt it was better to live for Ireland than to die for Ireland. This opinion caused even more friction, and the daily sight of men passing to and fro, to the kitchen, between hunger-strikers, with their eating utensils discreetly hidden beneath their coats, escalated the tension. Eventually, common sense won out and the strike was called off.

Michael's iconoclastic tendencies also came to the surface when, along with many others, he was excommunicated from the Catholic Church because of his Republicanism. He was refused Mass and the sacraments; in an act of youthful bravado, Republican youngsters walked defiantly out of the church. His stubbornness and single-mindedness are demonstrated by the fact that he abandoned the Church and, although some of his closest friends were priests, he was very critical of the institutional Church all his life. This broke his mother's heart and she was always praying for him and forever sewing miraculous medals onto his clothes, with no success. In those days a miraculous medal to Michael was like a cross to Dracula.

3. REBEL IN LOVE

JUST BEFORE CHRISTMAS 1923 MICHAEL WAS RELEASED FROM Gormanstown. At first he wouldn't believe the news brought to him by an excited prisoner; the hurt from the cruel tomfoolery and pranks of the men in the goods department still lingered. After several reassurances he gathered up his little library of poetry in Spanish, German and Gaelic in a parcel, signed some release forms and was quickly gone. Bewildered and unsure, he was again a free man. Once outside the camp he had difficulty in suppressing the desire to make a run for it. He stayed overnight in Dublin and arrived in Cork late the following day.

The homecoming was a bit of an anti-climax. Big Mick, who had never agreed with his son's politics, shook his hand and immediately retired to the pub. Minnie was overjoyed to have her 'little boy' home again, but it didn't take long for her to see that he had changed. Physically he had put on weight, but she quickly realised that his utter dependence on her was gone; the apron strings were well and truly cut. She cried quiet tears of understanding and told him, 'It made a man of you.'

Michael was also aware that he had grown and that things would never be the same again. It took him some time to get used to sleeping alone in his little attic again after nearly a year in the goldfish-bowl conditions of Gormanstown. Sifting through his orange box of books gave him the feeling of being reintroduced to old friends. While he was interned he had won first prize, worth seven pounds, for his Turgenev essay but he never received the much-needed money as there was no cash left in the fund. Daniel Corkery himself had also won that same prize many years previously.

As Michael had changed, so, too, had Cork. The city was in the throes of rebuilding. The young man didn't attend Sunday Mass now, much to his mother's dismay; news of this fact spread very quickly and he was taunted and avoided because of 'his loss of faith'. His refusal to go on hunger-strike was similarly frowned on and thrown in his face in Cork which was, after all, the home of Terence MacSwiney. MacSwiney's gaunt features after what was, in the end, a futile gesture may have influenced Michael's unusual yet extremely courageous decision. He tried in vain to find work but soon discovered that, having been on the losing side in the war, naturally enough, all the best jobs were given to the victors. To everyone's relief a general amnesty was declared in March and all prisoners were released (and also looking for work). After a month he got a job teaching Irish to the teachers in the nearby Protestant school, St Luke's. The wages were poor but he had improved as a teacher and he enjoyed the work. His boss, Mr Kenneally, was devoutly anti-religious; he was against every religion, but later surprised everyone by becoming a Catholic priest.

Michael struggled to get by; he was always broke, trying as best he could to write when he got the chance. At night he took long walks into the countryside until Daniel Corkery, aware of his plight, once again came to his rescue when he arranged an interview with Lennox Robinson, playwright and secretary of the Irish Carnegie Trust, who was looking for young people to train as rural librarians. The interview took place in the bar of the Glanmire Road Station and, after an in-depth grilling, Michael got the job. His mother packed his suitcase including a big holy picture of the Sacred Heart and, wearing his father's old trousers, he set off for Sligo.

It was a dream come true; at last he had enough books to read. His salary was thirty shillings a week and his digs cost twenty-seven and sixpence. He was left with practically nothing for cigarettes, and he soon discovered that it was more economical to post his dirty laundry home every week. Minnie washed it, giving her the maternal satisfaction of still looking after her son, and she posted it back each time including five shillings for himself. Again, God only knows where she got it. He very often bought books instead of food with this money, a practice which certainly didn't help his stomach problem. His short stay in Sligo was relatively uneventful; one of the highlights was a quiet celebration of his twenty-first birthday.

He was assistant librarian to Robert Wilson, a parson's son and convert to Catholicism. Just four years older than Michael, Wilson was an extremely kind and generous man. He was married to a stuffy

Englishwoman and Michael was regularly invited to their home for supper. He hated these evenings and was always self-conscious and uncomfortable when dining out, as he vividly describes at the beginning of this letter to Seán Hendrick tinged with tongue-in-cheek sarcasm:

> County Book Repository
> Sligo
> Dear Jack,
>   I am beginning this letter in what is for me the most unpleasant of moods, that which comes on me just before I go to fulfil my social functions as Assistant Librarian. I must spend an hour with the Wilsons, which means that I must make an unmannerly and noisy cup of tea behave itself while I dispose of it as gracefully as possible, modulate my Rabelaisian laughter to the dulcet mirth of my hosts, refrain from expressing the obscene sentiments which I feel when certain subjects are broached, and in general deport myself as little like a man of literary capacity as possible. There is I find a good deal in Lennox Robinson's remark about suppressed sex.
>   This is not to say, however, that I do not enjoy myself in the company of the Wilsons. As a matter of fact they are the most charming people one could wish to meet. I think you know me sufficiently by this time to realise that to anybody brought up to observe the rules of thought I shall always appear rather *outré*.

For years, Robert Wilson lived out the charade of a happily married man when, in effect, he was secretly gay. The trauma ended when his wife died and he happily and openly declared his sexuality.

In Sligo, Michael was a member of the sub-committee in charge of finance; this, in hindsight, is surprising because throughout his life he had a strong dislike of committees and treated them all with equal suspicion. He stayed at a house in John Street owned by an ex-officer of the Free State Army who was a staunch nationalist. When drink took hold of him and caused his Irish passion to rise, he opened his window and played 'The Soldier's Song' at full blast. Unfortunately, an equally loyal Protestant who lived directly across the street hurled insults and reciprocated by playing 'God Save the King' at an equally ear-shattering volume. With both anthems playing simultaneously practically every night, it must have been very difficult for the young Michael to write anything.

While he was in Sligo his boss Lennox Robinson was fired from his library position because of a controversial story he wrote in a new periodical called *Tomorrow*. In August 1924 'The Madonna of Slieve Dún' appeared and caused ecclesiastical consternation. The Church was immediately up in arms. In the story Robinson described how a single country girl thought that she had been visited by the Holy Spirit, in the same way as Christ's mother, and had given birth in similarly mysterious fashion. The country was shocked and, in the hail of indignation, Robinson duly lost his job. Michael was very worried about holding on to his own job, so this episode was a timely warning to him.

After some months, when he was just settling down in Sligo, he was suddenly transferred to Wicklow where a new library was to be opened. His fellow assistant had left a religious seminary for a life of books but later abandoned the library to go back to the priesthood. In a few short months the impressionable young Michael had worked with an anticlerical headmaster who became a priest, a married parson's son and convert to Catholicism who was secretly homosexual, and a librarian who opted for ordination. This insecurity and intellectual wavering in all matters to do with religion, nationalism and sexuality sums up the Ireland of the 1920s; it must have left an indelible mark on the budding young writer with his creative mind looking objectively at the whole scenario, and was surely a great source of material.

At first Michael was frustrated and disillusioned in his Wicklow library. He was very proud of his large selection of poetry books on display. The only problem was that not only did nobody ever come into his quiet little library but, to his utter disappointment, no one ever seemed to read poetry. Then, one day, a local man approached his desk.

'Excuse me, but could you ever tell me where I'd get a book on poetry, please?' he asked.

Michael was delighted. He pointed across the floor. 'The poetry section is over there in the corner,' he said.

The man thanked him and, for a few moments, browsed through several books before returning to the desk with a puzzled look on his face. 'There's nothing over there except a load of books on sayings and poems and all that kind of stuff,' he said.

The young librarian was equally confused. 'I thought you wanted a book on poetry?' he said.

The man scratched his head. 'No. I said "poultry" – chickens,' he replied, storming out the door.

Michael was left ruefully reflecting on the probability of another soul lost to his world of poetry.

The Wicklow library very nearly didn't open at all. Ever since that 'blasphemous' Lennox Robinson story, the hierarchy in Ireland frowned on books. It was feared that reading could be a potentially dangerous pastime and there was great concern about what the 'poor ignorant natives' read. At a vital committee meeting Michael, who was wise to the machinations of the Irish clergy, enlisted the help of a staunch nationalist and practising Catholic to help sway the vote in the library's favour. His fellow librarian in Wicklow, Geoffrey Phibbs, who was as enthusiastic about poetry as himself, was a Sligo Protestant with an English education.

Although from a completely different background, he became a great friend of Phibbs. Michael tried to teach him Irish and was amused when he began to occasionally use the pseudonym Seathrun MacPhilip. Phibbs was an instant, intuitive poet. There was no dilly-dallying with him as he dashed out up to half a dozen poems a day on any given subject; he never bothered about unimportant things like spelling or grammar; all that was left to his serious young friend. He had no special preference as to subject-matter and composed poems on pornography, unrequited love or just how he felt at that particular moment. But Michael toiled meticulously over each line, writing and carefully rewriting, until eventually he was happy with the end product. Sometimes, when they were working together in the library, Phibbs would suddenly grab a piece of paper and, within minutes, scribble out a quite brilliant poem. They became unlikely friends; the raw provincial and the educated Protestant; blood brothers; two young poets in love with poetry.

Michael still struggled on his meagre salary; one night every week he borrowed the library bicycle and cycled out to the Wicklow mountains to teach Irish. He received five shillings for this service. The pupil was an old teacher caught up in the wave of nationalism who was forced to learn Irish or lose his job. When Phibbs learned of Michael's lack of money, he wrote an angry letter to the library authorities. It worked: Michael's salary was immediately doubled. He couldn't believe the change in his financial situation and when he went home on holiday he discarded Big Mick's hand-me-downs and got his Aunt Annie's husband, Pat Hanlon from Glasgow, to make a new suit for him, his first since he was a child. He also acquired two new green shirts, surely as a result of Phibbs' influence. The old couple were both deaf and dumb. All his life his Uncle Pat seemed to spend most of his time popping in and out of their little house in Harrington Square. He was a natural wit and mimic and his nephew was always very fond of him.

Inadvertently, Phibbs introduced Michael to the Dublin literary scene. A week previously he had sent a scathing letter to the *Irish Statesman* attacking the editor, George Russell, Yeats and the Irish Literary Renaissance; but it annoyed him when Russell had only laughed at his letter, so he invited Michael to accompany him on the twenty-mile train journey to Russell's house in Merrion Square to give him a piece of his mind. Russell was better known as AE, an abbreviation of an earlier pen-name, Aeon, suggesting mankind's age-old, mysterious quest for truth: his constant theme. An Ulster Protestant from the fiercely pro-British town of Lurgan, he had acted in a most untypical manner by supporting the 1916 rising in Dublin. This did not go down too well with his Northern brethren. Michael, in a mood of light-hearted conspiracy, wrote to a friend looking for long-distance support:

> Phibbs has written a violent letter to the *Statesman* attacking the 'literary language' of our Dublin friends. The letter will appear in the issue of next Thursday and as both Phibbs and myself are going to write under both our own names and the names of kindly Christians that never existed, attacking the movement and defending it, we want your support. Get the paper (for one week only) and you will find Russell answering it. Then, in your most brilliant and final manner, dispose of the letter entirely (you can use a pseudonym only, let it be plausible – 'Augustine Delamore Baldwin, Sunnyside, Cork' will do). Then watch out and smite Augustine smite and thigh. At

any rate, help us to dispose of the Irish Literary Renaissance in a suitably undignified manner!

We reserve to ourselves the following phrase: 'Mr Phibbs has decided to constitute himself the Wordsworth of the Irish Literary Movement', and the enevitable reply that 'a man of Mr Anon's literary acumen should be aware that an individual can scarcely constitute himself into anything other than his component elements'.

I am holding on to *Ulysses* for you. I should be afraid to send it through the post but I shall probably see you on the 1st.

Slán is beannacht,
Micheal

AE was a big, bearded bear of a man who was generous to a fault. Phibbs was infuriated by AE's cheerfully indifferent response and thought him pompous, but Michael and he seemed to hit it off and, as he was leaving, he put a paternal arm around the young man's shoulder and asked him to send in something for publication. Michael was now writing more and more poetry and working hard on translations from the old Irish. That week he sent AE a verse translation, *Suibhne Geilt Aspires*, and it appeared in the edition of the *Irish Statesman* on 14 March 1925.

Suibhne Geilt Aspires was shown as translated by Frank O'Connor. It was the first time this pseudonym was used. He realised he was treading in dangerous water; a writer and a librarian, and with the Lennox Robinson dismissal in mind, he took his mother's maiden name, O'Connor, and his own middle name, Francis. (His confirmation names were Francis Xavier. He was confirmed at the very young age of ten, which showed that he was good at religion classes. Even though he missed school a lot, his mother would have ensured that he was well versed in his catechism. Around the time he made his confirmation he had high hopes of joining the priesthood.)

The *Irish Statesman* had a very high standard of journalism; Gogarty, Lennox Robinson, P.S. O'Hegarty and Seán O'Casey were regular contributors; even Phibbs condescended to write some blindingly critical letters to it.

AE called O'Connor his discovery; the young man was delighted with his overnight fame but from a more practical point of view the extra money was a big help. For the rest of that year, with plenty of encouragement from AE, he submitted translations, some controversial letters and a book review. The poor boy from Cork was making a name for himself and was quickly becoming accepted in Dublin's artistic circles. AE invited him to his home every Sunday evening and bombarded him with obscure European literature and Greek art and smothered him with affection and advice. Michael usually left burdened down with books of every description. AE, anxious to show off his protégé, introduced him to Lady Gregory, the playwright and co-founder of the Abbey Theatre, and William Butler Yeats, one of the greatest poets of the twentieth century.*

Yeats asked Michael along to his home for his Monday night get-togethers. The young librarian was now rubbing shoulders and holding his own with the likes of Osborn Bergin, Séamus O'Sullivan, Lennox Robinson, Sarah Purser, Francis Stuart and George Moore. Conscious of his background, nervous and inexperienced in the social graces (it must be remembered that just a year or two previously he had been a frightened young boy on the run, sleeping in ditches), he often spoke too loudly and too long to cover up his incurable shyness. It was frequently the same in female company. It must have been amusing to observe the twenty-one-year-old country boy impatiently getting his point across to the mercurial William Butler Yeats. But Yeats admired him greatly, treated him as an equal, and became a close friend, hero and father figure, and really appreciated his brilliant translations from Irish.

Although often bored in his Wicklow library, Michael really looked forward to and relished these weekly visits to the capital where books, poets, literature, the classics and all the relevant Dublin scandal were discussed, dissected and analysed in mischievous detail. He was just finding his feet when, suddenly, an important library position came up in Cork. AE begged him to stay in Wicklow because of its nearness to Dublin and said he felt it was a backward step returning south. Michael ignored him. His application was successful and to his delight he got the job. On 19 December 1925, at just twenty-two years of age, he became Cork's first county librarian. His salary of five pounds a week

---

* It has been said that Lady Gregory was in love with Yeats. He did regularly stay in Coole Park and she kept a special room aside so that he could write poetry in private. One day she was showing off to English visitors by allowing them to peep in the window at the great man. He was scratching his bottom at the time which shows that he was only human.

was more than anyone in Harrington Square had ever dreamed of earning. Big Mick, a lover of pensions, was very impressed that a pension went with his son's new job, but to his mother the title and his picture in the paper were reward enough. The years of selfless sacrifice had paid off. She was puzzled that her son wrote under a different name but she was very proud and gave him every encouragement. All the jealous, sniggering whispers about her useless, daydreaming son were well and truly buried. Big Mick, too, had a certain status in Harrington Square. He was now a respected, part-time docker with two pensions and a son in charge of the library. Although still a little dubious as to whether his son's job would last or not, he retired to the pub to spread the good news.

Michael settled in very quickly. With his newfound wealth and no rent to pay, he bought some furniture, a roll of lino for the floor and a gramophone. Minnie insisted on a new gas light in his room to make it easier on his eyes when writing. He wanted to really splash out and buy a new house in a different part of Cork. His mother was delighted but Big Mick wouldn't budge. Like a stubborn old soldier in the front line, he was entrenched in the Barrack Stream.

The opening of any new library was treated with suspicion by large sections of the clergy. The scandal of the Lennox Robinson incident was still fresh in their minds and most library committees were full of priests keeping a watchful eye on proceedings. The Church was genuinely worried. Books were looked on as an occasion of sin and a danger to the immortal soul.

Michael was delighted to be back in Cork. Once again he was in familiar territory and could call uninvited to his friends' houses, and he really enjoyed his long stimulating walks with O'Faoláin and Hendrick. But after just one month he realised that AE was right. He was bored stiff with the parochialism of Cork. It was one thing to be living in Dublin pining for home, but he had changed and felt stifled and longed for the intoxication of Yeats, AE, Phibbs and Grafton Street.

To compensate, he tore into his work. The city centre was still in the process of rebuilding and as yet there was no library building. For some months he worked from a temporary office in the courthouse. It must have been no easy job for a relatively inexperienced person to start a library from scratch. Amongst many other things he had to secure staff, books and a building. Although burdened with bureaucracy, he did eventually open his library over a shop at 25 Patrick Street. As expected, it was far from easy. He was soon to be embroiled in the politics of the Cork County Council. The mechanics of library life might have been quiet and pedantic in Sligo and Wicklow, but in Cork it was a completely different matter. To his utter frustration, what took five minutes in Wicklow took five months in Cork. Every decision he made had to be approved by a sub-committee of 110 people, and some members of the council would have nothing to do with him simply because he wore a green shirt.

On his first morning at work he went for a ten o'clock interview with the secretary of the County Council. The man was at Mass and turned up at eleven-thirty. Then, when Michael was trying to get some work done, the angelus bell rang and the secretary immediately knelt up on the table, lost in fervent prayer. That was the end of the interview. He left the room frustrated with the religious Irishness of the Irish. He had, reluctantly, in his possession a large library cheque. He wanted to bank it as soon as possible so, in his naïvety, he decided to be practical. That was another mistake. In his innocence, he lodged it in the nearest and more convenient bank which, unfortunately for him, was the 'wrong bank'; it was Protestant. The 'right' bank, the Catholic one, was some distance away. Several committee members objected and angrily accused him of trying to pocket the money. The whole fiasco was a comedy of errors and he nearly lost his job. (At that time, sectarianism was still prevalent. In Situations Vacant advertisements the proviso, 'No Catholics Need Apply', was displayed in many windows.)

His friendship with Daniel Corkery was also changing. While Michael, full of enthusiasm, had wider European aims and ambitions, the ever-gentle Corkery was a staunch Irishian but a provincial to the end. Michael was caught between two stools of language. He didn't know whether he should write in Irish or in English; Corkery favoured the former and advised him to stick with Gaelic, but Seán O'Faoláin, who now had his degree, was writing full-time exclusively in English.

Michael wrote non-stop, mostly poetry and translations, every night when he arrived home from the library. AE was delighted to publish everything he wrote. All through 1926 the *Irish Statesman* wasn't complete without a poem or an article by Frank O'Connor; one interesting translation, 'Celibacy', appeared in February. He was also a contributor to the *Irish Tribune*.

He became very ill again from overwork and bronchitis. His heavy smoking didn't help his lungs and Cork, with its valleys and marsh-like environment, only added to this problem. By July he was so sick that he had to miss work and rest for eight weeks. He took a short continental holiday which helped his recuperation no end. While relaxing and taking the sun on the Belgian coast, he had an acute attack of narcissism and impulsively purchased a large black-brimmed hat. When he arrived home he strutted up and down Patrick Street, complete with green shirt, black bow-tie and black hat cocked jauntily on the side of his head, much to the amusement and embarrassment of his friends. At long last he could call himself a poet. People now knew him as the man who was the head of the library and writing in the Dublin magazines.

He was becoming increasingly disillusioned with Cork. He was not one to be wasting his time with the mundane mechanics and the tedious technicalities of everyday library work, and the staff often sighed with relief when he wasn't in the building getting in their way. He was much more interested in people and spent all his time engrossed in animated conversation with them while, to the dismay of his assistants, the waiting queues grew longer and longer. He also kept a watchful eye on which books each borrowed, often sneaking a look when a particularly attractive girl returned a book after reading it. On discovering that it was a western or something he felt didn't do her justice, he would be deeply disappointed.

He was also beginning to spend more and more of his time out of the library. If people didn't come to him then he insisted on bringing books to them: Russian books, Greek books, any books. The library bought a van and every chance he got he travelled around the county, especially West Cork, and pushed books. He didn't care what the people read, even if it was only weekly magazines. He still felt claustrophobic in Cork and letters from O'Faoláin, who had gone off to Harvard University, only made him more frustrated. Two trips to Dublin on library business, where he met Phibbs, helped to ease the boredom.

On 8 August 1927 Hilton Edwards and Michael MacLiammóir brought a play, *The High-Steppers*, to Cork's Pavilion Theatre for a week. It was a huge success and after the opening Monday night a party was held at Mount Verdon Villa, the home of their old friend, Seán Neeson. Michael was one of the guests. He found that he had a great deal in common with MacLiammóir; they both loved languages, especially Irish, and during a long conversation MacLiammóir gave him every encouragement to revive theatre in Cork. Michael was inspired and, with the help of Seán Neeson and Hendrick, was instumental in forming the Cork Drama League. Opera House director J.J. Horgan was at the helm as president. Michael was appointed producer and Seán Hendrick was to be stage manager. The fact that Michael knew even less about producing than he did about being a librarian and that Hendrick knew absolutely nothing about stage managing a play wasn't given a second thought. As he was wont to do, Michael tore headlong into his job. He devoured every book available on every aspect of theatre and launched himself at this new task with a furious enthusiam.

The first decision was to find a suitable play. Lennox Robinson was approached and asked for permission to stage his comedy, *The Round Table*. Robinson agreed and rewrote relevant sections of it to suit them. He kindly waived all royalty rights which was of great financial help to the new group.

The next hurdle was a rehearsal venue. Seán Neeson stepped in and arranged a room in the Radio Eireann studio which was in a wing of the old Women's Jail in Sunday's Well, a place Michael had known only too well in different circumstances.

Finding a cast of fourteen was another problem. Many of them doubled up with two parts but he was finding it particularly difficult to cast Daisy Drennan, one of the main roles. One evening Geraldine Neeson brought along a pretty young girl to audition and, although she had a terrible stammer, she was a natural actress. Not alone did she get the part but that night Michael walked her home and from then on Nancy McCarthy became his leading lady.

The Drama League decided to be bold and put on Chekhov's *The Bear* as a curtain-raiser. Seán Neeson directed it and played De Courcy Drennan in *The Round Table* under the pseudonym Joseph Gilmour. His wife, Geraldine, appeared in both plays with Michael, who did just about everything else, including writing the programme notes. Rehearsals were long and intense; Michael demanded and got perfection. Eventually, the Cork Drama League made its début in Gregg Hall for two nights only in February 1928. In his programme notes Michael stated ambitiously that they hoped to aim high and stage six plays a year.

Their first venture exceeded all their expectations. The reviews were excellent. Several of the cast were mentioned for their performances and Nancy was picked out for special praise. One critic said, 'The acting was of a high standard and won much applause as the audience demonstrated its delight.' It was another cause for celebration to find that it was a box-office success. They made thirty pounds clear profit. It was decided to invest in a set of stage flats and, led by Michael, they painted them. He was happy enough with his début as a producer and, even though the group intended to give preference to Irish playwrights, he passionately wanted to spread his theatrical wings and experiment with the likes of Molière and Ibsen. Their first comedy went so well that he opted for a second, Chekhov's *The Cherry Orchard*. The opening night was set for April and, with practically the same cast, they went straight into rehearsals. The play was just coming together when, one night, while seeing Nancy home, he felt very ill and was rushed to the Bon Secours Hospital for an emergency operation to remove his appendix. The hospital was run by nuns and they were shocked when the patient refused point-blank to have confession and communion, as was the custom, before the operation. They called on Nancy to plead with him but she knew his stubborn streak better than most and told them that they were wasting their time. Michael dug his heels in and refused to see the priest. He was adamant that he wouldn't receive the sacraments now after being refused in Gormanstown.

The play was put on hold until he got back on his feet and after a delay of a few weeks *The Cherry Orchard* opened on 7 May for two nights with Michael again appearing and producing. It was critically acclaimed and received standing ovations. The Cork Drama League were on their way.

Then, a local priest, Father O'Flynn, who had founded the Cork Shakespearean Society in the Loft started attacking them in print. Lennox Robinson had praised the Drama League for their high standard and the priest reacted by publicly criticising Robinson. As could be expected, Michael jumped in to defend Robinson and he and O'Flynn exchanged four rather unfriendly letters in the *Examiner*, trading insults. Father O'Flynn said that Michael would go down to posterity at the head of the pagan Dublin muses. He accused him of putting on unclean and agnostic plays and referred to Seán O'Casey as a down-and-out Dublin playwright. He signed his correspondence 'The Producer'. Michael replied, using his name in Irish, stating that at least *Shadow of a Gunman* could be performed without the use of the blue pencil and that Shakespeare's plays were staged with all the dirty words crossed out. He signed off by saying that the masterpieces of the amiable and lofty Mr Shakespeare put him to sleep. Not to be outdone, Father O'Flynn reciprocated by remarking in a derogatory way that he was a 'Mike the moke' ('moke' is slang for donkey) and sarcastically headed his letter with a quotation from Byron, 'Fools are my theme, let satire be my song'. Seán Hendrick didn't stand idly by; he got his dander up and had a few well-timed little digs at the priest, signing his letters 'Spectator'. Ironically, for years, Michael had been an ardent student of the Bard and many years later he wrote a book on him, *The Road to Stratford*, which did very well. Although Michael and O'Flynn seemed to be at each other's throats, they were more alike than they cared to admit: they both loved theatre; they both loved Irish; but, of course, they were two proud, obstinate Corkmen.

By now Michael was hopelessly in love with Nancy McCarthy. She was to flit in and out of his life until the day he died. That summer they went off to Donegal together for three weeks. She told her father that she was going on a holiday with a friend – without saying who the friend was. Her father had ten children so he had enough on his mind. Off they went, all alone, but things didn't go according to plan. Nancy was apprehensive about their unchaperoned stay in Donegal and was tense and uncomfortable all through the holiday. Worse still, the weather was dreadful; it didn't stop raining for three weeks. Another dampener on the romance was that they stayed in houses three miles apart and Michael was drenched every night seeing her home and then trudging miserably back to his own residence in the pouring rain.

After a month he decided to bring her up to Harrington Square to show her off to his mother. She was the first girl he had ever brought home. Minnie was very wary of her; she was polite but conscious that Nancy might take her son away from her. Up until then she had been the only woman in his life. On that first visit she showed Nancy to the kitchen and made cocoa and biscuits and then discreetly disappeared.

Nancy was an extremely religious girl; she was a daily communicant. For eighteen months Michael met her every day outside St Peter and Paul's church after Mass. He proposed to her over a hundred times but, although she loved him, she just would not marry him. They walked all over the hills and dales of the city and talked incessantly. He pointed out all the places that mattered to him, told her of all the things that had happened there and generally gave her a deeper insight into and a wider appreciation of the recent history of Cork. He introduced her to art and literature and opened her mind to music, mainly Mozart, who was his favourite.

Nancy McCarthy was a captivating woman. The first time we met, many years ago, she was in a heated discussion with a priest over some religious disagreement. For an hour the argument waged to and fro until, eventually, the unfortunate priest threw his hands in the air in a gesture of defeat. 'All right. All right, Nancy. I give up. You're right,' he said in despair.

'I know I'm right, Father. I've been trying to tell you that for the last hour but you wouldn't listen,' she answered in triumph.

Another day, I spotted her walking her poodles near her home; at the time she was in her eighties. I crossed the Douglas Road and hurried after her. It was a cold winter day and she was well muffled up against the wind.

'How are you, Nancy? You're looking great,' I said.

She looked me up and down with a gleam in her eye. 'I'm not looking great and well you know it,' she said and strutted off like Helen of Troy and left me standing there in her wake. That was Nance.

The Cherry Orchard finished its two-night run on 8 May 1928. The next day Michael gave Nancy a poem called 'The Play'. It was long and dramatic and in it he poured out his undying love for her. He signed it '*Ich Liebe Dich*, M'. Still lovesick, he immediately wrote another two poems, 'The Sonnet' and 'The Hawk'. The latter was published in the *Irish Statesman* on 18 August 1928. In it, the word 'unattainable' jumps out at the reader.

THE HAWK

Profound, monotonous summer days
Too full to speak their peace
Brooded upon the hills
And on the ragged fields,
Pitted with filmy rock and hidden streams
That from the mountains break –
You murmured with a smile
'If deeper silence than their own can be
Surely it falls today upon the lake
At Gougane Barra and the holy isle.'

We lifted up our eyes and saw the hawk,
And suddenly my heart stood still,
He hung above a distant rock
On fluttering wings until
For very pride he hovered motionless
Remote and beautiful and dark,
And robbed the world of peace
And woke a world of anguish in my heart.

My foolish heart
That no remembrance keeps,
My heart that seeks you always while it sleeps,
My sorry heart
That wakes to find you still
Remote, still dear, still unattainable.

And still is dumb. I did not say to you
'When reason breaks
Our sky of summer blue
Its shadow makes
Life be where there should have been none,
And mother of that brood, the heart
Dwells with imaginations cold as stone,
Vivid as music, while she wakes.'

Still frustrated with the bureaucracy of his library work and its continuous small-town attitude, he applied for a new post in Dublin. Cork was closing in on him and the stifling parochialism was slowly choking him. He quickly came to realise that in Cork practically anything was accepted except success; success was frowned on. It was a case of local boy making good, but not *too* good.

When AE learned that a new library position was available in Dublin, he hounded the offices in charge of libraries and assured – even demanded – that Michael was the only man in Ireland for the job. He wanted his young discovery back under his literary wing again. Michael got the job and travelled to Dublin in September to undergo a medical.

Meanwhile, he had booked the Cork AOH Hall* to open the Drama League's programme on Monday, 26 November, with Ibsen's *The Doll's House*. As brave and experimental as ever, they decided to stage Robinson's *Crabbed Youth and Age* as a curtain-raiser. Again, the hard-working cast doubled up. By October, as rehearsals were in full swing, Michael got a letter officially notifying him that his application for the post at Dublin's Ballsbridge library had been successful. He still looked on it as only a temporary escape, a stop-gap, until he eventually returned home again.

By the end of November things began to go from bad to worse. Father O'Flynn came back to haunt him. One actress refused to say the word 'mistress' and wanted it crossed out. A fellow actor agreed with her because he was under pressure – he had a cousin who was a bishop. Michael nearly tore his hair out. Then, on the night of the dress rehearsal, the leading man mysteriously went missing. It later materialised that there had been veiled threats by Father O'Flynn. The actor was warned that if he went ahead and appeared in the play there was a strong possibility he would lose his job. Pandemonium set in. The show had to be postponed for one night while Michael worked furiously to learn the part. He gave a fine portrayal of Torvald Helmer, the leading male character, on the Tuesday night to high acclaim all round. Nancy was 'beyond praise' and said to be 'gifted' and 'outstanding'. Michael's acting was 'particularly fine' and the League were called 'a remarkable band of local artistes'. Interestingly, although the programme showed that the plays were down for only two nights, they decided to do an additional performance on the Thursday. The venture

---

* Ancient Order of Hibernia

didn't work out. The standard was excellent but, sadly, there just weren't enough theatre-goers in Cork and they lost heavily. That whole sorry experience, plus his lack of success with Nancy, is encapsulated in the humorously prophetic words of Seán O'Faoláin:

> To succeed in Cork you have to have the skin of a rhinoceros, the dissimulation of a crocodile, the agility of a hare, the speed of a hawk. Otherwise the word for every young Corkman is – 'Get out – and get out quick!'

4. THE PEMBROKE LIBRARIAN

ON SATURDAY MORNING, 1 DECEMBER 1928, MICHAEL ATTENDED a committee meeting at the Cork County Library to nominate his successor. Three priests, a Christian Brother and a teacher were present as he read out a letter from the Gaelic League who were unashamedly pushing their man, an Irish speaker, for the vacancy. Michael also wanted this man for the position but he had to be careful not to show his hand. The rest of the committee were reluctant at first; they didn't like being told what to do, but after a long and sometimes heated debate he finally swayed them to his way of thinking and his man got the job. Later that day, with a heavy heart, he packed his bags, including his green shirts and, with mixed feelings, left home. He realised, for the time being anyway, that Cork had stretched his patience to breaking point.

He decided to pay a visit to Wicklow before going on to Dublin, so he took the train via Waterford and Phibbs met him at the little station. By now Phibbs had married Norah McGuinness, a painter, but things were not well with the couple. Surrounded by a brittle veil of poetry, literature and painting, they were living in a hazy world of bohemian existence where free love, intrigue, illicit liaisons and live-in lovers were the accepted norm. Like true friends, Phibbs and Michael had no secrets between them. They frequently discussed, in minute, intimate detail, everything from scandal and sex to religion and writing; but Michael sensed that there was something amiss. His friend was unusually reticent and subdued; he was lifeless and acted like a man with the weight of the world on his shoulders. Phibbs confessed his troubled love-life and begged for advice. It came as something of a surprise to Michael that an educated, carefree man of the world like Phibbs should ask him for guidance in matters of the heart. He was flattered and tried to look wise but when it came to romance he was a complete novice. Although many years later he was to gain a notorious reputation, in reality he was a relatively late starter and didn't 'discover' women until he was in his thirties. He stated that, up to then, he had only ever kissed three women. His romantic entanglements were filled with platonic innocence, such as the innocuous teasing by the girls while he stayed in the French house during the Civil War.*

Another 'sexual' encounter was when he was seventeen. While attending a ceili dance in Blarney, a pretty girl in the corner happened to catch his eye. He took his courage in both hands and asked her if he could drive her home. She agreed and duly climbed aboard his bicycle. As he pedalled furiously, she stood on a bar which went through the back wheel and grimly hung onto the saddle for dear life. The rocky six-mile experience back to the city would not have been the most romantic in the world. At that time all the beautiful women in his life were either in his head, in Russian literature or in some steamy French novel. And Phibbs was seeking *his* advice; he must have been desperate! In January the unhappy couple left for London. This was a terrible letdown to Michael. The main reason he took the Dublin job was so he could be near his fellow poet and visit his bungalow as often as possible. Sadly, the Phibbs' marriage broke up and after a family row Geoffrey Phibbs changed his name to Taylor by deed poll. He went on to teach English in Cairo and later became a biologist; but he didn't forget Michael and posted him regular batches of poetry: good, indifferent, bad and brilliant.

Michael kept writing at a furious pace, mostly poems and translations, and sent them to the *Dublin Magazine* and the *Irish Statesman*. His weekly visits to AE and Yeats were resumed; there was a lot of catching up to do. He was now in Dublin, a great city of great writers and, more than anything, he wanted to be a writer.

He missed Phibbs and his old friend O'Faoláin who had married his childhood sweetheart, Eileen, but he had more immediate things on his mind: there was a library to be opened. On his first visit to the

---

* I once met a woman from the southside of Cork City who confided in me that she had gone out two nights with him.

'Well, what kind was he?' I asked.

'He wore black boots, long woollen socks, leather gloves and he was very tacky,' she replied.

When I asked her what she meant by 'tacky', she smiled coyly but refused to kiss and tell. He was at a very impressionable age and his clothes may have been an attempt to imitate the older and more flamboyant O'Faoláin. It must be remembered that when O'Connor was eighteen and struggling, O'Faoláin dressed in a suit, rode a motorbike, possessed his own bankbook and cultivated an audacious pencil-slim moustache. O'Connor acquired a similiar moustache the following year.

Pembroke District Library he was very disappointed; it was a small, old building. First of all, he had to find a staff and, even more important, a capable assistant. One of the first to apply was Dermot Foley, a fastidious, articulate young Dublinman, a trained librarian who took great pride in his thorough knowledge of the technical workings of a library. The interview with Michael was a disaster but he still got the job. Initially, he didn't get along with his blustering, impatient boss. For a while there were only the two of them in the building and Dermot felt under constant pressure because everything he did was deemed to be wrong. Michael usually swept through the library like a roaring tornado leaving everything scattered in his wake. He had a voice like thunder; it came up from the valleys of Cork and when he raised it even the windows seemed to rattle. They had met three years previously at a library convention in Cork. Dermot remembered the noble head and the unruly mop of hair thrown back like the wild mane of a stallion. That vibrating bass trombone voice was equally unforgettable.

Then, for no apparent reason, the animosity between them disappeared as Dermot slowly discovered that behind the tempestuous, dogmatic mask lurked a shy, nervous man. He decided that, no matter what Michael pontificated upon, he would smile, nod his head and apprehensively agree with him. He was very conscious that if they continued at the rate they were progressing, the library would never be opened in time. On each occasion when he felt he was just getting on top of the situation, Michael would come along with a flashing sword and blast all his plans and good intentions to smithereens; it was a bad place to be a dragon. But, determined and efficient, Dermot persisted in his methods and organisation and, eventually, he won Michael over to his way of proper librarianship. At the same time, he didn't realise the amount of pressure his boss was under and the tension didn't help his gastritis.

They became great friends and Michael was forever giving him books to read. After work he walked with him and talked in ceaseless animation about Cork. On one of these walks his vulnerability surfaced as he intervened when a young hooligan was beating an old woman. The youth turned and attacked Michael but his more streetwise companion quickly stepped in and sent the aggressor packing. Dermot became a regular visitor to both AE's and Yeats's homes and, although he was a fine speaker, he preferred to linger in the background and admire his friend's non-stop flow of brilliant invective. The only person who could really make Michael sit up and listen was AE, and he paid his young protégé a compliment by doing a beautiful pencil portrait of him.

On Friday, 27 September, the two men finally opened their library to the public. Michael's next step was to recruit a team of junior assistant librarians. He found it an impossible task. An excerpt from a letter to a friend in Cork dated 13 April 1929 sums up his feelings:

> I have disposed of an examination for junior assistants and come to the conclusion that Ireland is illiterate. Had my eye upon a most lovely girl whom I should have been glad to appoint but you should have seen her General Lack of Knowledge paper. Incredible. Marie Antoinette was a French lady who became religious and took to nursing soldiers during the war. (Another said she was a well-known author, and a third that she was a character in one of Mrs Henry Wood's novels.) Boswell was the founder member of the Salvation Army and died of a broken heart. ET 'I think T.M. Kettle is a member of the Rathmines UDC but there is of course the famous Captain Kettle.' Khyber Pass is in the Donegal Mountains and was fiercely defended by the Irish against the English soldiers. Alexandria, founded by Alexandria the Great, is a famous port in America, principally noted for its exports of cotton. Pepys is a character in a play called *And So to Bed.* Schubert was a great musician who wrote many beautiful sonnets.
>
> Holy God, me mind is like a bloody public lavatory! Give Kitty my love. I should like to write but what can one say that is better than saying nothing? And I should write so much more easily if I had not liked the old man! No, it's better to say nothing, however vacant that may appear.
>
> Corkery patted your show rather on the back, except for Nance McCarthy and Helen Nagle whom he pronounced dreadful. They should both be fired, he said. But he did obviously feel hopeless about it, he does! he

would! Sat with him for a whole hour and not a single spar. Two minds with but a – I feel virtuous! it is like the whore's night off.
Love
M

In Michael's first house his fellow lodger was a devout Catholic. This walking saint gently woke him for work every morning before going off to early Mass. He tried unsuccessfully to get Michael to attend church with him and then, like a true saint, explained that God would understand so he went to two Masses – one for himself and one for Michael. Then he asked him if he'd like to be a regular subscriber to a Catholic charity. Michael just laughed and refused point-blank so his friend contributed twice the sum of money. Michael eventually gave up in despair and moved to another flat.

The Pembroke District Library was now in full swing. Every day Michael walked to and from work with his head buried in a book; it's a miracle that he wasn't killed by a car. Although organisation wasn't one of his strong points, he turned out to be many years ahead of his time. Even though it was only a small library, he and Dermot were determined to put their own personal stamp on it. Conscious of his childhood difficulties in acquiring a decent book, he renovated an upstairs room and turned it into a bright children's department where there was a large selection of books he felt would be suitable for them. Determined to be a success in Dublin, he wanted his library to be different and adventurous. He introduced poetry and readings in the afternoons. Dermot usually helped out with this, and the children loved these dramatic, enthusiastic renditions almost as much as he did himself. Well-known personalities, especially actors and writers, were invited to come along and tell stories. These popular gatherings were normally packed. With his love of languages, he stocked the shelves with a plentiful supply of European books, mostly French, German and Russian. He insisted that the best books in the world were the books that most people wanted.

Unlike in Cork, they had a small, hard-working committee which was both flexible and open to suggestions. He got more daring and applied for money to buy records and start gramophone recitals in the children's department, and was pleasantly surprised when the committee looked favourably on this new venture. One day, when Dermot was quietly working in the lending department, the door burst open and an ecstatic Michael, waving a cheque for sixty pounds in the air, grabbed him. Before he knew it, they were on the tram to the city centre. They made their way straight to Pigott's, the country's premier music shop, where they splashed out on all the best known classics of the time. Michael brought along his own gramophone and, by adding their own collection of records, they soon had a fine selection. The musical gatherings proved to be very popular. For a while some people wanted the likes of Al Jolson but Michael was delighted when he discovered after a few months that the most requested records were Mozart, followed closely by Haydn and Schubert. Wednesday was library half-day and they had the building all to themselves, so Dermot, who was a trained musician, decided to devote that free afternoon to the formation of a children's choir. Youngsters from all over the area turned up for auditions. Michael took charge of the first rehearsal but the boisterous children severely strained his patience and his more tolerant assistant took over. He also tried to get a children's drama group up and going but he was refused permission though he did give weekly talks to the children on painting and classical music.

The staff were happiest when he remained in his little upstairs office reading, and when Yeats, AE or Lennox Robinson called they generally stayed there for hours talking literature. Their visits helped to give the Pembroke a reputation for being a modern and artistic library.

Sometimes Michael volunteered to help out at the lending desk; he was usually a menace in this technical area. Dermot did his utmost to be diplomatic and keep his boss away but it was like trying to hold a raging tide back; within minutes his meticulous system was turned totally upside down. The main problem was that Michael either ignored the basic rules or was just not bothered very much about library techniques. They were new to him and were a constant source of irritation. The catalogue was a completely different issue, however, because this contained all the information the reader needed about which books were in stock. He was annoyed and worried if someone asked for a book that wasn't in the catalogue. When he went behind the counter, things practically came to a standstill. He liked to talk too much to people, which caused chaos. It was a very busy library, and in no time the queues were out the front door until Dermot diplomatically managed to coax him out of the way back up to the sanctuary of his office. Other days he liked to mingle discreetly among the readers, speaking to them, recommending this book or that book, sussing out which titles were left untouched, which were chosen, and he was even more interested in who chose what. Again, he kept a particular eye on what the pretty girls read and was forever peeping surreptitiously over their shoulders and quietly trying to change and improve their reading habits.

Back in the autumn of 1929, as the Pembroke District Library was preparing to open, the Irish Government ushered in the Censorship of Publications Act. The Censorship Board was to hound Michael for the rest of his life. It was determined to finally put a stop to any 'unwholesome' books 'contaminating' the country. Ireland became the laughing-stock of the literary world. Just about everyone and everything was immediately banned; and it was accepted that you really weren't anybody until you were banned in Ireland. The Church and State combined to rule with a fist of pious bigotry – even Tolstoy was banned. Michael was a regular victim of the Censors and often received extra special attention from the Censorship Board. The period between 1930 and 1960 was a bad time to be a writer in Ireland; artistically they were handcuffed; objectivity was choked; creativity was stifled; ignorance reigned supreme. The list of books that suffered from this dictatorial, narrow-minded régime is endless.

Early in 1930, with plenty of encouragement and advice from AE, Michael started seriously to tinker around with short stories about his experiences in the Civil War. A few months previously he had a story called *After Fourteen Years* published in the *Dublin Magazine*. He was to read that same story on BBC Radio in 1938. He had experimented with one other short story before this; it was called *War* and AE published it in August 1926; but over the previous two years the *Irish Statesman* had become involved in a long-running court battle about an alleged libellous article. It dragged on between 1928 and 1930. There was no outcome but the costs were crippling and, tragically, on 30 April, after eight years of highly influential existence, the *Irish Statesman* ceased to operate. AE was heartbroken. Michael's last two contributions were a poem, 'The Stars were Astand', on 5 April, and an article, 'Joyce – The Third Period', a week later. A letter in the *Catholic*

Bulletin commented on the 'moral rottenness of the *Irish Statesman*' but its demise left an enormous void in Dublin literary circles which wasn't really filled until the emergence of *The Bell* many years later. From a practical point of view, what had become a major source of income for Michael was now gone. In a long letter to Nancy, he said, 'The death of the *Irish Statesman* may force me to seek a market in the USA.'

For the first six months of 1930 he was off sick for eight weeks and all through that summer he was very ill with his old gastritis problem. It seemed to be lurking, ever present, just waiting to manifest itself at the slightest hint of tension. His yearning for Nancy and overwork in the library only added to his anxiety.

Minnie was worried and decided to pay him a visit to help him to recuperate. She stayed for almost two months and mothered him back to good health; it was to be the first of her many visits. She spoiled him, tidied his flat, washed his clothes and cooked for him and, for several weeks, his delicate stomach survived on just baby food. At times like this Minnie realised that she really had two children to spoon-feed: her son and her husband. While Michael basked in comfort with his mother, Big Mick pined for his missing wife. She sent him daily accounts of his son's condition but eventually word reached Dublin that Big Mick was on the drink and Minnie's presence was urgently required back in Harrington Square. For years the O'Donovans resented these trips to the capital and looked on them as a form of desertion. Secretly, Big Mick prayed for the day his son would marry and leave him with his wife all to himself.

By 1931 the Pembroke District Library was the talk of Dublin; there were 33,000 people in the area and an indication of how busy they were can be seen that in the twelve months of that year over 136,000 books were borrowed. Europeans living in the city who couldn't buy books in their own language were regular visitors. Michael and Dermot were both delighted with this development. The boss and assistant relationship was now long gone; they accepted each other as equals and were like two over-enthusiastic children, proud of their achievements. It was their own unique library and they felt like two young pioneers, full of enterprise and hope, setting out on a long journey.

Sadly, Ireland wasn't yet ready for them; they went too far too quickly and officialdom frowned on their grandiose notions. At the end of the year, in a new Act, the Pembroke township was brought under the umbrella of Dublin Corporation in an extension of the city boundary and their beloved library lost its independence and individuality. Michael was shattered and cried tears of bitter frustration on Dermot's shoulder. Worse was to follow: his own assistants were removed and replaced by strangers from the Central Library; the choir was dispensed with; and instead of the stimulating poetry and storytelling sessions, there were boring lectures on the Gaelic League; half the time the lecturers didn't even turn up and the children quickly disappeared, never to return. Then a posse of religious do-gooders raided the library and removed all books on Russia, and there were many anonymous complaints that readers were getting a copious supply of 'dirty' books. It was a laughable situation. Numerous upright citizens volunteered to read all the books to ensure that Irish purity was protected. It was jungle law: if there was the slightest doubt about any reading material then it was immediately removed from the shelf. A depressed and disillusioned Michael confessed to the ever-elusive Nancy in a letter: 'I've got a job and I'm going to sit on it.'

He hid his anger and disappointment and toiled non-stop on finishing his short stories, hurling himself at them with a furious energy; woe betide anyone who interrupted him, as for every page he typed he tore up ten in exasperation, cigarette ashes flying in every direction until, at last, he threw a critical eye over the end product.

One day, out of the blue, a letter arrived at his flat stating that the *Atlantic Monthly* had agreed to pay him $140 for his short story *Guests of the Nation*. He grabbed the astonished landlady, kissed her and danced her round the room, and then practically ran all the way to work where he took Dermot completely by surprise and twirled him round the library to the amazement of the startled onlookers. On the spur of the moment, like two eager boys playing truant from school, they decided to escape to Glendalough in the Wicklow hills to celebrate. In their unbridled happiness, however, they forgot to bring enough money with them. Dermot had to get the bus back to Dublin, borrow a few pounds, and send it on to Michael in Glendalough.

Having success with one story was one thing but he now had a collection of new stories and he couldn't find a publisher to take a chance with them; he realised that he wasn't well known enough. Then, as ever, AE came to his rescue. He stepped in and wrote to his own publisher, Harold Macmillan, and fervently recommended Michael, praising him to the high heavens, comparing him favourably to James Stephens and ending by giving him a personal vote of confidence.

Macmillan wrote to Michael, enclosing an advance cheque for thirty pounds, and agreed to publish his book of short stories. The title was *Guests of the Nation*, after the first and probably the best story in the collection. Eleven of the fifteen stories had a war theme. The author's painful involvement in the Civil War was still fresh in his mind and writing these stories, getting them off his chest in a way, exorcised the spirits and the torment of that whole experience. *Guests of the Nation* itself is undoubtedly one of the finest anti-war stories ever written. Even Osborn Bergin, accepted as being the greatest of the Celtic scholars, and a man who was practically impossible to please, told his colleague, Professor Dan Binchy, that it was a story that deserved to live. It involves two kindly British soldiers who are hostages in the Troubles. In time they form a friendly relationship with their captors, but the overriding politics of the situation demands that they be executed. Anything else would be seen as weakness. The soldiers understand that it has to be done. At the end they are shot and their bodies dumped in a nearby bog. There is a strong underlying message stressing the futility, the tragedy and the stupidity of war.

He also included *After Fourteen Years*, written some time back in the *Irish Statesman*, and *Procession of Life*, a sad tale set in the docks of Cork where an old watchman, a lady of the night and a young boy (Larry) become unlikely friends. They are three lonely souls contemplating the cruelty of life; Larry, locked out by his father, is lonesome and just idly passing time while enjoying the excitement, the danger and the closeness of the woman; the woman is sad and lost and reflecting on what might have been; and the tired old man is dreaming and spinning yarns of his far-off, long-gone youth to a willing audience.

Guests of the Nation had a unique freshness about it and Michael was delighted with the rave reviews. He didn't forget his old mentor and sent Daniel Corkery a signed copy. It hurt him when he got no response. Just three years previously he had been quick to jump in and defend Corkery when Father O'Flynn had insulted him in the *Examiner*. Michael was also disappointed that his book received very little recognition in Cork, which only fanned the flames of his love-hate relationship with his native city. Up to this point, Michael still considered himself a poet; but the unexpected success of his first book set him thinking. He started immediately on his second.

All his old fire and ambitions for the Pembroke Library had now turned lukewarm. Although suffering from the constant bureaucratic handcuffing, he did his best under the trying circumstances and went through the daily motions of running a library. He wrote a staggering amount of letters, from complaints about the numerous windows not being cleaned properly to the constant stream of protests to City Hall about the damp state of the supply of firewood for his library fire.

Michael, still very ill, developed large boils on his neck, which his doctor thought might be a form of cancer. Worried by this, he went to see Dr Oliver St John Gogarty for a second opinion. When Michael explained about his doctor's diagnosis, Gogarty, a well-known wit, poet and throat specialist, uttered the immortal words, 'He wouldn't know cancer from a pain in his ass.' Gogarty, a close friend of James Joyce, was an amazingly eccentric and versatile character. He was a writer, poet, professional footballer, champion cyclist, archer, aviator and senator. The only thing wider than his circle of friends was his circle of enemies. He wore a fur coat and travelled around Dublin in a yellow Rolls-Royce. Michael Collins often stayed in his house and, later, Gogarty embalmed Collins's body when it was brought to Dublin after his death in the Civil War. Once, Gogarty was kidnapped by Republicans but escaped by diving into the Liffey. On another occasion, in a restaurant, he drew a sketch on the tablecloth and then cut it out. This left a big hole in the cloth and when the manager arrived on the scene he demanded seventeen shillings and sixpence. There was a libel case over his autobiography, *As I Was Going Down Sackville Street*, at which Beckett appeared as a witness.

When he wasn't ill, Michael could be the life and soul of any party. The actor in him came out. He was an excellent mimic and loved to tell stories and recite long, dramatic passages of poetry to an appreciative audience. During these good times he was game for anything. He often sang to himself in his office – in fact, he could be heard across the street, until Dermot abandoned his busy post and ran upstairs to beg him to stay quiet. The frustrated readers couldn't concentrate with all the noise from above. For a man who was so excitable, he could also be unbelievably patient and dignified when dealing with some of the irritatingly trivial complaints of library life.

He surprised Dermot another day by buying a few old dance records and insisted that his friend visit him that evening. When Dermot arrived at Michael's flat at the appointed time he got the shock of his life; the carpet was rolled up in the corner and Michael, like an exuberant teenager, was frantically skipping around the room with his arms around Mary Manning, a noted writer and the Gate Theatre's publicity manager. As clumsy as ever, he trampled all over the unfortunate woman's feet until he finally tripped over himself. He wisely decided to retire from dancing that very night.

Not long afterwards, he got a mad longing to try tennis but that proved to be an even bigger disaster. He just wanted to bash the ball about with no real plan and stubbornly ignored all the rules and the fact that the different white lines were there for a specific purpose. His poor eyesight was another drawback and he drove Dermot to distraction by continuously claiming points when the ball was clearly out. His sporting career lasted two weeks.

The friendship between the two young librarians blossomed and they even played around with the idealistic concept of setting up their very own little bookshop in Grafton Street, hoping that it would be a rendezvous for poets and writers. But Dermot was growing more and more disillusioned that their library wasn't theirs anymore. The officialdom of Dublin Corporation held a firm grip on the reins and made sure that it was a 'safe' Catholic library. Around this time Michael harboured notions of being a full-time writer but there was no way he would just give up his ample library salary of £250 per annum; he couldn't afford to. At the end of 1931 a position became vacant in Ennis Library. Dermot applied for it and got the job. With mixed feelings and a certain reluctance, he left Dublin. Michael was depressed. He missed Phibbs, Nancy and his mother and now Dermot was gone. After his departure Dublin was a lonely place for him. They kept in contact by letter. Dermot called at Dublin whenever he could and Michael paid a flying visit to Clare when the opportunity arose. He didn't drive, having neither the patience nor the inclination, so Dermot hired a car and they set off around Michael's favourite part of Ireland: the Cliffs of Moher and the wild natural beauty of the Burren.

With Dermot's departure, Michael became immersed in AE's and Yeats's get-togethers. His circle of literary acquaintances had widened considerably; not only was he fraternising with AE, Robinson and

Yeats, his three amoral Protestants, but he was now hobnobbing with the likes of Robin Flower, T.F. O'Rahilly, Richard Best, F.R. Higgins and Edmund Curtis, all eminent men, and he was particularly friendly with the novelist Joseph O'Neill. The boy from the slums with barely four years of schooling behind him had come a long way.

Although these sessions were supposed to be evenings of serious discussion on books, theatre, Celtic translations and the general arts, in effect, especially with his theatrical acquaintances, they were often nights of shameless tale-telling, back-stabbing and scandal-mongering character assassinations. It didn't take Michael long to realise that he had to be careful what he said about anyone. He knew that there was a strong possibility, before the night was over, that it would be repeated, exaggerated, told and retold with mischievous relish all over Dublin. Although he was never slow in voicing an opinion, when it came to his academic associates, especially those involved in Celtic studies, he could be an avid listener and a lot of their intelligence and knowledge rubbed off on him. But his theatre/writer friends were a complicated, eccentric bunch, full of cliques; some of them spent so much time betraying confidences it was a wonder they had any spare time to write anything. Lennox Robinson was usually half-drunk and only attended in body. Fred Higgins was Yeats's best friend yet he was a notorious gossip – even Yeats wasn't safe from his lethal tongue. At times he wasn't aware of the hurt he was causing and when confronted about it he protested and repeatedly stressed that every time he left Yeats's house he felt like a thousand dollars.

Michael looked up to both Yeats and AE but he had two completely different relationships with them. He would do anything for the big, kind, warm-hearted Ulsterman. In a way, AE, as a father figure, was a replacement for Daniel Corkery. From the very start he helped Michael's career in every possible way. Once, in the early days, he praised him in his own *Irish Statesman* under the pseudonym YO. And he wasn't the only young writer AE helped. In 1926 the Harkness Fund was offering travelling fellowships to the USA for suitable candidates. Seán O'Faoláin applied but needed a reference; AE immediately stepped in without giving it a second thought and strongly recommended him. O'Faoláin was in no doubt that without AE he wouldn't have spent two years studying in the States. Many of his associates, especially Yeats, considered AE boring, and occasionally this was true, as he could be set in his ways, predictable and repetitious; but sometimes a casual phrase or a pertinent word by Michael jolted his train of thought, causing him to flash into life and all the old boyish enthusiasm flooded back in a burst of brilliance. Michael loved him when he was like this.

Osborn Bergin, professor of old Irish at UCD, was AE's dearest friend. Michael was extremely fortunate to have someone of the stature of Bergin to turn to for advice and help, just as he would later be able to do with Dan Binchy. In turn, they also appreciated his natural feel for the structure of language and his instinctive grasp of Gaelic translations. In 1927 AE was responsible for bringing Michael and Binchy together when he arranged a meeting at the offices of the *Irish Statesman*. At first the two young men didn't get on but later they became great friends.

Yeats and AE went back a long way; they were like two old cronies who argued a lot, but AE could be deeply hurt by Yeats's criticism. They first met as teenagers at art school in Dublin and, despite many quarrels, they retained a close, if at times rocky, friendship all their lives.

Michael had a certain affinity with Yeats. As a boy he admired him – he was the ultimate poet, all the things he longed to be: suave, immaculate and wealthy. Coincidentally, they had a lot in common: like Michael, Yeats had poor eyesight; he was forever calling people by their wrong names, thus creating enemies all over Dublin, and he, too, had been bullied at school because he was a thin, awkward and nervous pupil who concealed his shyness with an arrogant attitude. He found that his lack of academic achievement was a heavy burden and he was constantly reminded of this. Another reason why Michael held him in such high esteem was the fact that he steadfastly refused the offer of a knighthood and the trappings and the honour that went with it; Yeats insisted on remaining an Irishman.

It's easy to understand the admiration Michael had for Yeats; after all, he had had a hugely successful forty-two-lecture tour of America in 1903; the following year he had been the main motivator in the formation of the Abbey, Ireland's national theatre and he had received the Nobel Prize for literature in 1923. In many ways, this was the making of him, because up until then he had not been well-off. He was unaware of his success until the editor of the *Irish Times*, Bertie Smyllie, who had known about it since that morning, phoned him late at night to congratulate Yeats. He went on and on about the coveted prize and the honour it brought to himself and his country until the impatient Yeats emotionally begged, 'How much, Smyllie? How much?' That night he celebrated with a plate of cooked sausages. Yet it shows the esteem Yeats had for Michael when he very often 'stole' his poetry translations. Michael was aware of this; it was the 'in' joke at the time, but he took it as the highest compliment. Whenever he pointed this out to the great man, Yeats reacted with a smile and informed him that poor poets borrow but great poets steal.

They really had a father/son relationship. If Yeats was ever quiet or unresponsive, Michael would stage a mock quarrel just to make him come out of his shell. One evening O'Faoláin and Michael were visiting his house when he was finishing a poem. He read it to them and asked O'Faoláin if he liked it. O'Faoláin said that he did and praised it accordingly, but Michael, tongue in cheek, said that he hadn't an earthly clue what it was about, so Yeats went meticulously through the poem line by line. Just as they left Fred Higgins appeared and the following morning he told Michael that Yeats had got a great kick out of the whole incident because, in his opinion, O'Faoláin hadn't really known what the poem was all about and he was certain that Michael understood every single word. Yeats paid him another compliment when he said that Michael did for Ireland what Chekhov had done for Russia.

Michael had now compiled seventeen translations from the old Irish spanning a thousand years of the Celtic middle ages. He put them together in a delightful little book called *The Wild Bird's Nest*. It was published in 1932 by Elizabeth Corbet Yeats of Cuala Press. There were only 250 copies printed and there was a lengthy introduction by AE praising Michael and dwelling on many aspects of ancient mythology:

> There is a character in the Irish poetry translated by Frank O'Connor which is in much of the literature in Irish, and which persists in Anglo-Irish literature of our time. I do not think this Irish character has been well understood. It arose partly out of the isolation of Ireland as an island, and partly because Ireland was never part of the ancient Roman empire. Those ancient Romans were great builders but

they were also great destroyers, and they obliterated in England, France and Spain almost all traces of the culture which preceded their own. In Ireland, never subject to the Latin domination, there are rich survivals of a culture almost unaffected by the later European. It continued the primaeval culture of imagination which was, I think, the culture of the world before the Greeks came with the beginnings of philosophy and science. People simply imagined things about the universe, and what do we not owe to that imagination which discovered above this world its heaven worlds and its god worlds, and populated them with pantheons of divinities. How dark would nature seem to us, how arid our literature and art, but for the imagination of our Graeco-Latin ancestors and their tribes of gods, nymphs, naiads, dryads, hama dryads, oreads, fauns and satyrs. India and Persia had their own divinities; and in Ireland the imagination of the ancestors created images which are as beautiful as any to the artist mind: Angus, the Celtic Eros, a beautiful young man circled by dazzling singing birds, his messengers which he sang into the hearts of young men and girls and whose kisses brought love and death; Lug who comes over the waters on a winged horse out of the Land of Promise; Mananan the sea god with his boat, the Ocean Sweeper; Lir with his transformed children and the hosts of the Sidhe, all clear-cut, bright and beautiful to the imagination.

AE goes on to talk about philosophical systems, bleak cynical moods and Greek mythology. His long foreword and style of writing are an insight into the character of the man. He ends by again touching on O'Connor:

Those who come after us on a later wave of time cannot realise the quickening of imagination which came to us of an earlier generation when the labour of scholars revealed to us that almost forgotten literature in Gaelic. The early sagas as raw material for the imaginative artist are, I think, equal to anything in Greek mythology. The lyric poetry is of very fine quality. The evidence is in these translations by Frank O'Connor. Many people have turned fine poetry in one language to very indifferent verse in another. But no one, I think, has ever made fine poetry out of bad originals.

The miracle of silk making out of a sow's ear is still as ever unbelievable.

The three best known of the seventeen works in *The Wild Bird's Nest* are the long translation, *The Lament for Art O'Leary*, an unusual staccato-type piece. The second is the brilliantly bitter-sweet *The Old Woman of Beare Regrets Lost Youth*, a moving account of an elderly woman crying out for her long-lost girlhood. Again, it is quite long. Here are the first few verses:

I, the old woman of Beare,
Once a shining shift would wear,
Now and since my beauty's fall
I have scarce a shift at all.

I am ebbing like the seas,
Ebbtide is all my grief;
Plump no more I sigh for these,
Bones bare beyond belief.

It is pay
And not men ye love today,
But when we were young, ah then
We gave all our hearts to men.

Men most dear,
Horsemen, huntsmen, charioteer.
We gave them love with all our will
But the measure did not fill;
When today men ask you fair,
And get little for their care,
And the mite they get from you
Leaves their bodies bent in two.

The third was the outstanding *Kilcash*. It is difficult enough to change a work, especially ancient prose, and make it rhyme in a different language when the writer has also to remain true to the original. Not only did Michael do this with brilliance but very often his translations were better than the originals. Most of the Gaelic texts he worked on were drab and pedantic; they were hundreds of years old, but he had the uncanny ability to breathe new life into them, which made them more attractive to the modern reader. *Kilcash* manages to capture the exact mood. The following is the complete text in all its rhythmic beauty:

What shall we do for timber?
The last of the woods is down.
Kilcash and the house of its glory
And the bell of the house are gone,
The spot where the lady waited
Who shamed all women for grace
When earls came sailing to greet her
And Mass was said in the place.
My cross and my affliction
Your gates are taken away,
Your avenue needs attention,
Goats in the garden stray;
Your courtyard's filled with water
And the great earls where are they?
The earls, the lady, the people
Beaten into the clay.

Nor sound of duck or of geese there
Hawk's cry or eagle's call,
Nor humming of the bees there
That brought honey and wax for all,
Nor the sweet gentle song of the birds there
When the sun has gone down to the west
Nor a cuckoo atop of the boughs there
Singing the world to rest.

There's a mist there tumbling from branches
Unstirred by night and by day,
And a darkness falling from heaven,
And our fortunes have ebbed away;
There's no holly nor hazel nor ash there
But pastures of rock and stone,
The crown of the forest is withered
And the last of its game is gone.

I beseech of Mary and Jesus
That the great come home again
With long dances danced in the garden
Fiddle music and mirth among men,
That Kilcash the home of our fathers
Be lifted on high again
And from that to the deluge of waters
In bounty and peace remain.

One day, Michael met someone who was to be his close friend for the next twenty years. Seán O'Faoláin invited him to visit Leonard McNally's coffin. (McNally was the informer who infamously betrayed Robert Emmet.) A Mitchelstown man, Father Tim Traynor, gave them a guided tour of the vaults of Adam and Eve's church where the body was buried, and, much to Michael's delight, he gave the coffin a hefty kick as they passed it, sowing the seeds of their friendship. The two men actually had a lot of mutual friends including O'Faoláin, the Buckleys from Gougane Barra, Nancy McCarthy and that wonderful sculptor Séamus Murphy. Their friends were well aware that Michael and Traynor had tempestuous streaks in their characters; yet when the two did get to know each other – when Tim was curate of the nearby Star of the Sea church – they surprised everyone by getting on unusually well.

In many ways they were two of a kind, and both were very close to an over-affectionate mother. Tim's mother became a young widow who scrimped and saved and showered him with unselfish love. He was a ruggedly handsome man who gave as good as he got, but when he was a child his mother had made sure that he kept away from the rough boys in the town, dressed him in an Eton collar and, with her hard-earned few pennies, paid for violin lessons for him which set him apart from the other boys. She, too, had high hopes for her son. Eventually, he went to University College Cork and every Saturday he travelled home to see his mother; but one weekend he didn't feel like making the journey to Mitchelstown. To get out of going home he told his mother that he was studying in Cork but instead went to the seaside resort, Youghal, for a day out with some friends. Unfortunately, his mother, with nothing to do, also decided to go to Youghal for a break. As Tim and his pals strolled along the strand he got the shock of his life when his mother passed by. She nodded silently, smiled but later scolded him by telling him that he had 'no word'.* Like Minnie, she lived to see the day when her son made it. She was a very proud woman when he was ordained at the Pro-Cathedral in 1925. When she died, conscious of her sacrifices, Tim felt that as a final tribute he should do the reading at the burial. Friends advised him against this but he insisted on going ahead. But it proved to be too much for him and he broke down in tears. Another priest took over and finished the ceremony for him.

Father Tim was an unusual priest in many ways and he and Michael were an unlikely duo. At times he felt trapped by his vocation and Michael often teased him and tried to tempt him out of the priesthood, but in those days it was unthinkable for a priest to leave. All his adult celibate life he pondered and brooded on what might have been: whether he would have made a good husband and father, or if he would have succeeded as a businessman.

Although he was ordered by his superiors to stay away from Michael, they called regularly at each other's homes. Father Tim lived near the church in Leahy's Terrace and, during one visit, Michael thought he recognised a photograph in the living-room. It was of a pretty girl who had lived near him in Dillon's Cross and he had once had a crush on her; but Father Tim, in his younger days, had also had his eye on her and one evening he walked her the three miles home from UCC to St Luke's, holding her hand all the way, which was tantamount to a proposal of marriage. The girl had since died and Father Tim kindly gave her picture to Michael as a keepsake. He felt that it was appropriate; after all, he was a middle-aged priest.

Surprisingly for those days, for a man of the cloth, Tim enjoyed a drink and owned a car; he sometimes drove down to the Curragh and if ever he fancied a horse Michael put the money on for him – the

---

* 'didn't keep promises'

clergy weren't allowed to gamble. He got very annoyed when people put him on a religious pedestal; all he wanted was to be one of the boys. He hated it when all normal conversation immediately ceased when he entered a room and he was treated with an over-polite respect. To Michael's delight, he was a dreadful man for gossip, and it was normal in those times for the piously religious people, especially women, to reveal the most intimate and often innocent details of their private lives. He gave Michael the seed of many of his stories. One was *The Holy Door* which was about a woman who couldn't stand the sight of her husband and whenever he went to bed with her she gritted her teeth, closed her eyes, and imagined he was Rudolf Valentino. Another, *The Frying Pan*, a confession by Tim, turned out to be a hilariously puzzling account of a priest who was madly in love and longed to be married to the wife of an old friend – who, in turn, wanted to be a priest.

Tim Traynor was both a determined and stubborn man. One day he got a mad urge to try to get his hands on a relic of St Brigid for his church. He soon discovered that the only known relic of the saint was a thighbone which was in a convent in a remote village in Portugal. Undaunted, he set off to the continent to track down the cardinal who was in charge of the convent. He eventually did this but, unfortunately, the holy man would have nothing to do with him. Day after day he visited the cardinal's residence but the monsignor who was his secretary gave Tim one excuse after another. Almost a week crept by and he began to get desperate but, being a good Corkman, he refused to take no for an answer. He hated the thought of going back to Dublin empty-handed so he tried his luck just one more time. The same monsignor came out and, again, it was a litany of excuses. Father Tim said a small prayer, took a pound note from his pocket, and gave it to him. There was an immediate change in the monsignor's attitude and he asked Tim into the waiting-room. Within minutes the cardinal materialised but when he heard what Father Tim wanted he proceeded to give him the poor mouth* about how bad things were in the village and if anyone was to interfere with the relic then the people would get very angry. Father Tim said another small prayer and took out his wallet. Suddenly, the cardinal grabbed it and in a flash there was a five-pound note gone. The man disappeared quickly and in no time he returned with a letter of permission for Father Tim to break the

---

* 'to protest one's poverty'

thighbone of St Brigid and take a piece of it back to his church in Dublin.

Michael loved that story mainly because Tim was so serious and thought that there was nothing at all funny about it, and when he indignantly told him that there was no way you could buy an Irish bishop for five pounds, Michael made it worse by bursting into derisive laughter.

Whenever Tim Traynor got the chance, he escaped with Michael to Gougane Barra in the rugged mountains of West Cork. He stayed in a room over the bar, got rid of his priestly collar and wore civilian clothes. Some nights he worked behind the counter of the pub and argued boisterously with the customers, especially if they didn't know that he was a priest. He cursed and swore in colourful invective with the best of them. He loved his holidays there as he was treated like a normal human being and he could be as argumentative as Michael. What gave him most pleasure was the honesty and humanity of the locals who gave him no special privileges and treated him as one of their own. It was a huge change from his lonely existence in Dublin where old men doffed their hats in respect and he had to endure the embarrassment of women standing up and offering him their seats.

Every spare moment he had in Gougane Barra was spent in a small whitewashed cottage owned by Tim Buckley, a famous local tailor, and his wife, Ansty. He revelled in their company and they, in turn, treated him like a son. The tailor was a charming, walrus-moustached, lovable old rogue who spent his entire day sitting on a rock minding the farm, which consisted of one black cow, and watching the traffic, which was non-existent. Ansty, who was equally remarkable, usually passed the time by scolding him although she was well aware that he took no notice of her. The tailor was a crippled old rascal with a twinkle in his eye and the gift of eloquence. He often boasted that when he was a child his mother took him on a visit to kiss the Blarney Stone but, instead, he took a bite out of it and, ever since, he had never stopped talking. He was king in his cosy little cottage, taking centre stage, sitting on a butter-box by the turf fire, and for hours he held forth on sex, religion, the price of whiskey and the state of the human race.

Michael was particularly fond of the kind old couple. They had a simple, unpretentious naturalness about them; their door was always open; their home was always full; there were no questions asked;

everyone was welcome. Not only were Tim Traynor and Michael regular visitors there, but Nancy McCarthy, Séamus Murphy, Seán O'Faoláin and Father Michael McSwiny, a priest who was banished to Kinsale by the Bishop of Cork for not toeing the line, could come and go as they wished. With an audience of local characters as well as visiting dignitaries and tourists from all over the world, the garrulous tailor could be spellbinding; the conversation overflowed with richness and no one left that cottage thirsty.

One such tourist, Eric Cross, an Ulsterman, was a regular caller and became very friendly with the couple. He wrote a lovely little book about them, *The Tailor and Ansty*. Michael felt both honoured and delighted to write the introduction to the book. The tailor was like an excited schoolboy about the whole thing, but the Irish Government immediately stepped in and banned it for being indecent and obscene. The old couple couldn't comprehend how anyone could find their simple account of life in rural Ireland offensive in any way; but worse was to follow. They were victimised and isolated by the very neighbours who had been glad to accept their generous hospitality over the years. Misguided louts attacked their home. One evening three priests made it their business to visit the tailor and roughly manhandled the poor old cripple to the floor by his fire and made him burn his copy of the book. Luckily, Michael wasn't present; in all probability, he would have physically defended his friend.

Even today, over half a century on, when reading the book it is difficult to understand why it was considered indecent or what was obscene. Was it the way the tailor described the time, when he was a much younger man, that he travelled to Belfast looking for work? He was unfortunate enough to come across a group of belligerent Orangemen who recognised his broad Gougane Barra accent, grabbed him and ordered him to denounce the Pope. Being a good Catholic, he refused. They then held him by the ankles, upside down, dangling from a bridge high above the raging Lagan and repeated the request. Under the circumstances – he couldn't swim – he felt it wise to agree with them and readily insulted the Pope. This whole incident was more humorous than vindictive, but the Irish Censorship Board misinterpreted the gist of the story and, through fear, ignorance and prejudice, decided to ban the book.

What was to follow was a disgrace. Michael and his friends were furious and publicly made their feelings known. Tim Traynor was frustrated; handcuffed by his religious vows, he had to stay quiet. It was unheard of for a priest to criticise the government. But the whole sorry business didn't stop there. It went all the way to the senate when, ironically, a Protestant, Sir John Keane, tabled a motion condemning the Censorship Board; to show how innocent the book really was, he wanted to read it to the senators but they recoiled in sanctimonious hypocrisy at the thought of pornography being forced upon them. The spokesman for the government was a friend of Eamon De Valera, the infamous Professor William Magennis. The government wanted Magennis on the board of the Abbey Theatre but an angry Yeats refused point-blank and threatened to close the theatre first if they tried to force the issue. Magennis pontificated with unbending arrogance. He said that the tailor was obsessed with sex and he called Ansty a moron with the mental age of a five-year-old child.

Old friends, O'Faoláin and Hendrick, weren't slow in joining in the fray. Michael wrote a passionate letter to the editor of the *Irish Times* which summed up the general feeling:

> Dear Sir,
>
> Nothing in years has so shocked me as the ban on *The Tailor and Ansty,* Mr Cross's faithful transcript of the memories and fancies of an old Cork *Seánchaidhe.* For as long as most of us remember, the home of Tailor Buckley and his wife have been the haunt of students of Irish; priest and layman; of writers, painters and scholars. Whatever the great-hearted old couple had – and it was little enough, God knows – they gave like princes, and in that little cottage of theirs there was always music and poetry and legend and good talk for whoever cared for such things. Their little home had become famous, and people wrote from distant countries to remind them of their existence. And now, at the end of their days, an Irish Minister, acting on the advice of an Irish Censorship Board, has proclaimed that the gay and wise and fantastic talk that delighted so many is 'in it's general tendency indecent'. This is not an occasion to discuss the rights and wrongs of censorship. The verdict is as cruel as it is false,

but I believe it was arrived at without thinking of the pain it must cause. Of course, if Mr Cross or any of the Tailor's friends who read the manuscript could have imagined such madness, the book would not have been published during the lifetime of himself or Ansty. But the harm has been done, and now I can only beg those members of the Government I know and the Catholic writers and artists whose opinion will weigh against that of any committee to do all they can to undo it while there is still time. The Tailor and Ansty are the last of their kind; they represent dead generations of Irishmen and women and we of the new Ireland should show them at the end something of their own great charity and courtesy.

Yours etc.

Frank O'Connor

But William Magennis won the day and, after a lengthy and savage attack on the book, Sir John Keane's motion was heavily defeated. Tim Buckley and his wife couldn't comprehend the treatment they had received. Behind all the tailor's old gruff and outward bravado he was a very sensitive man and deep down the whole experience hurt him badly. The affair went on for years and had a profound effect on them. Michael, Nancy, Séamus Murphy and especially Father Tim visited as often as possible. A good friend, Guard Hoare, also kept an eye on them when he could. After almost ten years the Irish Government appointed an Appeal Board and one of the first books to be unbanned was *The Tailor and Ansty*. It was discovered to be neither indecent nor obscene; but by now the old couple were long dead. The tailor had died at the age of eighty-five after a short illness. Sadly, when he died, Guard Hoare was cycling from Ballingeary with a bottle of whiskey for him.

Friends came from far and near for the funeral and the neighbours forgot the old ignorances and sat around the coffin in grief and disbelief that he was gone. They knew in their hearts that Gougane Barra would never be the same again. Ansty was heartbroken. At the wake Nancy put her arm gently around her distraught friend and led her to another room while the body was being placed in the coffin. She said to Nancy, 'Look out, girlie, and see if there's anyone crying for him.' Ansty's health deteriorated and she died shortly after in a workhouse in Cork. The old couple are buried together in the nearby graveyard. Séamus Murphy made a beautiful headstone and Michael chose a suitable epitaph from Shakespeare's *Much Ado About Nothing*: 'A star danced and under that I was born.'

Their great friend, Tim Traynor, whom the tailor called 'The Saint', is buried close by in the island cemetery behind the tiny St Finbarr's church. He died penniless ten years after the deaths of Ansty and Tim; the Church rules stated that he be buried in the city but his friends somehow granted his dying wish: that he be buried in his beloved Gougane Barra. For years, Bishop Lucey of Cork, an old-fashioned, no-nonsense clergyman, refused to allow a headstone at the grave but Nancy approached him and eventually Father Tim's relatives and friends from Sandymount and Killester were given permission to erect a monument symbolically surrounded by a rosary of plaques in Irish embedded in the ancient wall where worshippers came from all over the world to pray and 'do the rounds'. He lies in peace with the idyllic background of a bright blue sky looking down on the timeless, shimmering glass lake and the grey richness of the rocks intermittently spattered in the vast purple heather. Even today the locals still remember him affectionately as 'Father Tadgh'. Years later, as a final tribute to Tim Traynor, Michael wrote about this poignant event in a beautiful story, *Mass Island*.

Early in 1932 Michael finished *The Saint and Mary Kate*. He was very happy with it; in fact, he was quite satisfied that it was the best thing he'd ever written. When his mother visited him, he read her extracts from it. She was both horrified and delighted with her son.

It must be remembered that this was his third book in just one year and he was feeling the pressure. Still lovesick, he wanted to dedicate it to Nancy but she asked him not to; she felt that it wouldn't be appropriate. Eventually, he dedicated the book to his mother. He also had a rather unusual epigraph from St Theresa inside:

Let nothing disturb thee,
Nothing affright thee,
Everything passes,
God is unchanging.
He who has patience,
Everything comes to him;

LEFT: Michael O'Donovan was born in this house on 17 September 1903 (photo courtesy Richard T. Cooke)

BELOW: A typical view of Cork's Northside in the 1920s. Shandon Steeple is in the background (© *Cork Examiner*)

OPPOSITE PAGE: Michael's beloved mother, Minnie

RIGHT: Michael's parents, Minnie and Big Mick

BELOW: Cornmarket street market, where Michael and his mother often shopped

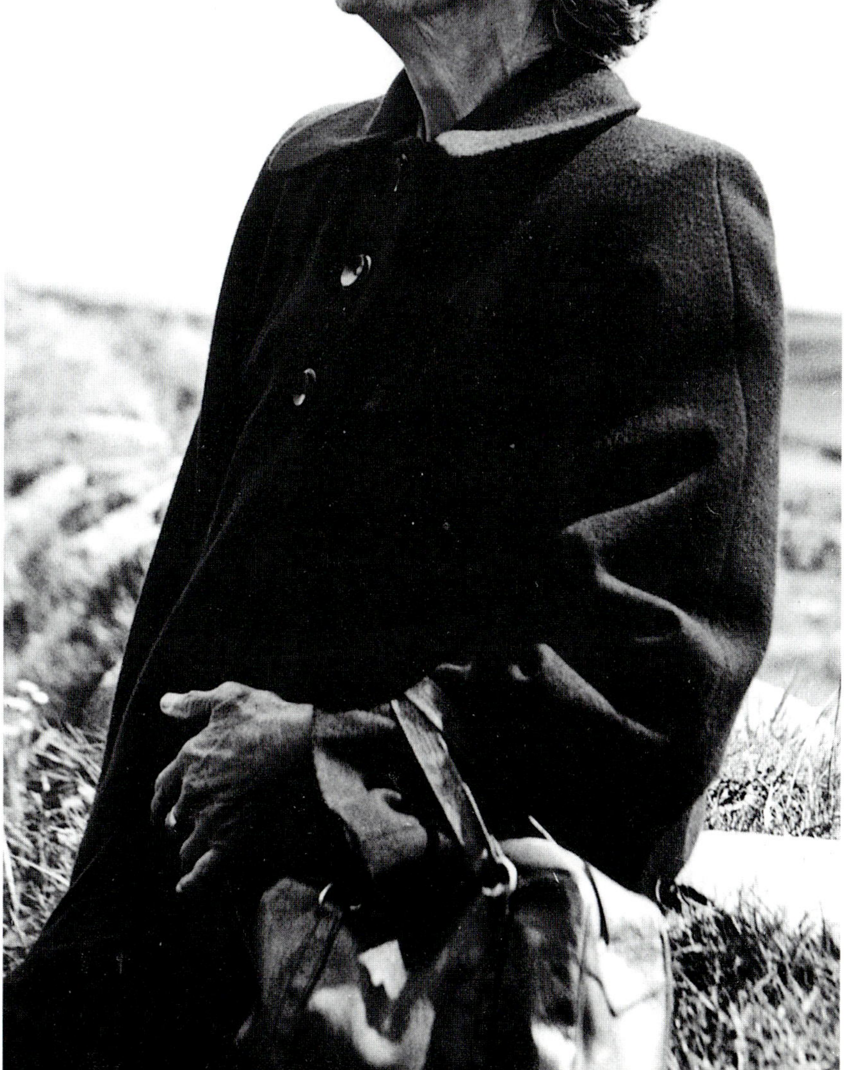

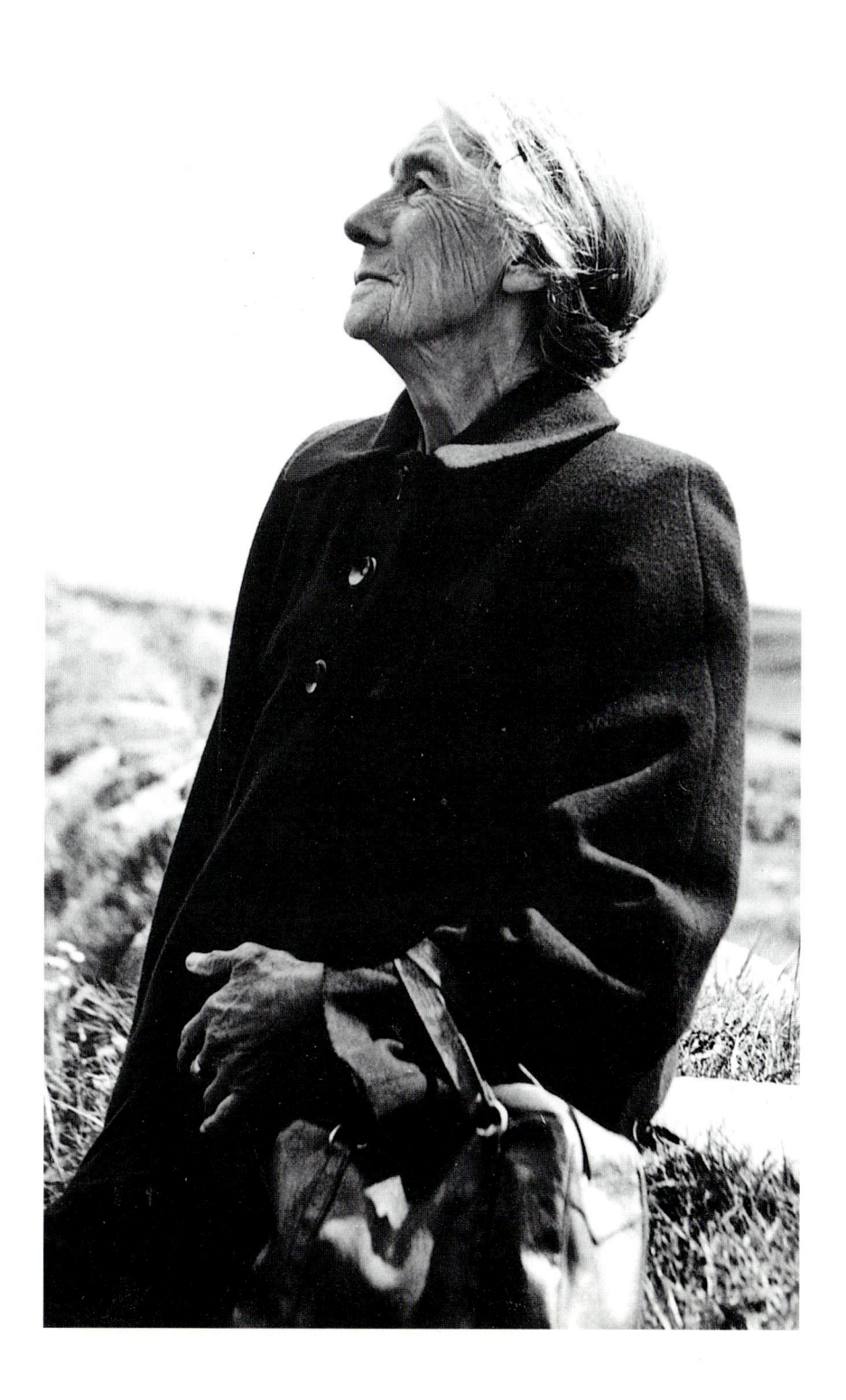

ABOVE AND RIGHT: The ruins of Cork the day after the Burning (© *Cork Examiner*)

LEFT: General Michael Collins
(© *Cork Examiner*)

BELOW: Cork's Women's Jail, where Michael O'Donovan was imprisoned during the Civil War
(photo courtesy Richard T. Cooke)

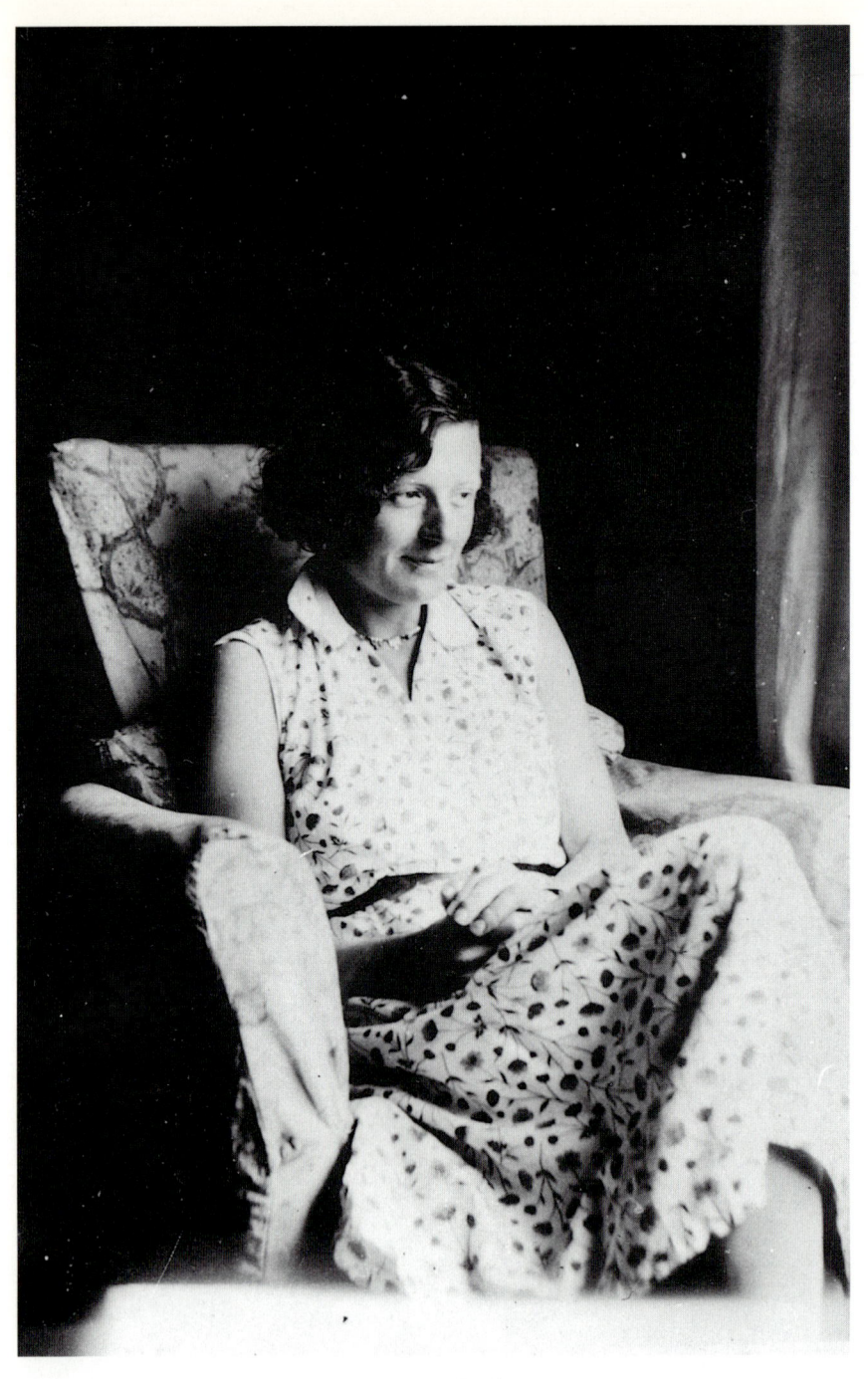

Nancy McCarthy

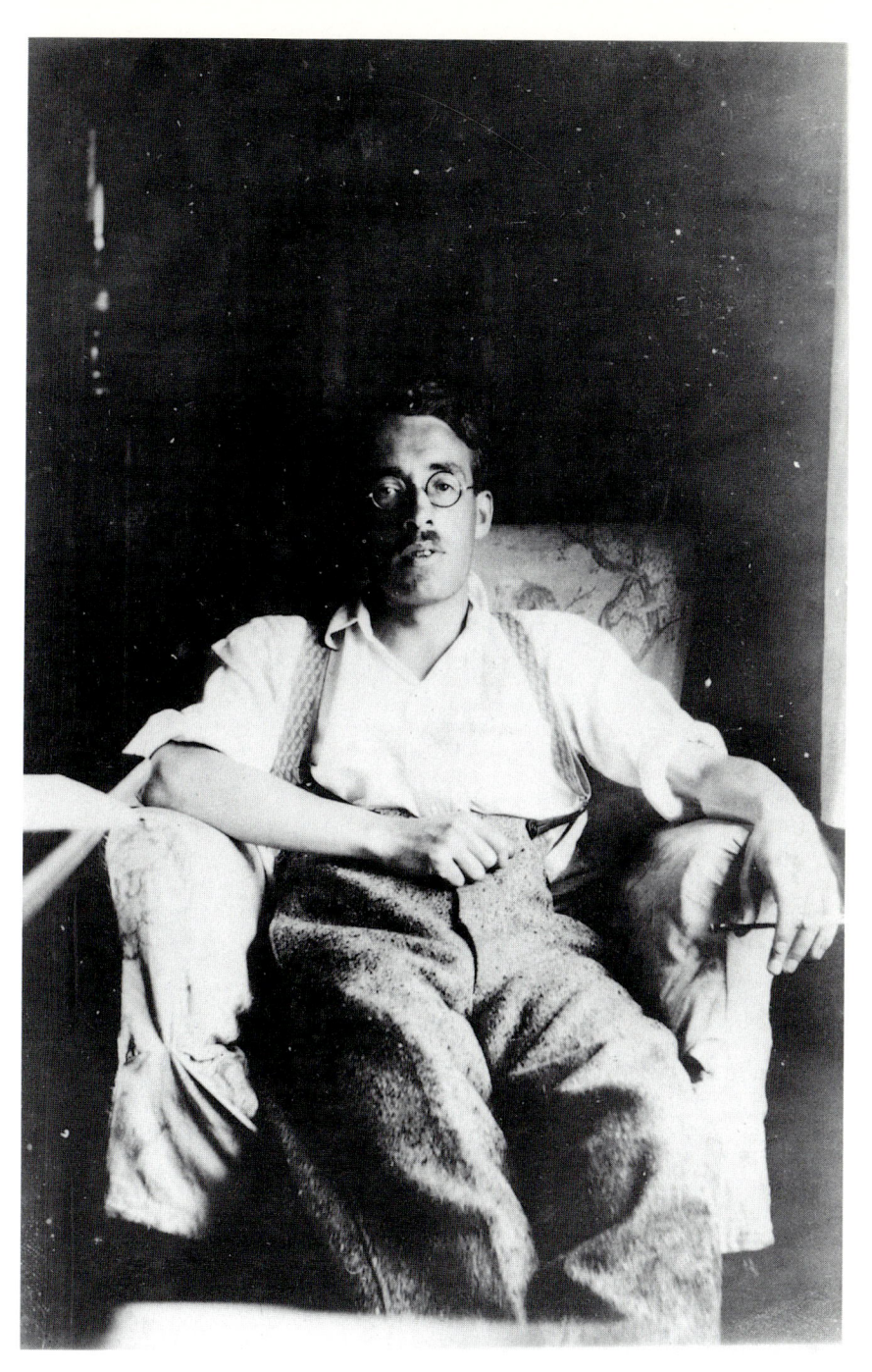

Michael O'Donovan

RIGHT: Nancy in her chemist's shop and (BELOW) in later years with her beloved poodles

He who has God,
He lacks for nothing–
God, only, suffices.

St Theresa

The Saint and Mary Kate was set in a large, slum tenement house (The Doll's House in Batchelor's Quay, Cork, demolished in 1966). It deals with, among other things, the trials and tribulations of Mary Kate McCormick and Phil 'The Saint' Dinan who have been friends since childhood. It is a tale of unrequited love. Phil is an excessively pious young man and Mary Kate is a highly passionate woman (Michael and Nancy in reverse rolls?). Once again, Harold Macmillan, future prime minister of Britain, was the publisher and, although it was thought by many to be a beautiful book, it didn't do as well as expected. It topped the Irish best-seller list for one week but was much more successful in Britain and the USA than it was in Ireland. There was a typical Irishness about the way a critic who was blind drunk denounced it as a disgraceful book at a library convention in Cork at which Michael was present.

Yeats was genuinely delighted for Michael and wrote to all and sundry highly recommending it. AE was in mourning for his wife, Violet, who had just died and he wasn't in his usual good spirits; but after reading *The Saint and Mary Kate* he heaped enthusiastic praise on Michael who, in turn, felt for his old friend and called on him whenever he could, to try and cheer him up. Knowing how strongly Michael felt about the events of the Civil War, AE suggested he write a biography of Michael Collins. The idea appealed to Michael for two reasons: firstly, in spite of the fact that he was anti-treaty and that they had fought on opposite sides in the Civil War, he greatly admired the character of Collins; secondly, he had recently become more and more disenchanted with De Valera, his censorship and his government.

For many years, Yeats had been trying to get a strong body of writers to join together to help and encourage young writers and to show solidarity against the Catholic Church and the Censorship Board. This finally happened in 1932. Over twenty of Ireland's top writers turned up when the Irish Academy of Letters held their first meeting. T.E. Lawrence, the illegitimate son of an Anglo-Irishman, wanted to be a member. He said, 'I'm Irish and it's a chance to admit it publicly.'

George Bernard Shaw was elected president, Yeats was vice-president and AE drew up the rules and constitution and was a willing secretary; Michael and O'Faoláin were also present. Seán O'Casey and James Joyce weren't interested and Daniel Corkery refused to become a member because, still brimming with nationalism, he felt it should be confined to writing in Irish.

Initially, the meetings were fairly innocuous, consisting of speeches, meals and presentations but, unfortunately, it wasn't long before little groups and cliques began to form and consented to privately disagree on different points of literature. On other occasions, under the influence of alcohol, the debates became more open and more heated. Dr Gogarty, for example, had been so kind to Michael when he was sick; yet, with a razor-sharp tongue, he made an unprovoked attack on the young writer at one dinner.

In the event of a book being banned the group indignantly took up arms and vigorously protested against the evils of the Censorship Board, but they never really had any success. Essentially, it was Yeats's dream and Yeats's academy. He gave it credibility; he had a calming influence and an aloof dignity; everybody looked up to him. At a banquet held in his honour in August 1937 – he was now in his seventies – he stood up and made a short yet beautiful speech. Here is a small extract.

> For a long time I had not visited the Municipal Gallery. I went there a week ago and was restored to many friends. I sat down, after a few minutes, overwhelmed with emotion. There were pictures painted by men, now dead, who were once my intimate friends. There were the portraits of my fellow workers; there was the portrait of Lady Gregory, by Mancini, which John Synge thought the greatest portrait since Rembrandt; there was John Synge himself; there, too, were portraits of our statesmen; the events of the last thirty years in fine pictures: a peasant ambush, the trial of Roger Casement, a pilgrimage to Lough Derg, event after event: Ireland not as she is displayed in guidebook or history, but Ireland seen because of the magnificent vitality of her painters, in the glory of her passions.

Yeats died on 28 January 1939. The Academy lived on but it missed his guidance and was never again the same without him.

AE was a creature of habit and he hated it when Michael broke his routine by going off to Ennis, Gougane Barra or Cork. He did everything in his power to fix his young friend up with a woman. He tried to get him to marry and settle down permanently in Dublin. He even arranged for him to have a meal with a beautiful French girl, but it went all wrong. The young couple knew what AE was up to, resented it, and never really got on. By now Michael had several women friends including his dancing partner, Mary Manning, AE's secretary; the actresses, Irene Haugh, Ruth Draper and Meriel Moore; and the singer, Anne Crowley, from Bantry in West Cork. For a while he was crazy about Meriel. Once, when she was in a play at the Gate, he managed to wangle a small part in the play just to be near her. He was also very close to his landlady, Molly Alexander, who looked after him like a mother. Ethel Montgomery, a married woman almost twice his age, was another regular visitor to AE's home and Michael was taken by her vivacity, her laughter and her devil-may-care attitude to life. With regard to women, he was certainly playing the field and had no intention of making any firm commitments. Fate, however, had other plans for him.

5. THEATRE OF DREAMS

THROUGH ILLNESS, MICHAEL O'DONOVAN MET HIS FOURTH AND final father figure. He was feeling very sick one day and, in despair, he visited the nearby dispensary. He was ushered into the surgery by Dr Richard Hayes. Michael liked him at once and they eventually became great friends. Tall and distinguished, Richard Hayes was twice Michael's age – just as Corkery, AE and Yeats were. One of the weaknesses of a mother's boy seemed to be the dependence on a much older substitute father.

Richard Hayes was a talented, complex individual. Born in Bruree, County Limerick, he was a close boyhood friend of Eamon De Valera. He fought with Thomas Ashe in the Easter Rising of 1916 and was sentenced to death, but this was later commuted to twenty years penal servitude. Released in the general amnesty in 1917, he was re-arrested in 1918 and while in Reading Jail he was elected a TD for East Limerick and sat in the first dail. Dr Hayes supported the Free State side. He was medical officer in the Earl Street dispensary from 1916 to 1920, but his salary was withheld for four years until the election of a Sinn Fein board of guardians when he received what was owed to him. He hardly ever spoke in the dail and resigned in 1924. He was an authority on Irish military emigrants and wrote several books about the Irish in France. He refused the exalted post of governor-general, the king's representative in Ireland, but was a member of the Irish Academy of Letters, a director in the Abbey Theatre, a film censor for fourteen years, a graduate in literature from the National University of Ireland, and the French Government made him a member of the Legion of Honour.

He regularly called at Michael's house and they strolled along Sandymount Strand, the doctor erect with gleaming walking-stick punctuating the smooth sand, elegantly sucking on his pipe, lifting his hat and bowing to passing women. Everyone knew him and the loquacious young writer by his side, puffing cigarette after cigarette.

Tim Traynor and Richard Hayes did not get on; the latter, whose brother was an equally famous priest, disagreed with Tim's behaviour and felt that he didn't act like a proper priest. When he was with Michael, he constantly had little digs at Traynor – just as Tim continually warned Michael against the doctor. Michael got great fun out of all this and mischievously played one against the other, but behind it all he liked Richard as much as he liked Tim and needed the friendship of both men.

In December 1931 Michael surprised everyone by applying for a vacant library position in Cork. The chance to be reunited with the elusive Nancy McCarthy was probably behind this decision. He travelled to Cork with high hopes but he knew almost from the start that he was fighting a losing battle. The interview was unsuccessful, mainly because of ecclesiastical pressure on the committee. One particular priest vehemently opposed Michael's application for the post. In the end it was Denis Cronin, his old assistant, the very man whom Michael and the Gaelic League had helped just a few years previously, who got the job and a disappointed Michael returned at once to Pembroke.

In the late spring of 1932 he again felt unwell and Dr Hayes ordered him to take a long rest. He wanted to leave Dublin for two reasons: one was to avoid the vast crowds and the irritation of the Eucharistic Congress which was about to take place; and, secondly, he badly needed a break from work to get back on his feet. He rented a house in Glengarriff, in West Cork, for himself and his mother for six weeks. He was delighted when AE and Osborn Bergin decided to take a holiday and join him for the duration of the Congress. The weather was perfect and the three men swam in the sea every day and relaxed and enjoyed the beautiful surroundings. AE was in fine form; he painted most days and reminisced about the time he had spent in the Glengarriff area back in his student days. Even Big Mick, normally a confirmed home bird, joined them for a fortnight. He went for long walks with his son up the twisting boreens and over the mountains of West Cork, but after three days he became homesick and couldn't wait to get back to the Barrack Stream. He had an obsession about the safety of his house when he was elsewhere. Before leaving home he steadfastly locked and bolted and double-checked every window and door, barricaded his front gate with barbed wire and ensured that every neighbour in the square kept a vigilant eye on his unprotected castle.

Nancy joined them for a few days, staying in a nearby hotel. The good weather and the company of the two older men created a carefree atmosphere and the young couple got on exceptionally well. Before Nancy left for Cork they got engaged when she finally, if apprehensively, agreed to marry him.

When his parents went home and Bergin and AE returned to Dublin, Michael set off on his bicycle on a tour of West Cork. He stopped off to see Michael Collins's home near Clonakilty which rekindled his interest in writing a biography of the charismatic leader.

When Michael eventually returned to Dublin, his batteries recharged, he was suntanned, refreshed and raring to go. Although *The Saint and Mary Kate* did quite well at first, he was generally disappointed with the lukewarm response of the Irish critics. It didn't help when Seán O'Faoláin's book, *Midsummer Night Madness and Other Stories*, appeared and got excellent reviews. It may have been his underprivileged childhood but, in many ways, Michael was his own worst critic. Ever sensitive, he was slow to accept good critiques and often highly suspicious when he was the object of praise. His way of overcoming criticism was to be more determined and work even harder at his next project. He finished a story he was working on – *There is a Lone House* – and it was published in the journal, *The Golden Book*, in January 1933. There was a brief excitement when it was decided to make a film of *Guests of the Nation*. A couple of well-known Dublin actors thought it had the makings of a good movie. Michael helped in any way he could, and offered his advice with the script and observed the action with a keen interest as they shot the film in the Wicklow Mountains.

AE, who was still affected by the death of his wife, was becoming increasingly disillusioned with the Irish political situation; he passionately hated De Valera and blamed him, rightly or wrongly, for the state of the country. To add to his frustration, he could do nothing about it. He felt naked, stripped of his power, like a toothless tiger since the demise of his *Irish Statesman*. Michael met him almost every day and did his best to cheer up his old friend. They had long, intimate conversations and for a while AE came out of himself, but his health was not good; he was nostalgic and he became deeply depressed and often discussed death. Then, for a man who was such a creature of habit, he made the highly unusual decision of moving to London to live. He sold his house and proceeded to give away all his personal possessions. Certain people materialised like vultures and unashamedly played on the old man's generosity; his house was practically stripped. At first, Michael found it extremely difficult to go to the house to say goodbye but, through Fred Higgins's perseverance, he reluctantly made an appearance. AE begged him to accept two beautiful broadsheet drawings done by Jack Yeats and one of his own paintings, a tree by a lake. Trying to make conversation, Michael asked, 'What is that tree?' AE replied, 'It's just a tree.' Michael was deeply saddened by the whole experience and in August AE left for London. They kept in contact by post but Michael missed their regular get-togethers and life was empty without him.

Michael kept busy, taking notes and working on the Michael Collins book. Piaras Beaslaí had already written a biography of Collins in 1930, but Michael hoped to make his a more up-to-date, detailed and in-depth account. One of the many problems he encountered was that people in the know were very slow to part with information. It seemed as if they were afraid. Even in death Michael Collins retained a certain mystique.

This was where Michael's friendship with Richard Hayes was extremely helpful. The doctor opened many doors for him; Hayes's heroism in 1916 was still talked of and his influence in high places was legendary. No one knew more about Michael Collins than his faithful right-hand man, Joe O'Reilly; he had been in the big man's shadow day and night. But the problem was that O'Reilly would talk to nobody about those turbulent days. After just one word from Richard Hayes, however, he agreed to a series of meetings in his home with the eager Michael. Paradoxically, Joe O'Reilly talked a lot but said nothing. Then one night Michael struck gold. In the course of conversation he asked O'Reilly how Collins acted when he had to have someone shot. Suddenly Joe O'Reilly became Michael Collins. He jumped up, stormed savagely around the room, cursing, swearing and gesticulating. To his amazement, O'Reilly behaved like Collins for the next two hours. This experience was an invaluable insight into the character of the dead leader.

Father Tim Traynor also did his bit and worked very hard to help with the biography; he arranged several revealing interviews with members of Michael Collins's secret assassination squad. But it was Richard Hayes who set up a series of meetings with government minister Seán MacEntee, army general Richard Mulcahy, and W.T. Cosgrave, a former head of government. The most important man kept an obdurate, aloof silence: Eamon De Valera.

Michael's long-distance romance with Nancy McCarthy wasn't working out; at the best of times their relationship was rocky until, in 1934, Nancy eventually broke off the engagement. He was devastated. His health deteriorated dramatically and he suffered a nervous breakdown. It was something he had never expected. Seán O'Faoláin and his wife Eileen stepped in and kindly looked after their old friend and nursed him back to good health. They insisted that he move in with them to recuperate. It was a slow, painful convalescence, helped by a short holiday in Glengarriff. It took him a long time to get over it. All their lives, Michael and O'Faoláin argued fiercely and sometimes bitterly about everything from politics to the origins of communism, but they were never closer than at this sad time and the O'Faoláins were the epitome of kindness and patience.

Nancy McCarthy had finally decided that marriage to Michael would never work out. They were great friends but, in many ways, they were very different. She was one of ten children and her family situation ensured that no one had any airs or graces or false notions of grandeur. He was the exact opposite: an only child loved, spoiled and protected by an adoring mother. In hindsight, Nancy's decision was probably the correct one. Michael always clung to the notion of marrying Nancy and going back to Cork to live. In effect, she made up his mind for him. The umbilical cord was finally and irrevocably cut. Dublin was now his stamping-ground and he rarely visited Cork again.

For the next few years he once again threw himself into his work, turning out short stories literally by the dozen in a prolonged burst of creative energy. Some of his stories were translated into foreign languages and he now had a much broader market of newspapers and magazines for his work: *Yale Review, Everyman, Harper's Bazaar, Ireland Today, Atlantic Monthly, London Mercury, Bookman, Life and Letters, Esquire* and *Lovat Dickson's Magazine.*

Early in 1933 George Moore, one of the foremost men in the thirty-five-member Irish Academy of Letters, died just before his eighty-first birthday. He was immediately replaced when the poet Patrick Kavanagh arrived in Dublin. Kavanagh had an even more rural background than Michael but he was extremely outspoken, sincerely honest and had an equally raw brilliance. At this time, theatre was thriving in Ireland, especially in Dublin; in fact, it was generally accepted that Dublin was then the theatre capital of the world. They were prolific times, with a constant stream of new plays by new writers being produced at the two principal venues, the Abbey and the Gate. First nights were hugely exciting and sometimes controversial occasions. Tickets were usually sold out weeks in advance and it was the most fashionable thing to be seen mingling with celebrities at these events. The Abbey opened in 1904 and had a policy of concentrating on Irish plays by Irish writers. It went through the troubles of the early Seán O'Casey plays and survived the riots at John Millington Synge's *Playboy of the Western World*.* (Coincidentally, Padraig Colum, poet and great friend of James Joyce and leading activist against Synge in the Abbey riots, was a regular guest performer at Michael's weekly poetry readings at the Pembroke Library.)

Those two young geniuses, Michael MacLiammóir and Hilton Edwards, founded the Gate in 1928 and they were a breath of fresh air. Like two magicians, they experimented with original European and American plays, different lighting techniques and innovative sound effects and production ideas as well as producing foreign playwrights and Shakespeare. They regularly toured to unusual European venues such as Spain and even went to Cairo.

These first nights were big social occasions, spiced with gossip and scandal, and there was often as much drama in the auditorium as on stage. Some of the first-nighters were T.C. Murray, Lord Longford, Seán O'Casey, Paul Vincent Carroll, Seán Lemass, Peadar O'Donnell, Joe O'Reilly, Maurice Walsh, Sir John Lavery, Cathal Shannon, Liam O'Flaherty, Leslie Howard, Patrick Kavanagh, Sir John Betjeman and several other dignitaries including the Abbey directors.

The ordinary theatre-goers took the plays very seriously, but they also kept one eye on how Yeats or Lady Gregory reacted to a certain scene, or if someone like the Abbey director Brinsley MacNamara slept through the second act, or if Lennox Robinson had had a drink or two

---

* It was felt that O'Casey had insulted Irish Nationalist self-esteem and Catholic notions of chastity. Synge's play had used the word 'shift' (i.e. a female undergarment); it was also considered that his female characters were an insult to Irish womanhood.

before the performance. These animated audiences were hard to please; if they didn't like what they saw, they just got up and left. But if they were satisfied, they gave a genuine standing ovation and might demand up to a dozen curtain-calls and an appearance by the author on stage. One night an unfortunate patron who applauded at the wrong time was immediately ejected, and another night an Abbey actress who had given a fine performance as a cruel woman was followed on her way home by some of the audience and verbally attacked.

But not every play was successful: in one, *Men Crowd Me Round* by Francis Stuart, the house was practically empty and took in just six pounds for the first two nights, which was very sad for a writer who was a member of the Irish Academy of Letters.

This was the golden age of Irish theatre. The actors were world class, and various brilliant names spring to mind: Arthur Sinclair, Ria Mooney, Denis O'Dea, Sara Allgood, Noel Purcell, Frank Fay (of whom Yeats was a great admirer), Barry Fitzgerald and his brother Arthur Shields, Fred O'Donovan, Maire O'Neill, Maureen Delaney, M.J. Dolan, Meriel Moore, Sybil Thorndyke, Eileen Crowe, Robert Speaight, Agnew McMaster, Ann Clery, Phyllis Ryan, Joe Linnane, Jimmy O'Dea, Hilton Edwards, Michael MacLiammóir, Margaret Rutherford, Dan O'Herlihy, James Mason, Orson Welles, Cyril Cusack and even F.J. McCormick who, at this time, was probably the greatest actor in the English-speaking world. Sir John Gielgud also produced at the Gate.

There was a healthy, if sometimes petty, rivalry between the Abbey and the Gate. Many observers felt that the Gate was Dublin's artistic centre and that the Abbey was merely a theatre for tourists and visitors. Certainly the Gate, which was a much more intimate theatre, had a young, vibrant following. MacLiammóir and Edwards had an unbelievably hardworking and versatile company; their aim was to put on a different play every fortnight. One week MacLiammóir, who was also a noted playwright, did the set, costumes and produced, while Edwards performed on stage. The following week they would reverse the roles.

In spite of the rivalry, MacLiammóir often guested with the Abbey and, in return, the Gate was never slow to put on something by Lennox Robinson. In 1932 the Gate produced *The Cherry Orchard* with Sara Allgood as Madam Ranevsky, the part played by Geraldine Neeson in

Michael's Cork Drama League; and, for horseshow week, one of the most important weeks of the year, they did a magnificent *Romeo and Juliet*. MacLiammóir was an outstanding Romeo and Meriel Moore performed one of the most acclaimed Juliets of all time.

Through Richard Hayes, Michael became more and more interested in theatre. Hayes was a compromise candidate nominated as the government representative on the Abbey board just to keep the infamous Senator Magennis out in the cold. At first he declined the offer; he felt that he knew nothing about theatre, but Michael appealed to his vanity and his sense of fair play by persuading Yeats to call on him personally to practically beg him to accept the invitation. Hayes graciously stepped into the breach.

For the next few years Michael became embroiled in the politics of the Abbey, where life-long friendships were ending and starting on a daily basis. Lennox Robinson was also very helpful. He was a morbid, moody and sometimes brilliant playwright and, although he had initially treated Michael harshly, he now took him under his wing and regularly brought him along to the theatre, introduced him to the actors and even got permission for him to sit in on rehearsals.

The people of Dublin unreservedly loved the plays of Seán O'Casey but he was the writer the critics loved to hate. In 1930 he was very angry when the Abbey refused to produce his new play, *The Silver Tassie*. Instead, it went on in London with Charles Laughton playing the lead role and was a tremendous success. In 1932 it came as no surprise when O'Casey rejected the offer to join the Academy of Letters. Yeats expected it. Seán O'Casey never really forgave the Abbey for the snub or that Yeats had played a big part in that rejection. Everything O'Casey wrote was guaranteed to create controversy in the Abbey. *The Silver Tassie* was no exception. The Abbey actors toured extensively but in April 1933 De Valera asked them not to take an 'objectionable' O'Casey play to the USA. They ignored him and the government responded by insisting that a note be put in the tour programme stating to all intents and purposes that they did not represent the Irish Government.

In July 1935 there was a storm when ashtrays were placed in the Abbey and smoking was allowed; but the following month there was a hurricane when *The Silver Tassie* was staged. The public loved it, but the press slated the author. One American critic labelled him 'the whore-minded O'Casey'. Both laymen and priests were up in arms against it. The clergy resented the 'filthy' language. One of the Abbey directors, Brinsley MacNamara, the only Catholic on the board, made a long statement in the *Irish Press,* saying that he was completely against producing the play and strongly opposed to some of the language, which he called 'obscene and wantonly offensive' to Catholics. He had tried in vain to have the unpleasant parts omitted and was under the impression that he had succeeded until he saw the show. He also criticised the audience for their 'almost insane admiration' for O'Casey's 'vulgar and worthless' plays. The actors and producer, too, felt the wrath of his pen. MacNamara had tried unsuccessfully to get his fellow directors to view *The Silver Tassie* through his Catholic eyes. An angry O'Casey, like Michael and O'Faoláin, was a great man to write to the newspapers. He penned a strong letter with a sting in its tail.

> Finally, I am in no way whatsoever ashamed of one single solitary word or phrase appearing in *The Silver Tassie,* and the storm of abuse that the play has received only convinces me that *The Silver Tassie* is a greater play than I thought it to be. Thank you.
> Seán O'Casey

The Abbey actors resented the public attack on them by one of their own directors and contemplated going on strike. Eventually, all the hullabulloo petered out when MacNamara resigned from the board. The one good thing to come out of the fuss was that the Abbey, which up to then had been in the doldrums and losing the war of ticket sales against the Gate, was catapulted back into the limelight, and the nightly 'House Full' signs were most welcome.

Michael had been in continuous correspondence with AE and was aware that his old friend was living a sad and lonely life in England – and that he was rumoured to be dying; Dr Hayes had confided to Michael that he thought the old man was suffering from cancer. The American President, Franklin D. Roosevelt, invited AE to the US. Although very ill, he embarked on a punishing forty-four-stop lecture tour of the United States which was to hasten his death. He passed away peacefully on 17 July 1935 in a Bournemouth nursing home. He was sixty-eight. His body was brought back to Dublin and, on the following Saturday, after a huge funeral, was buried in Mount Jerome Cemetery. As his old foe, De Valera, stared solemnly across the grave, Michael, with tears in his eyes, said a final sad farewell to his dear friend. AE was described perfectly as a child-genius; the man was truly a genius with the open kindness and generosity of a child. His death left a vacuum in Michael's life.

At the end of February 1935, yet another letter written by Michael and O'Faoláin appeared in the *Irish Times*. They were highly critical of the Abbey directors' policy and their attitude to new plays by Irish writers. Although Michael wrote this as an outsider looking in, he was intimately aware of the goings on in the inner sanctum of the Abbey. Richard Hayes kept him well informed of all the relevant juicy bits of greenroom scandal. The aging Yeats was striving determinedly to keep up the high standard of the theatre. Lennox Robinson was coming under fire; his drinking didn't help. Yeats was tempted to fire Robinson but took an easier option in April by adding three new members to the board: Ernest Blythe and Fred Higgins and Brinsley MacNamara, who was to last only a few months. At the end of July, just a week after AE's funeral, Hugh Hunt arrived from England as artistic producer. The wily Yeats had gradually and painlessly robbed Robinson of most of his power. Now the problem was that the Abbey had two producers when it could hardly afford one. As well as the Gate, the opposition was growing; two new theatres, the Peacock and the Torch, were up and running and doing well. One of the biggest worries in the Abbey was shortage of money.

Michael continued to write steadily, mostly translations and short stories, but now he was asked to read his own work on radio. Throughout 1935 his unmistakable voice was instantly recognised as he read his stories. Although often nervous, he was a natural and popular performer.

Then, in April, he became very ill and hardly ever left his flat. One day Dermot Foley made a surprise visit from Ennis to see him. He found his old friend withdrawn, drained and lonely. The persistent Dermot dragged him out for a walk. He suggested a visit to the Central Criminal Court where a controversial case about a woman accused of poisoning her husband was in progress. The galleries were crowded with inquisitive onlookers. The defendant, a small woman in a shawl, sat impassively in the dock. One of the barristers who knew Michael approached him and told him that, in his opinion, she would probably get away with it, as women in her situation were usually found not guilty. There was a remarkable change in Michael; his illness was forgotten and his temperature came back down as he strode urgently back to his flat, persistently puffing on a cigarette, his mind racing. Exactly one week later he met Dermot and read to him *In The Train*, a wonderful story about a woman who poisoned her husband. It was published in *Lovat Dickson's Magazine* two months later.

When Brinsley MacNamara resigned from the board in September, after only five months, Michael was invited to join the Abbey board of directors as his replacement. He was delighted but worried, because MacNamara was a friend of his. Up until then his only involvement in theatre had been his brief, exciting, groping in the dark adventure with the Cork Drama League – which ended in a shambles. It was a giant and frightening step for him to become a director of Ireland's national theatre. Yeats knew that he wouldn't be around forever and was apprehensive about the theatre's future when he was gone. He once intimated that Michael would be his successor in the Abbey and, likewise, O'Faoláin in the Academy of Letters. How wrong he was.

Michael was a librarian by day and had now become involved in the Abbey on a nightly basis with a group of men much older and more experienced than himself. In many ways he was very different from them; he was impatient to get things done, and done quickly. As ever, he was direct – too direct at times – and full of enthusiasm. But, behind it all, he was nervous. At his first meeting in the boardroom, the portraits of Lady Gregory and Synge staring down at him were a timely reminder of the importance of his position.

Initially, he was an innocent in the antics of boardroom politics which were slow, traditional and often devious. His one ally on the board, Richard Hayes, was of little practical help: his function was to keep a watchful eye on finances and he openly admitted that he knew even less than Michael about the workings of the Abbey.

Michael may have been thrown in at the deep end and slow to respond at first, but he learned to cope very quickly and in no time was fully acclimatised. His biggest fault was his naïve honesty. Whether he was right or wrong, he gave his opinion with a veracious bluntness. He soon realised that, sometimes, he had to bite his tongue and watch what he said about anyone or anything. Lennox Robinson seemed to survive in his own world and was apathetic towards new writers' submissions for review. When it came to intrigue, poet and fellow board member Fred Higgins was a master. He was everybody's friend and derived immense pleasure from openly confessing that whenever something went wrong in the Abbey he got out of it by shamelessly blaming the rookie Michael. For several years Michael was blamed for everything from bad decisions and poor productions to choosing unprofitable plays when, in fact, he was completely innocent.

Within a relatively short time there were three young additions to the Abbey: Michael, Hugh Hunt and Russian set designer Tanya Moiseiwitsch. The intention was that this new blood would help revitalise the theatre and give it a fresh modern image. Hunt, only twenty-four, took to Michael immediately, mainly because he was by far the nearest in age to him. There was a mutual respect and Michael enjoyed the fact that Hunt, with his clipped Oxford accent, was completely ignorant of the history of both Ireland and the Abbey. They went for long walks; Michael always seemed to do this with a new acquaintance as if he were sizing up the character of a potentially interesting friendship.

The Abbey actors were well used to the old tried and trusted methods of producers like Lennox Robinson. They hardly needed a producer, in fact; they were so flexible, talented and experienced they could put on a play all by themselves. But Hugh Hunt introduced different methods and held much longer and harder rehearsals. The artistic Tanya Moiseiwitsch added original, colourful and inventive sets to liven things up. Hunt knew that he and his new-broom style of producing were under pressure but his first few plays did exceptionally well. Then came the crunch when he boldly decided to attempt *The Playboy of the Western World*. He was to prove conclusively that an unassuming Englishman could do a good job on the old favourite. The audience had never seen a *Playboy* performed quite like this and the theatre was packed. Cyril Cusack was outstanding as Christy Mahon but some of the diehard traditionalists didn't like what they called an irreverent English version.

When all the hullabaloo had died down, and with plenty of encouragement from Michael, Hunt wanted to stage a Yeats play. Yeats, who wasn't well, had just returned from a holiday and heard greenroom gossip about the unconventional *Playboy* and refused to give Hunt permission to perform any of his plays. Later he relented and gave them *Deirdre*. One of the biggest breaks with tradition was Hunt's controversial casting of an English actress, Jean Forbes-Robertson, as the female lead. He also invited Michael MacLiammóir to play opposite her.

The theatre was tingling with excitement on the opening night. Tickets were long sold out and it was standing-room only. Yeats surprised everybody by attending. When the play ended it was greeted by thunderous applause. An angry Yeats left immediately; he was so furious he refused the repeated calls for a speech from the author. Michael, who had been unable to attend, was told that the audience loved the play and was amazed at Yeats's reaction. On the following night he had to go and see for himself. Again, the audience were ecstatic but he had to agree with Yeats: he thought it was dreadful. The problem lay in the cultural tension between Yeats's text and the attitude taken by the young English producer. Yeats felt that the undignified treatment of the text, plus the miscasting of MacLiammóir and the very sophisticated Forbes-Robinson in the main roles of Naisi and Deirdre, was nothing short of calamitous. On the other hand, the audience seemed to like the upbeat approach to what was now a somewhat hackneyed play. On the third night the distraught Yeats turned up again and wanted to pull the plug on his play. Eventually, he allowed it to run for only one week. Paradoxically, it was one of the most popular box-office successes in the history of the Abbey.

In a heated board meeting later, Yeats castigated Hunt. Michael, who had just given Hunt a two-year contract, sprang to his English friend's defence. Fed up with the constant bickering and conspiracy, Hunt wanted to resign but finally agreed to do a series of 'safe' plays. Yeats got his way and Hugh Hunt was forbidden to ever produce anything by him, Lady Gregory or John Millington Synge in the Abbey.

If Hunt was a man of theatre, Michael was a man of books; he didn't take to playwrighting easily, was never really confident when writing for the stage, and felt it was the least effective string to his artistic bow. Still, he was genuinely delighted and encouraged by Hunt's success. One day a chance remark by an actor friend, who thought that the story *In the Train* had all the dramatic ingredients to make a good play, sparked his imagination. Half afraid to try it himself he asked Hugh Hunt for advice. For three weeks the two of them threw all their energies into hammering out an acceptable play. At first, Michael didn't understand or agree with some of the stage gimmickry of his collaborator but they both compromised and trusted each other's individual expertise. Finally, by the spring of 1937, the script was finished. Hunt had the good fortune to assemble a talented cast and they went into immediate rehearsal.

Although Michael was not a natural theatre man, it was impossible to keep him away from rehearsals. He sometimes read a passage from the script in the way he felt it should be done and surprised the actors with the high standard of his performance. But increasingly he was getting in everyone's way. He practically hid down at the back of the theatre, out of the way, carefully watching every move. When there was something he wasn't happy with, it drove him mad. Finally, one such evening, his patience ran out and, exasperated, he stormed up onto the stage and in no uncertain terms told the leading lady that Nancy McCarthy in Cork would act her off the stage. He was barred from all future rehearsals.

Despite all the teething troubles, *In the Train* opened in a blaze of excitement at the end of May. The opening night was like a gathering of the clans; all the well-known first-nighters were there. Young Hunt was coolness personified and took it all in his stride, but before the show Michael was a bag of nerves. Like an expectant mother hen, he fretted and fidgeted all over the place and couldn't keep still for a second as he anxiously accepted handshakes and best wishes from his fellow directors.

He needn't have worried. The play was an outstanding success and at the end the audience rose as one, unified in thunderous applause. Michael responded as the calls of 'Author! Author!' rang out through the auditorium. He appeared shyly on stage, briefly thanked the audience and the cast, picking out Ann Clery, Denis O'Dea and the inimitable F.J. McCormick and finished by paying special tribute to Hugh Hunt. He was delighted with his first attempt as a playwright but, although he was always fascinated by the theatre and had many more excursions into it, this was never where he achieved his greatest success.

At last, in 1937, his biography on Michael Collins appeared. *The Big Fellow* was published by Thomas Nelson and Sons Ltd. A labour of love, it had been a long and demanding task; he was relieved that it was finally finished. For years he had been fascinated by Collins the human being. Many myths had grown up about him but Michael wanted to portray the man: the drinking, swearing, generous yet sometimes bad-tempered and ruthless man. It was a difficult book. Michael Collins was a complex character; a many-sided individual with a story to fit each different mood. Michael was well aware that undertaking a biography of such a man was an impossible task; a thankless job. One of the problems was that he was too near to that whole momentous period. Many of the players in *The Big Fellow* were still alive and the bitterness had not yet gone away. Civil War politics reigned supreme; ex-gunmen still roamed the streets of Dublin and old sores had not yet been healed and Michael Collins still had an aura of mystique and mystery – even his enemies admired him. But he was an extremely sensitive subject.

The Big Fellow got a mixed reception, criticised in some quarters and highly praised in others. Yet today, over sixty years later, it stands out as an accurate, well-researched and intimate account of that harrowing chapter in Irish history. *The Big Fellow* is the book Liam Neeson said had the greatest effect upon him when he was preparing to play the part of Collins in Neil Jordan's film.

In May Michael was ill again with violent stomach pains. Very worried about what seemed to be a never-ending problem, he decided to consult a specialist in Switzerland. Before he left, however, he wrote to his mother and she came to his Northumberland Road flat to stay with him and look after him.

All through her life, having been orphaned so young, Minnie was never sure exactly what age she was; she looked and acted much younger than she really was, but Big Mick had a sneaking suspicion that she was 'a couple of years' older than him. During that visit, much to her husband's delight, it was discovered that in fact she was four years older than him. She was seventy-two but refused to claim her old-age pension because of vanity. The needless loss of this weekly income nearly drove Big Mick to hysterics.

Michael recuperated, but Minnie lingered on in Dublin and on 18 July she celebrated her first-ever birthday party with her first glass of champagne. She went out to greet her son, who was returning from an after-lunch stroll, and fell down a flight of stairs. There was a sad irony in the fact that the stumble may have been the result of that first and only drink when all her life she had witnessed at close quarters the effect alcohol had on other people. Her son was in shock as his mother lay there in terrible pain. Dr Hayes arrived at the scene immediately and feared the worst. For reassurance, he called another doctor and they both agreed that she had suffered several serious fractures, which was very ominous for a woman her age. It also emerged that she had endured chronic appendicitis all her life but had kept this news to herself. The idea that his mother had had this dreadful physical condition for all those years and had carried on without complaining, and had never spent money on a doctor or a hospital, made it even worse for Michael.

At first it was feared that she would never walk again. After nearly two weeks in the Eccles Street Nursing Home, Michael insisted that she stay in his flat, as Big Mick in Cork was in no condition to look after her. She found it strange to have her son there, lovingly tending to her every need, even helping to dress her and brush her hair.

He got word from Cork that his father was back on the drink, so he decided to take Minnie with him to Switzerland. Although she was still weak on her feet, the holiday turned out to be a wonderful experience. To Michael it was a dream come true; a fulfilment of all the promises he had made to a loving mother as a daydreaming young boy. One day in the beautiful Swiss Alps as Minnie sat resting in the sun, looking down at the breathtaking view, sheltered from the fresh mountain breeze, he asked her if she liked it. She smiled wistfully and replied, 'It would be a grand place to hang out the washing.'

After what was a miraculous recovery, Minnie, with tall tales of the continent, returned once more to the mundane drudgery of Harrington Square and a sulking husband, his pride hurt, who yet again felt that his son had borrowed his wife for far too long.

On returning to Ireland, Michael attended a party in Dublin where he met Evelyn Bowen, a Welsh actress. She had come to the capital to study the mechanics of the Abbey with the intention of forming a similar theatre in Wales. She had a young son, Paddy, and was married to a celebrated English actor, Robert Speaight, who was currently touring the United States with T.S. Eliot's *Murder in the Cathedral*. She had heard of Michael and when they met she found him charming; he seemed to have a fatal attraction to actresses and started going out with her. His growing reputation gave him an aura of maturity and self-confidence in the company of women. The gossip-mongers had a field day and before long their relationship was the talk of Dublin, because not only was Michael a man of the theatre, forever in the limelight, and a well-known writer who seemed to thrive on controversy and the odd public dig at the institutional Church, but he also held down the respected position of head librarian in Ballsbridge. True to form, he ignored them, laughed at them, and got on with his life.

In August the traditionalists in the Abbey decided to stage *The Playboy of the Western World* again and, as Hugh Hunt had been forbidden any involvement in the production of works by Synge, the task of producing was given to Fred Higgins. Higgins was many things, including a fine poet, but he was never a producer. The whole undertaking was a complete disaster.

The following month the Abbey players were once again offered a tour of America. Before they left, De Valera gave a farewell dinner for them. He still tried, unsuccessfully, to influence the choice of plays performed by the Abbey. Michael was the main spokesman for the board. He gave a long passionate speech and ended by reiterating the chronic need for more young Irish writers.

At the end of September the cream of the Abbey actors set sail for New York. From the very beginning the tour was a shambles. Fred Higgins was in charge and just about everything that could go wrong did go wrong.

Michael was left at the helm in Dublin with what was, effectively, only a second-string group of players at his disposal. He knew that the theatre was crying out for good commercial plays. Still basking in the relative success of his first venture, he decided to write another play. While researching the Collins book he had touched on a dramatic incident which fascinated him and he found himself unable to get it out of his mind. Back in 1882 Lord Cavendish and his under-secretary Thomas Burke were savagely attacked and stabbed to death in the Phoenix Park. The organisation which carried out this assassination called themselves the Invincibles. Michael wasn't particularly interested in the actual murder; what fired his imagination was how it affected the killers, Joe Brady and Tim Kelly, and their families, several of whom were still living in Dublin in 1937. To many, the Invincibles were looked on as brave, honourable Irish heroes upholding the dreams and ideals of the true Fenian movement. To others, they were nothing but callous murderers. Uncertain how to tackle the thorny subject, Michael approached Hunt for his theatrical opinion. Unfortunately, his friend knew absolutely nothing about the incident but Michael's enthusiasm rubbed off on him and he agreed that it was possible that there might be the makings of a play there. For a month the two men threw themselves into the project with a vengeance. Michael didn't always agree with some of Hunt's theatrical tricks but after much trial and error and painful rewriting they felt they had something worth while. Hunt cast the play. He was lucky to get Ann Clery as the nun and Cyril Cusack played the delicate role of young Tim Kelly, the ex-choirboy who was inveigled into the Invincibles.

To Michael's dismay, he was completely barred from rehearsals. Hunt's knowledge of Irish history was negligible and Michael was worried that his interpretation of what remained a controversial and sensitive issue might spark off trouble. Ireland was still a country shrouded in festering martyrdom, and over-patriotic gunmen with itchy fingers lurked impatiently in the shadows.

The night before *The Invincibles* opened, Joe Brady's sister called to the theatre and innocently offered Hunt and Michael the suit and crucifix her brother wore when he was hung. She thought it might help the authenticity of the play. Surprisingly, this kind offer was refused, a decision which Michael deeply regretted for years after.

At the opening night of *The Invincibles* there was more than the usual first night tension. The audience was littered with dignitaries but there were quite a lot of strange faces. Rumours were rife that ex-volunteers were going to stage a demonstration. The thought of violence frightened Michael and it didn't help matters when Yeats's old girlfriend, the Nationalist icon Maude Gonne, turned up. As the curtain rose he nervously sat and waited, supported on one side by old friend Dermot Foley, and on the other by Evelyn Bowen.

To his relief, the audience immediately loved it. They were surprised by the unusual entrance of the paperboys, who mingled briefly with the crowd, calling out about the Phoenix Park murders. An uneasy Michael felt that this theatrical trick didn't work but the engrossed audience were impressed. They uniformly hated James Carey who had informed on the Invincibles and near the end the atmosphere was electric as the two prisoners awaited their execution. Tim Kelly quietly sang 'Hail,

Queen of Heaven' to Joe Brady in the cell next to his. The audience spontaneously joined in and gave an emotional rendering of the hymn.

When it was all over, there were numerous curtain-calls and a delighted Michael again singled out Hugh Hunt for special praise. During the run of *The Invincibles* the Abbey was packed. Yet, to his bitter disappointment, the critics gave it a mixed reception.

Fred Higgins was still in the US on the ill-fated Abbey tour. One night when Michael was walking with Yeats to his bus-stop, the great man turned and asked him if he would like to become the managing director of the Abbey. At first he was startled and didn't know what to say. He knew that business in the theatre had picked up a lot recently, mainly due to Hugh Hunt, and was in the black for the first time in years, but running the country's national theatre would be a huge responsibility for a thirty-three-year-old, as well as being a thankless and time-consuming position. Although the challenge appealed to him, he would have refused anyone but Yeats. Very soon he was to discover that running a busy library by day and a theatre by night left him with very little time to write. It was obvious to everyone that he was overdoing it. Richard Hayes, who was seeing him on a nightly basis, was increasingly worried about Michael's chain-smoking, continuing loss of weight and his alarmingly high blood pressure, for which he stubbornly refused to take medication.

Shortly after *The Invincibles* finished at the Abbey, the Actors' Guild held a debate in the Gate about the potential problem of a demonstration in the theatre. Lennox Robinson castigated Michael and Hunt for the insensitive theme of their recent play. He felt that the subject of the hanging of Irishmen whose relatives were still alive and living in Dublin was dangerously close to the bone. What infuriated Michael was the fact that Robinson hadn't objected in any way before or during rehearsals; he even offered help or advice, but waited until after the event to criticise. Michael held an emergency board meeting and demanded Robinson's immediate resignation. At that heated meeting Robinson felt that, slowly but surely, he was being pushed towards the back door.

As ever, Yeats the peacemaker stepped in and suggested a solution to a potentially nasty situation. He offered Michael the olive branch of a written apology from Robinson. This was grudgingly accepted; a generous apology by post helped to smooth his ruffled feathers.

Luckily, he didn't know that it was the wily Yeats who had personally written and sent the apology on Robinson's behalf.

The first-choice Abbey troupe had now been in America almost ten weeks, and the remaining actors found work hard to come by. To add fuel to the smouldering fire, Seán O'Faoláin had written a play for the Abbey, but he caused an uproar when he said he wanted Evelyn Bowen to play the lead role. The Abbey actors didn't like this one bit and threatened to go on strike. An indignant delegation approached Hunt and insisted that an Irish actress be given the part. They felt that there was unfair favouritism at work: Evelyn's relationship with Michael was well known. Finally, the quarrel ended when it was agreed that open auditions would be held. Evelyn still got the part.

She Had to Do Something opened at the end of November. It was booked out but only received a lukewarm reception from the first-night audience. Evelyn as Maxime Arnold and Cyril Cusack as Neddy were praised for their performances. When called on for the customary speech, O'Faoláin was jeered by some patrons. Instead of ignoring it, he unwisely turned on them and then had a go at the Catholic Church and its narrow-minded outlook on theatre in Ireland. The treatment he received after *She Had to Do Something* convinced him that writing for the theatre was not for him. Sadly, his performance only put Michael and the Abbey under even more pressure.

Michael had now been almost ten years in Dublin but he retained many of the faults of the provincial. He could still be naïve and at times he had the subtlety of a sledgehammer. It wasn't in his nature to be devious or unscrupulous in any way or form. He was too trusting for his own good and he often spoke without thinking; everyone knew where they stood with him.

Fred Higgins returned from America and joined forces with his friend Lennox Robinson. Board members Blythe and Richard Hayes often took their side in some of the boardroom squabbles, especially when Yeats was missing.

Undaunted, Michael typically worked himself to a standstill and came up with yet another play, his third in nine months. *Moses' Rock* had the political split caused by Parnell in the Irish Party at Westminster as its background. Again, Ann Clery as Kate O'Leary and the versatile Cyril Cusack as Ned Hegarty were the principal players. As before, controversy plagued Michael because he dared to touch on the taboo subjects of sex outside marriage, and Catholicism and Nationalism. Although well performed, and capably produced by Hunt, the play didn't fill the theatre like his first two but, paradoxically, the critics hailed it as his best yet.

The immense pressure he was putting himself under could be seen at the end of *Moses' Rock* on the opening night when he collapsed in the theatre. Luckily, Dr Hayes was at hand and ordered him straight to bed. Although he was six foot tall, he weighed less than ten stone; he was now quite gaunt in appearance. After comprehensive tests, Hayes grimly told him that in his opinion he had cancer and gave him five years to live. Michael was shattered. This diagnosis hung guillotine-like over his head for the rest of his life.

As he lay dejected in bed for four weeks, frustrated with his enforced inactivity, he gave a lot of thought to his future. In his own mind he knew that things couldn't continue as they were. Eventually, Harold Macmillan, who had published his first two books and become a good friend of his, made up his mind for him and pushed him in the direction he secretly wanted to go. He strongly advised Michael to be either a librarian or a writer; through illness and overwork it was impossible to do both. Worried about the gamble of living adequately on the uncertain earnings of a writer and reluctant to throw away the reasonable but steady wages of a librarian, on 1 April 1938 at thirty-four years of age, after fourteen eventful years in the library service, he retired with a pension of seventy-five pounds a year.

Michael's relationship with Evelyn Bowen was now much more than a passing flirtation. It was common knowledge that they were practically living together. Both Church and State frowned on this. He was ever conscious that his domestic situation undermined his position at the Abbey and caused embarrassment to his fellow board members. He found the daily friction of living in Dublin impossible. In order to escape the spotlight, he and Evelyn and her son, Paddy, moved to nearby County Wicklow, a short train journey from the capital. They rented a small farm in the rustic village of Woodenbridge, deep in the Wicklow mountains. It was a writer's paradise. Isolated and secluded, it was a peaceful and perfect setting for a troubled man struggling to find himself.

Marrying was out of the question. Her own marriage to Speaight was in tatters; just two months before they moved to Wicklow Speaight arrived in Dublin to see his wife about an annulment. The whole, seemingly inextricable, situation was to drag on for another year.

As well as starting a new life with Michael, Evelyn had also to take on his delicate, eccentric and often angry stomach. Her first priority was to find some way of making him put on weight. She acquired a scattering of hens and planted a garden full of vegetables. This ensured a daily supply of fresh eggs, a variety of fresh vegetables and plenty of fresh air. With a regular diet of wholesome, nourishing food Michael slowly began to thrive. His mother travelled up from Cork for an extended holiday and, between them, the two women pampered him back to good health.

With no library salary, he now had to write to live. He settled down to do what he was best at – writing short stories. Like the nearby Vale of Avoca, there was a slow, steady trickle of creativity. He was still wrestling with his half-written novel, *Dutch Interior*.

Back on his feet, he again made his presence felt in the Abbey and the Irish Academy of Letters. The Academy meetings were often acrimonious and controversial, especially if Gogarty was in attendance. In February Austin Clarke resigned, having attacked Yeats.

Michael found it difficult to deal with having almost too much time to write. He finished that fine story, *Mac's Masterpiece*, which was published in the *London Mercury*. He also kept himself busy by working on radio. He had a natural radio voice, especially when reading his own stories; in fact, he did more than just read them – never content with half-measures, he performed them with gusto. He was also getting more invitations from the BBC as a panellist discussing the arts.

He settled down in his new role as 'husband', man of the house and country writer and was at peace with himself. After some time a pattern developed, and writing, walking and reading filled his day. There were regular visitors to break up the routine: his mother, Dermot Foley, novelist Elizabeth Bowen and Richard Hayes. He dreaded it when Hayes called because each visit was a reminder of his illness. Hayes didn't like Evelyn and eventually his visits became few and far between, and he and Michael drifted apart.

By now Michael was becoming increasingly disillusioned with the greenroom gossip and the bickering disagreements within the Abbey boardroom and, in June 1938, he tendered his resignation. Yeats immediately begged him to change his mind. Yeats, who was also very ill, quietly explained that he saw Michael as his successor in the Abbey Theatre. The board members were not enthusiastic about Yeats's plans and Michael himself was uncertain about the whole matter.

In early December the failing Yeats went off to Menton in the South of France to rest. With a renewed burst of energy Michael finished his fourth play, *Time's Pocket*, and it went on in the Abbey on St Stephen's Day. Again, it had a background of the Fenian movement and the story raised eyebrows in certain circles: Nance left her drunken husband and went to live 'in sin' with the man she really loved, a Fenian just released from prison. Ria Mooney was excellent as Nance and F.J. McCormick stood out as the country poet. An ecstatic audience on opening night gave *Time's Pocket* eight curtain calls but the critics didn't share their enthusiasm. On 6 January Michael attacked the critics in a stinging letter to the *Irish Times* and the following week a similarly scathing letter by O'Faoláin defending his friend and *Time's Pocket* appeared in the *Independent*. The critics duly responded with even more brickbats.

Michael was frustrated with the slow progress of his novel; he seemed to be getting nowhere. Evelyn was now pregnant and Speaight had filed for divorce on the grounds of adultery. The whole sorry mess became a fiasco and dragged tediously and painfully on. They paid a visit to Wales to see Evelyn's parents and wait for the court decision. While staying in Chester, Michael corresponded with Yeats. He knew that Yeats was very ill in France, yet when he received news of his death he was deeply shocked. His loss was irreplaceable and it put all the childish quarrel-mongering in the Abbey into perspective. That night Michael couldn't sleep and spent the long hours of darkness walking the walls of Chester, soul-searching and mourning the passing of his great friend, hero and father figure.

Two weeks later, on 11 February 1939, he married Evelyn at the Chester Registry Office and they immediately returned to their little farm in Wicklow.

His position in the Abbey had now become impossible. Yeats had appointed him editor of *The Arrow*, the Abbey publication, but Robinson, Hayes, Blythe and Fred Higgins had taken control of the board and succeeded in isolating him. The calming influence of Yeats was sadly missed. Michael felt helpless. On 12 May he wrote an angry letter of resignation to the Abbey Theatre.

Now, no longer bothered by his library problems or the intricacies of the Abbey, he was at last a full-time writer. Although he was still fighting an uphill battle with *Dutch Interior*, his book of translations, *Fountain of Magic*, which he had been working on for ten years, was published. He dedicated it to William Butler Yeats. Austin Clarke gave it a poor review in the *Irish Times* and Michael and O'Faoláin, once again, gave as good as they got with a flood of indignant letters to the paper in reply.

Meanwhile, Evelyn entered the Leinster Nursing Home in Dublin. On 18 July she gave birth to a son, Myles. This put Michael under more pressure to write. He now had to provide for a wife and family. When the mother and baby arrived home to Woodenbridge, his peaceful existence was shattered. There was a constant stream of well-wishers; even Father Tim turned up to congratulate his old friend. Deadlines were missed and, to make matters worse, his father decided he wanted to visit Wicklow to see his new grandson. When Michael heard of the proposed visit of Big Mick, panic set in, and when he met the train at the little station he was shocked to find his father very drunk. He knew that Minnie would never have allowed her husband get on the train in Cork in that condition. But Big Mick was as nervous about meeting his son as his son was about meeting him. He had got off the train in Waterford for three hours where one drink had led to another. Michael somehow got him home to bed but early in the morning Mick went staggering off into the darkness looking for a drink to cure his blinding headache. His son eventually tracked him down and it was decided there and then that he would be better off back home in Cork.

This sad experience must have triggered off long-submerged memories of his childhood, he had seen his father in this condition a thousand and one times. Big Mick knew that he wasn't welcome in Wicklow and later that day he made the long, lonely journey back to the Barrack Stream. Michael was never to see his father alive again. He died on 13 March 1942 at the age of seventy-three. With the relative wealth of a part-time docker with two army pensions, he was a regular at the numerous early-morning pubs on the dockside. He never recovered from a long, lingering bout of pneumonia, which he had ignored with his son's stubbornness. It was only after he was dead that

Minnie told Michael of the pneumonia. She always felt that he never really understood his father. Although the combination of alcohol abuse and illness had taken their toll, Minnie, loyal to the last, never blamed her husband.

Michael made a flying visit to Cork for the funeral. He was generally ignored by most of the O'Donovans at St Patrick's church, to which the coffin had been brought. To his annoyance, the ceremony was carried out with obscene haste. The officiating priest was in a terrible hurry because he wanted to get away to see a Gaelic football match in nearby Glanmire. At the tiny graveyard in Caherlag, Michael was even more annoyed at the speed of the burial. He went to the bar, bought a round of drinks for his cousins and immediately left Cork. When he was told later that the football match was nearly over when the priest got there, he was delighted.

Shortly after the funeral, Minnie closed the door of her little house in Harrington Square and went to live permanently with her son. She was almost seventy-seven, yet in many ways she was starting a new life. Her moving in with him meant a lot to Michael. It gave him a chance to repay her years of unselfish devotion and she was to be a constant Cork presence for him. For Minnie, the move from the Barrack Stream was a big change. As usual, she took it all in her stride and for the remainder of her life she doted on her son. Every year, on the anniversary of her husband's death, she withdrew into herself for days, prayed for him and had novenas and Masses said for him and worried about where he was. For some time she couldn't believe he was gone – that big, awkward, clumsy baby of a man who could barely fix his tie by himself; she often had to stand on a chair and knot it for him.

Three weeks after the birth of Myles, Michael agreed to give a lecture on John Synge in the Gresham Hotel. The Dublin hotel was packed and the evening was a great success. An excellent public-speaker, he fell back on his acting experience and could always be relied on to give an animated, dramatic performance rather than a lukewarm lecture. No one slept while Michael spoke. It surprised many to find that, behind all that seemingly effortless and confident virtuosity, there stood a shy, nervous man. Even though he was never a drinker, he sometimes gulped back a quick double whiskey to calm his nerves before attending the most innocuous of meetings.

Around this time, audiences in the theatre began to fall away, mainly because of the growing popularity of films. Dublin was becoming cinema-crazy. While he lectured in the Gresham, the Theatre Royal was packed to the rafters with up to 80,000 people in the space of one week to hear Gene Autry, the singing cowboy, and the city practically came to a standstill with thousands more waiting outside the Royal, hoping to catch a glimpse of the film star.

Although his relationship with the Abbey was well and truly finished, Michael still kept a quiet eye on the theatre scene in the city. At the end of August, when the volume of visitors to see the baby in Woodenbridge was down to a trickle, he was delighted to see that his old mentor, Daniel Corkery, had a play on at the Abbey. *Fonham, the Sculptor* was a tragedy in three acts. The play was full of poetic speech and beautiful dialogue but it was only a moderate success.

6. THE WAR YEARS

THE DARK CLOUDS OF WAR WERE HOVERING OMINOUSLY OVER Europe. Throughout the summer of 1939 Germany had been flexing its muscles; sabre-rattling was the order of the day and when a meeting between Hitler and Chamberlain abruptly broke down there was a foreboding of doom. Things came to a head in September with Germany's attack on Poland. Britain declared war, Ireland declared itself neutral and for the next five years life changed dramatically in the country. The British and American markets for Michael's work all but disappeared. With the restraints on his earnings he worked long hours in perfecting the constant flow of short stories. An air of depression prevailed yet it didn't seem to affect Michael as he penned the following ditty:

England! Had you but a good diuretic at this hour
Mr Chamberlain seeks to appease
While Hitler continually opposes.
Neither of these gentlemen sees
A solution as clear as their noses.
You simply transpose
'Appease' and 'appose'

Now you will see
'Appo' and 'Appea'.
Erase an 'a' and an 'e'
And one double 'p'.

Well – you can't but agree
That 'a-po-'s for 'a-pe-e' !
But these gentlemen don't,
Or they can't or they won't.

Can it be they don't know
That the place where to go
For 'a pee' is 'a po'?

As the war progressed, travel became impossible. When Michael wanted to go anywhere, even long distances, he went by bicycle. He was getting more and more interested in old ruins, especially the ancient churches and castles scattered all over Ireland. Evelyn, who shared this enthusiasm, sometimes accompanied him on these marathon journeys, taking notes and photographs of these neglected relics of a different era.

Radio Eireann were aware of the high praise he had received for his broadcasts on the BBC all through 1938 and they stepped in and invited him to read his own stories on the radio in November. He was delighted but still apprehensive about these live broadcasts. By now the people of Ireland were familiar with his easily identifiable voice.

At the end of that year he penned a fiery, sarcastic letter to the *Irish Times*. It contained a tribute to Yeats and a few well-aimed digs at the Abbey.

> Lynduff
> Woodenbridge
> Co. Wicklow
> 18 December 1939
> Sir,
>   I have just seen a notice of the London production of *The Unicorn from the Stars* 'to commemorate the death of the greatest lyric poet of the age', as the promoters put it. One might be tempted to believe that the directors of the Abbey Theatre had not yet heard of Yeats's death if it were not that they have marked it by the publication of a theatre magazine graced by some admirable cartoons (cartoons being, as everyone knows, the appropriate way of marking a great national grief). From several references in this magazine it would appear that the directors knew Yeats was a poet. But the supposition that they neglect his work because they fear it might become too hackneyed is disposed of by the fact that his last play, finished a few

days before his death, and crowning the great series of Cuchulain plays, has never even been produced by the Abbey Theatre. What, then, can one say but that the directors have disgraced themselves again?

I am glad that the anniversary of Yeats's death will be celebrated elsewhere in Dublin. I understand that the production of a new play will make such a celebration impossible at the Abbey, but surely, with two such admirable companies as the theatre possesses, it should be possible at the conclusion of the run of a new play to produce a Yeats's memorial programme. Or must we say that it takes more than twelve months and the example of England to remind the directors of their most obvious duty?

Yours, etc.

Frank O'Connor

He got more daring with his cycling excursions; one day it was a short skip to Wexford to look at some old castle or a quick hop down to Waterford to inspect that famous monastery, Mount Mellary. Other weekends it was a tortuous expedition around the rugged Kerry coast to see the primitive dwelling-places of the religious monks or a spin across the flatlands of County Limerick. On one such trip to Limerick, Dermot Foley introduced him to a pharmacist, Stan Stewart, who was an expert on local archaeology. They became staunch friends and whenever Michael and Evelyn were in the area they stayed at his house. Stan, much older than his new friend, was a kind, easy-going man who, in contrast to the non-stop activity of Michael, preferred to relax and chat over a quiet pint.

On these cycling treks around the country the couple were often followed by plain-clothes police. Michael was getting special attention. The Irish Government was baffled and very wary of him. De Valera couldn't make up his mind whether Michael was a communist, a Nazi or a spy.

One of the most important aspects of these journeys to some of the remotest parts of Ireland was that Michael picked up countless ideas and material for his writing. Lonely people were eager to tell him their stories and, when he wanted to, Michael could be a great listener.

At last, to his relief, he finished *Dutch Interior*. With the dedication

ABOVE AND LEFT: The writer seeking inspiration

TOP: Daniel Corkery, who introduced Michael to the Irish language and was a huge influence in his life
ABOVE: Eileen and Seán O'Faoláin

ABOVE: The Tailor, Tim Buckley, and his wife, Ansty
RIGHT: Father Tim Traynor
BELOW: Beautiful Gougane Barra in West Cork

CORK DRAMA LEAGUE

President : J. J. HORGAN, Sol.
Producer : FRANK O'CONNOR.
Secretary & Business Manager : DONAL CRONIN.
Stage Manager : SEAN HENDRICK.

The Cork Drama League has been founded in the hope of providing for Cork a local theatre which will adequately express the best of Southern thought and emotion. English drama—no matter how significant it may be in its own setting, or how important it may seem in countries where it has been absorbed by the national theatre—can have no beneficial effect upon a country which is subjected to cultural influences only from one source.

The Cork Drama League proposes first of all to perform Irish plays, and more especially plays by local authors; it proposes secondly to give the best of the American and Continental theatre, of Chekhov, of Martinez Sierra, of Eugene O'Neill and those other dramatists whose work, as a result of the dominating influence of the English theatre, is quite unknown in Cork.

For this purpose the League asks for subscriptions. If a hundred subscribers can be found, each to subscribe a guinea, the League will be in a position each year to produce some half-dozen fine plays. In this, its promoters believe they have taken up what should prove no very ambitious task, since they are sure there are in Cork at least five score people who care sufficiently for beautiful things to provide what funds are necessary for the project. Already they have received much help and they trust that the League's first performance will ensure them what else may be required.

Monday and Tuesday, February 20th & 21st, at 8 p.m.

THE ROUND TABLE
A Comedy in Three Acts by LENNOX ROBINSON.

CHARACTERS :

Mrs. Drennan	...	DAISY BREEN
De Courcey Drennan	...	JOSEPH GILMOUR
Daisy Drennan	Her	NANCY McCARTHY
Bee Drennan	Children	SYLVIA CLINCH
Jonty Drennan		DONAL CRONIN
Christopher Pegum	...	P. W. O'RIORDAN
Mrs. Pegum	...	KATHLEEN JENKINS
Miss Pegum	...	KATHLEEN MURPHY
Miss Williams-Williams	...	GERALDINE NEESON
Philip Flahive	...	FRANK O'CONNOR
Fan Franks	...	CATRIONA NI LAOGHAIRE
Two Men	...	J. CRONIN & E. BARRY
An Elderly Woman	...	KATHLEEN MURPHY
A Railway Porter	...	J. CRONIN

Play produced by FRANK O'CONNOR.
Acts One and Two are in the Drennan Drawing Room.
Act Three is a Railway Station Waiting Room.
Time is the present.

THE BEAR
A Comedy in One Act by ANTON CHEKHOV

CHARACTERS :

Luka (a footman)	...	DONAL CRONIN
Popova	...	GERALDINE NEESON
Smirnov—"The Bear"	...	FRANK O'CONNOR

The Scene is a Drawing Room in Popova's House.

Orchestral Selections by Messrs. J. Collier and E. O'Donovan.
Scenery kindly supplied by the Committee of the I.C.I.C.Y.M.A.
Furniture by M. A. Ryan, House Furnisher, Mac Curtain Street.

TOP LEFT: These steps at St Patrick's church are vividly described in *First Confession.* The young Michael made his own first confession here
TOP RIGHT: The Doll's House, Bachelor's Quay, Cork.
The Saint and Mary Kate was set in this old tenement house
ABOVE: The Cork Drama League's first production
(courtesy Cork Museum)

TOP: A typical demonstration and one reason why so many of Michael's books were banned
LEFT: At Trinity

TOP: Osborn Bergin, Michael and AE
ABOVE RIGHT: AE in 1903

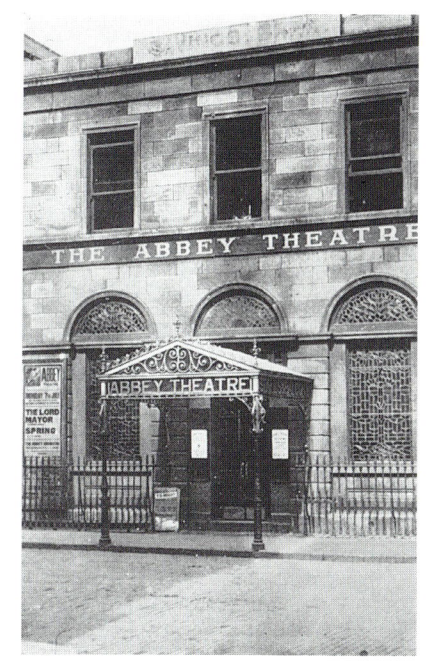

TOP LEFT: William Butler Yeats
TOP RIGHT: Dr Richard Hayes
(courtesy National Library)
LEFT: The Abbey Theatre, Dublin

TOP LEFT: Michael holds his baby daughter, Hallie-Og
TOP RIGHT: With Harriet and Hallie-Og in New York and (ABOVE) in France

'To My Wife', it appeared in June. The reviews were mixed but worse was to follow. In July the book was banned. He had expected this and surprised everyone by not kicking up a fuss – not even one letter to the press. He just shrugged, accepted it and got on with his writing. His fifth play, *The Statue's Daughter*, was finished but he was finding it difficult to get it staged. As controversial as ever, it was about a national hero with an illegitimate daughter, and people shied away, afraid to be associated with it.

The war had also put a severe dent in Seán O'Faoláin's literary income. He met Michael and Denis Johnston several times that summer and in the course of conversation they discussed the idea of bringing out a new magazine in Dublin where writers could get their work published regularly. Although the market was very limited, they knew that it would be a great incentive for aspiring young writers. Generally, O'Faoláin was the guiding influence. He had the clinically objective mind of an editor. The new magazine was called *The Bell* and was modelled on AE's *Irish Statesman* and they agreed that it would appear monthly. It became the single most influential magazine in Ireland during and after the war and young writers like James Plunkett, Brian McMahon and Brendan Behan got their first break in *The Bell*. Other regular contributors were MacLiammóir, Anthony Cronin, Kate O'Brien, Lennox Robinson, Eric Cross, Séamus Murphy, Benedict Kiely, Jean-Paul Sartre, Myles Na gCopaleen, Brinsley MacNamara, Peadar O'Donnell and Liam O'Flaherty.

For Michael and O'Faoláin, it was a much-needed platform for their poetry and their opinions, and it was a vital voice in their fights against the common foe: the Church, the State and the Censorship Board. The first issue included *The Long Road to Umera*, a story which Michael had previously read on the radio. His main function was as poetry editor and, like the *Irish Statesman*, *The Bell* had a wide range of writers and an even wider range of subjects, publishing a variety of articles, new poets, essays, book reviews, political comment and short stories. One of the strengths of *The Bell* was its high standard of journalism; the magazine was flooded with submissions and only the very best were published.

In September Michael went to London to do a broadcast for the Home Service. They were delighted with his performance and invited him back to do a series of programmes but he was deeply shocked by the state of the bombed city. The relentless German bombing raids made it a dangerous place to be. He agreed to return in Christmas week but then said he would only do the BBC broadcast from Dublin. A lot of political strings were pulled. De Valera was furious over this arrangement and tried everything in his power to stop it. Neutrality was an extremely delicate subject and Michael had a reputation for causing trouble. Eventually he was given permission to go ahead with his talk from Dublin. It was entitled 'Across St George's Channel' and in it he vividly described the sirens, the fear, the mayhem and the sad deaths of the young boys killed in London during the Blitz.

De Valera didn't trust Michael and at the end of the autumn when he went cycling up around the Cliffs of Moher he was followed everywhere by a posse of diligent Special Branch detectives. Although Evelyn was eight months pregnant with their second child, she accompanied her husband and, as they gathered stories and happily poked amongst the old ruins, every move was carefully watched and noted.

On Wednesday, 27 November, Evelyn gave birth to a little girl at the Leinster Nursing Home. The child was called Liadain because at the time her father was working on a translation of a medieval Munster poetess of that name. She had one unexpected visitor to the home. Geoffrey Phibbs, now Geoffrey Taylor, turned up out of the blue to congratulate Evelyn.

A few days before Liadain was born, there was chaos at the third night of a play in the Gate. *Roly Poly* was a daring play Lennox Robinson had adapted from a Guy de Maupassant story set during the Franco-Prussian war and transferred to the present time. It was stopped by the authorities on the grounds that it breached neutrality. Micheal MacLiammóir came on stage and explained that everyone could get their money back at the box office on the way out. Then Robinson appeared and told the startled audience that he had taken over the theatre for the night and they could all remain as his guests. So they stayed and saw the play. The next morning a messenger called on Robinson informing him that the cultural attaché at the French Embassy was very angry and demanded to fight a duel with him. Robinson wisely refused.

*

In early January 1941 things were happening fast in Michael's life. Fred Higgins died suddenly and when Ernest Blythe was appointed as his successor some people forecast that it was the end of the Abbey. A few days later James Joyce died in Zurich after an operation. His death meant the silencing of one of the most controversial Irish literary voices of the twentieth century. Then Richard Hayes, still a director in the Abbey, became Ireland's new film censor. All this must have been on Michael's mind as he took the boat to England once more. At first the Irish Government were slow to give him permission to travel. They were worried that his comings and goings to a country at war might be misinterpreted by Germany and they were afraid of possible repercussions. Countries were capitulating all over Europe and the government had a genuine fear of a German invasion. The harsh reality of war was brought home to Ireland when Belfast was heavily bombed in April. Eventually the authorities relented and gave Michael a temporary travel permit.

The BBC had offered him a month's work doing a series of broadcasts on different aspects of the theatre. This was right up his street. They allowed him free reign to talk about his own views on acting, actors, critics and Shakespeare. He blossomed in the freedom of choice and was unusually relaxed and in full command of himself, although it must have been an ordeal interviewing household names like John Gielgud and Tyrone Guthrie. The BBC were so impressed that they wanted to take him on as a full-time staff member. To get the job, he was required to take a relatively simple examination in general knowledge. To his horror he suffered a panic attack of nerves and his mind went completely blank. Needless to say, immediately after the test he knew all the answers. The BBC were surprised at his failure but they still offered him work all through the war. It is idle to speculate what direction his life would have taken had he passed that exam. Some years before, Osborn Bergin bemoaned the fact that Michael wasn't caught at an early stage and put through the mill of academic discipline. But he would surely have turned out a different man and his genius would have been blunted. He was such an unschooled intuitive writer that he regularly made learned professors shake their heads in disbelief. Especially when grappling with a particularly difficult translation, he seemed to strike gold.

It was around this time that Michael became almost obsessed with the meaning of dreams. Years previously he had been mildly interested in this subject, mainly because he learned of Yeats's and AE's fascination with the occult. O'Faoláin had heated disagreements with him on the definitions and symbols of the unconscious. Michael felt confident that dreams were messages sent from the brain and accepted them as material for many of his stories. For years he kept a pen and notebook by his bedside, at the ready, and took detailed notes of all dreams. Once, Nancy McCarthy's brother, a mutual friend, brought a potion back from Sweden and offered a bottle to Michael and O'Faoláin. This medicinal liquid was supposed to induce dreams. The two men eagerly agreed to try it out. Some time later the friend met them and enquired if there had been any reaction from the medicine. A disappointed Michael replied that it had had no effect on him. O'Faoláin said that it had done absolutely nothing for his dreams but that it was a wonderful laxative.

The Bell was now thriving. Just as he had with Dermot Foley when they wanted their own special library, Michael, the hard-working idealist, now wanted *The Bell* to be their own unique magazine where they could express themselves without fear, write their articles and encourage new poets to be bold and brave and be damned with the consequences. Patrick Kavanagh came into this category. His provocatively brilliant poetry became a feature in *The Bell* and, in many ways, Michael took him under his wing. At times Kavanagh had the same arrogant stubbornness as Michael; once, he boldly got up and walked out after the first act of a famous play in the Abbey just because he didn't like it. Everybody noticed but he couldn't care less. O'Faoláin did a great job as *The Bell*'s editor but Michael, who continued to do heroic work in the poetry section, found the isolation of Wicklow a major stumbling block. He, Evelyn and the children moved to the city and rented a house at 57 Strand Road. There he had one room completely to himself where he could write undisturbed. All his life he insisted that nothing should interfere with his writing and woe betide anyone who broke the creative flow. Sometimes when that special moment, that magic spell, was gone it never returned.

Michael was overjoyed that he had done so well in London, yet he was relieved to arrive home in one piece. Everything was strictly rationed in Ireland, so he always made sure he returned with a plentiful supply of cigarettes, which were more readily available in England. A letter to Seán Hendrick shows that people were very kind to him and the facetious postscript below is typical of his attitude towards any form of bureaucracy.

> 57 Strand Rd
> My dear Jack,
>
> Thanks for the fags. With the aid of these, of a ham presented by another kind soul, a pound of tea by a third, a bottle of port by a fourth and of sherry by a fifth, I got through Christmas in the bosom with the maximum of fortitude. Actually, nothing could have been more welcome. Christmas *sans* fags – !
>
> From your note I deduce accurately that you left Dublin without seeing O'Faoláin, that you then wrote to him and that himself and Eileen put two and two together and concluded that Evelyn and I had persuaded you not to call on him. I should have warned you that he describes E as a witch and imagines all sorts of deep intrigues of which she is the source. He's wrong as the dear child has about as much guile as would suffice a Corkman for a conversation about the weather, but every man to his fancy. If I'm right the best thing you can do is write me a letter I can show to Wilson, describing what's been done and what the verdict is and I'll go and see him. I don't know him, but he is a writer, and he did get fined £200 for helping some RAF lads to escape so he must be all right. Write soon or late, as I expect to be in England at the end of the month. Since I saw you I've been preparing a broadcast in Wales which is Ireland plus and where the horror of bilingualism is fully visible. A Welsh scholar and poet I talked to said Wales could never have a literature till they dropped the damn language – and he could scarcely speak English.
>
> Do try to explain to Cross that if attacking the Censorship simply meant going out with my little tool box and removing it there would be no discussion necessary. The Censorship will not be removed until either clerical

pressure has been removed from the two political parties or a foreign power reminds us that we didn't get our freedom to establish another little fascist tyranny and Dev comes rushing round to O'Faoláin and myself begging us to explain to the world that Ireland is really a democratic country where every man can say what he pleases.

I have now discovered why I always wanted a house on Sandymount Strand. It's the nearest I can get to England.
Ever
M

P.S. As my letter will probably be opened, I'd better make it clear that I shall be seeing Wilson not about some plot for overthrowing the government but about a deaf child. Irish people are *so* imaginative.

For over a year now he had encountered nothing but trouble and strong resistance in his efforts to stage *The Statue's Daughter*; everyone was afraid to take a chance. The Abbey asked him to rewrite sections of it. He refused point-blank. Several prominent actors were requested not to attend auditions for parts. Finally, the Dublin Drama League, which had just been revived, decided to stage *The Statue's Daughter* as their first production for twelve years. After many hiccups the play went ahead on 8 December at the Gate. Michael Farrell, who was the theatre critic for *The Bell*, was roped in as producer.

When the curtain rose on the first night, the Gate was only half-full. The performance started at 7.30 and most of the audience turned up half an hour late. Although they enjoyed it, some seemed embarrassed by the theme: talk of Catholics marrying Protestants and the disgrace of a national hero with an illegitimate child; and all this by an author who just had his last book banned for indecency. Yeats's wife, Georgina, was secretary of the Dublin Drama League and may have had something to do with the decision to perform the play. She also got him to become a member of the Cuala Press board of editors, a position he used to publish Kavanagh's poetry.*

The commotion over *The Statue's Daughter* was just dying down when there was more trouble. He wrote an article called 'The Future of Irish Literature' which appeared in *Horizon*, a popular monthly

---

* Cuala Press was established at Dundrum, County Dublin, in 1902 by Evelyn Gleeson

magazine, in January. Kavanagh's poem about the Great Hunger appeared in the same issue. If the pieces had appeared separately, they might have got away with it, but together they hadn't a chance. They were two marked men. Michael's article touched on contraception which, along with illegitimacy, divorce and abortion, was a taboo subject. *Horizon* was immediately banned and the vice squad raided Kavanagh's flat to check up on him.

Michael was steadily making a name for himself on radio. His voice was now heard quite regularly; in January, for instance, three of his stories were broadcast. Then, all of a sudden, the honeymoon was over. Radio Eireann wanted nothing more to do with him. Although he had agreements to work for them, nobody would see him, nobody would talk to him and he was completely ignored and out of work for the next six months. Things were bad but he could still fall back on his work for the BBC, or so he thought. He explains his predicament in another letter to his friend in Cork:

> 57 Strand Rd
> Dear Jack,
>   As I don't suppose you have 12/6 to spend on a book of thirty pages, I'm sending you the proofs of Paddy Kavanagh's poem which may or may not be prosecuted for indecency. I have been barred from the Dublin Radio Station on the strength of my contribution to *Horizon* with a resulting tightness of purse strings which prevents us blowing money on one of our usual jaunts. I shall be in London for the next two weeks doing a story and a broadcast on 'What is an Englishman'. My mother calls the Strand 'the Glen' [a play area near the Barrack Stream] and says 'Evelyn, I'm taking the baby down the Glen.' She has also identified four or five respectable Dubliners as old neighbours and tells us that she saw 'Mrs Harrigan' or 'Mr Frost' so she is, as you might say, settling down as far as a Corkie can by assimilating everything to the superior culture.
>   Evelyn sends regards.
>   M

It had been several years since Michael had been in Cork and in June he decided to take Evelyn on a cycling trip to his native city. They took the coast route through Waterford and Youghal. As they walked down Summerhill after a quick tour of the Barrack Stream, Michael was delighted when he bumped into Nancy. She was on her way to Blarney. She wore solid walking-shoes and a serviceable raincoat and couldn't help but notice that Evelyn was all dressed up in her Sunday best. When Michael introduced them, Evelyn embarrassed Nancy by her reluctance to shake hands with her. Eventually, Nancy made her excuses and went off down MacCurtain Street. Typically, Michael found the confrontation between the two women highly amusing.

The following month he travelled to London to do a broadcast of his story *Song Without Words* for the BBC. His visa was valid and up-to-date yet he was stopped on the pier at Dún Laoghaire. The Special Branch had special orders to block him leaving Ireland. He was angry and embarrassed and left totally in the dark. His search for an explanation from the authorities was met by a blank wall of silence. He explored every avenue but was met with a frosty indifference. In effect, he was officially blacklisted from work in Ireland and wasn't allowed to leave the country. Getting desperate, he wrote to everyone, including Harold Macmillan who had considerable political clout. Macmillan's hands were tied, however; he could do nothing. Michael's friends bombarded the newspapers with a non-stop flow of irate letters. O'Faoláin used *The Bell* to attack the Government but all to no avail. The Church, State and Censorship Board continued to make a powerful enemy, and by September Michael and his family were almost destitute.

One night they had a surprise visitor to their home, sent by the formidable Archbishop of Dublin, John Charles McQuaid. Michael was reading in his room so Evelyn innocently sent the man upstairs. A few moments later she heard a roar from above. She knew from experience that this meant her husband was more than a little upset. Afraid, she ran up the stairs to find him furious. Evelyn's long drawn-out divorce and the couple's eventual marriage in a registry office were still a sore point with the Church and McQuaid, who was well aware of Michael's plight, had sent the messenger with an offer of immediate work if the couple separated. No thought was given to the children. The fuming Michael was on the point of throwing the unfortunate man out when the more composed Evelyn stepped in and made a suggestion. She coolly stated that if she was offered a job she would agree to discuss a separation. As far as Evelyn was concerned, her suggestion was merely a ploy, but it was certainly effective: two days later she was given a position in Radio Eireann and for fourteen weeks she worked around the clock. At the end of December, when her term with Radio Eireann was up, she was offered another job. For years Michael had been at loggerheads with the Church and the 'bloody country'. He hated hypocrisy and bigotry of any kind. This latest episode was a stern reminder of the power of the Church and only galvanised his obstinate stand against what he considered to be unfair meddling in his private life.

Michael now had five mouths to feed, including his mother. In a prolific burst of energy he cycled around the ruins of Ireland collecting material for his new book, *Irish Miles*, and he worked on articles, translations, short stories and poetry for *The Bell*. The financial return for all this activity was relatively poor. He was bored, angry and frustrated with his enforced imprisonment in Ireland. To make it worse, his wife now had a regular job and she was earning more than he was. Disillusioned, he poured out his heart in a letter to Stan Stewart. This small excerpt is an indication of his feelings at the time:

> Blast Ireland, Blast Catholicism, Blast Protestantism. I spent ten years trying to save this country from itself when I should have been saving myself from this country.

Then Hector Legge, editor of the *Sunday Independent*, asked him if he would write a weekly column telling the people what was wrong in Ireland. The only condition was that he had to use a pseudonym. At first he refused on principle but later changed his mind; he was almost broke. They agreed that no one was to know, and for the next two years one controversial article after another by the mysterious Ben Mayo shocked the country. Michael revelled in his secret role as the conscience of the Irish people. His closest friends – O'Faoláin, Seán Hendrick and even his mother – didn't guess the true identity of Ben Mayo; but Ben Mayo had a field day: nobody was safe from his fiery pen. He wrote almost a hundred articles and some still have relevance today.

At one stage he thought he'd never get out of Ireland. Fed up, he wrote a highly interesting letter in 1942 to Seán Hendrick. It must be remembered that he had now been confined to the country for almost twelve months:

> 57 Strand Rd
> Dear Jack,
> By this time you'll probably have seen Paddy Kavanagh if you are not actually on the point of wanting to murder him and me with the dint of boredom. But as he is going to write about Cork he might as well get it from you and Murphy,* and if you can get him to stop lecturing you and talk naturally, you may get some amusement out of him. He wants to see the Tailor, and, as he wrote a stinking review of [*The Tailor and Ansty*], I think the Tailor ought to be encouraged to massacre him for the good of his soul. You should try to go with him and see. I am in the slough of despond myself, not having been out of the country since January and with my passport expired. My only hope now is a speedy end of the war and a little house in Hampstead. My new book of stories is due this autumn. I gave up writing for *The Bell* when O'F started sending me letters, written by the office boy, beginning Dear Michael and ending per and pro S. O'Faoláin. Among the forms of hallucinations of grandeur I never before heard of a man that thought himself a limited company. My great consolation is the eighteenth century to which I recommend you. Over the long weekend we cycled in the rain to Portarlington, a wonderful little town.
> You might try reading Swift. The modest proposal for eating the children of the Irish poor would certainly delight you, and I think you'd probably enjoy his suggestion that the English employed people to shit round corners in order to suggest that the Irish had enough to eat. A great man, even though Corkery has discovered that he's not Irish.
> Why don't you take up architecture as a hobby? It's the only art we have and the only one we never bother to look

---

* Seamus Murphy, the sculptor and author of the book, *Stone Mad*

at. Also it has the advantage of keeping one moving and seeing things, instead of settling into the comfortable middle-aged feeling that it's all more or less as one suspected.

Why don't you come up for a few days?

God bless,

Michael

In January 1944, after a flurry of behind-the-scenes negotiations, Michael was officially given the all-clear to go to England. He was promised a job by the BBC working on scripts. For several years now England had been good to him, and during the war he, in turn, was a good friend to Britain. In effect, the scripts he wrote were propaganda speeches for a film studio.

Although the country was in the throes of war, he found life there pleasantly different; he enjoyed his escape from sanctimonious narrow-mindedness; there was no ecclesiastical harassment and he appreciated the easy-going attitude of the British to both his life and his writing. They just accepted him for what he was.

He made sure to take his notebook with him wherever he went, aware of the vastness of the country and the different culture of its people. He listened a lot and, though generally the English were not as naturally talkative or as friendly as the Irish, he did manage to squeeze out the seeds of a few interesting stories which he used later. He was away from home longer than expected and time crawled by but Evelyn was kept well informed by long, detailed letters. He missed Sandymount, his family and his cycling trips. In April his collection of short stories, *Crab Apple Jelly*, was published by Macmillan and received excellent reviews in the *Irish Times*.

He became friendly with Larry Morrow who had worked with Evelyn in Radio Eireann. His heavy schedule kept him busy during the week but he found the weekends boring. One weekend Larry introduced him to Joan Knape, a friend of his girl. There was an immediate attraction between them and very soon Michael and Joan became inseparable, which certainly made for trouble in his marriage. Considering the times and situation they were in, their coming together was unintentional but understandable: two lonely people caught up in circumstances beyond their control.

Three months had now passed. He did a fine broadcast on James Joyce for the BBC and an interesting series of lectures on the theatre. Much to Evelyn's annoyance, Michael lingered on in England. He insisted that work was work and that it had to be taken when available, but she was getting more concerned about Joan; she knew all about the affair from the stream of letters she had received from her ever-honest husband.

At the end of September, after eight months, he arrived back in Dublin. Evelyn and the children were delighted to have him home again. Myles was now six and Liadain was nearly four and they had missed their father and the clickity-clack of his typewriter. However, the reunion was shortlived as he had to return to England two weeks later to continue working on more speeches. Shortly after arriving in London he met up with Joan. To his horror she was pregnant. He wrote at once and told Evelyn. A month later he arrived back in Sandymount a worried man; it was bad enough facing Evelyn but facing his mother was far worse. He was shrouded in guilt and regret and there was a palpable tension in the house.

As usual, in times of strife, Michael seemed to be at his prolific best. He practically locked himself away in his room, on automatic pilot, lost in his private world of literature. He rewrote stories, composed articles and put the finishing touches to several short stories for *The Bell* and completed that magnificent translation, from Gaelic, of Brian Merriman's *The Midnight Court*. It took a long time to finish but working on Merriman's bawdy old poem must have given him immense pleasure. To many it still stands today as one of his finest achievements. He expected an outcry on its publication and he wasn't disappointed. It is a long piece, lengthy enough to be a book on its own, all about a poor frustrated woman in a terrible state for the want of a man.

Of all his translations, Michael was surely at his superlative best with *The Midnight Court*. While always trying to stay true to the original, in many ways a translation has to be a completely different poem. It is a delicate undertaking. There is a wafer-thin line and, like a tightrope-walker, Michael, with perfect balance, manoeuvred along that tightrope with an outrageous brilliance. Here is a small example of its mischievous irreverence:

A starved old gelding, blind and lamed
And a twenty-year-old with her parts untamed.
It wasn't her fault if things went wrong
She closed her eyes and held her tongue;
She was no ignorant girl from school
To whine for her mother and play the fool
But a competent bedmate smooth and warm
Who cushioned him like a sheaf of corn.
Line by line she bade him linger
With gummy lips and groping finger,
Gripping his thighs in a wild embrace
Rubbing her brush from knee to waist
Stripping him bare to the cold night air,
Everything done with love and care.
But she'd nothing to show for all her labour;
There wasn't a jump in the old deceiver,
And all I could say would give no notion
Of that poor distracted girl's emotion,
Her knees cocked up and the bedposts shaking,
Chattering teeth and sinews aching.

Ah, you must see that you're half insane;
Try cold compresses, avoid all strain,
And stop complaining about the neighbours,
If every one of them owed her favours,
Men by the hundred beneath her shawl
Would take nothing from you in the heel of all.
Covetous, quarrelsome, keen on scoring,
Or some hairy old villain hardened with whoring;
A vigorous pusher, a rank outsider,
A jockey of note or a gentleman rider–
But a man disposed in the wrong direction
With a poor mouth shown on a sham erection!

He had a stroke of luck when Evelyn innocently took a chance and sent the story, *News for the Church*, to *The New Yorker*; it was a story that had been rewritten and renamed several times. *The New Yorker* accepted it and this was to be the start of a long and valued friendship with that highly influential magazine.

On 8 May 1945 the war ended as abruptly as it had started. When peace broke out there was a wave of euphoria in Britain. The bombing stopped and a relieved nation picked itself up and tried to get back to normality. Back in Ireland the blacklisting of Michael was lifted and, sadly, Ben Mayo was dispensed with, but, to compensate he did eleven articles for the *Times* over a period of six months. His propaganda speeches also finished with the war.

In June Joan gave birth in London to a baby boy, Oliver. Although very worried about her well-being, he couldn't get to see her until November when he crossed over to England to do a regular column for the *Evening News*. He stayed in her home but the relationship was ambiguous; they were both confused and uncertain and the atmosphere was one of cool indifference. He finished his brief spell with the *Evening News* and returned once again to Dublin. They kept in contact by post but Joan became very ill and found it difficult to cope with the six-month-old baby on her own. Evelyn kindly invited her to stay with them in Dublin until she recuperated. Joan accepted but that created another problem: how to explain Joan's arrival to Minnie. They made up all kinds of excuses but when Joan eventually turned up at the door Minnie took the baby in her arms, glanced at her son, and smiled. That wise eighty-year-old knew straightaway who the father was. So, not counting his mother, Michael lived happily at 57 Strand Road with the two women in his life and Minnie spoiled Oliver with daily doses of love and attention. Evelyn and Joan got on reasonably well with each other. At times, though, the situation bordered on French farce and Michael wisely stayed out of the way upstairs in his room. During Joan's visit he enjoyed his role as king of the castle with three adoring women attending to his every need.

After two months Joan felt well enough to return to England with the baby. A month later Michael followed her to London to do some newspaper work. That was to be the pattern for years to come; he was commuting between two women but irrevocably married to his writing. He felt caught between doing the right thing for Joan and a sense of duty to Evelyn, who was pregnant again. After two weeks he was back in Dublin and settled down to finishing *Irish Miles*, an unusual travel book dealing with the ruins in every corner of Ireland.

For quite some time no publisher had dared to touch *The Midnight*

Court but at the end of 1945 it was finally published by Maurice Fridberg. As expected, it was banned by an incensed Censorship Board. This was no surprise to the author, yet it frustrated him. To add to this, all the travelling to and from England was getting to him, but the *Evening News* helpfully suggested that he could do his column for the paper from his home in Dublin.

In the spring of 1946 Macmillan published *Irish Miles* which, if nothing else, showed the writer's versatility. It was very different from the usual Frank O'Connor work: a lighthearted travel book punctuated by two dozen glossy pictures and told in an informal way. He was disappointed that it did not do as well as he expected and, with the banning of *The Midnight Court*, the outlook in the O'Donovan household was pretty gloomy.

To add to his worries, at the end of June Evelyn gave birth to a boy who was named Owen. As usual in times of need it seemed to trigger off a burst of creative energy. Throughout the last six months of 1946, in a frenzy of determination, he wrote nine short stories, all of which were accepted and published. He also compiled a collection of his best new and old stories for a forthcoming book, and he toiled over a book on Shakespeare which he had been working on for over a year.

One of the highlights of that summer was the visit of two young scholars from America, John Kelleher and Richard Ellmann. Ellmann was writing a book on Yeats. These two young academics had heard about Michael and were very familiar with his work, but when they met him they were in for a culture shock. They were surprised by the enthusiasm and passion of the man, his wide literary knowledge and his overwhelming eloquence. At times, when he was in full flow, they could hardly get a word in. Michael became extremely friendly with both men and later dedicated the volume of short stories entitled *Traveller's Samples* to Kelleher.

The trips to the BBC usually lasted about a fortnight but in December 1946 he sailed from Dublin for what turned out to be a six month stay in Britain. Within a month of his arrival there, he asked Evelyn, the three children and his mother to join him. They duly arrived and the family lived in a country cottage in Lyme Regis. He settled down as best he could in his new surroundings but found that the lack of privacy hampered his writing. He wasn't overburdened with work but was faced with a great variety of different tasks: scriptwriting for a documentary, a BBC programme on Yeats and a broadcast in Edinburgh. The only regular work he could depend on was his newspaper column for the *Evening News*.

Michael didn't know it but around then, to some observers, there was a subtle change in his writing style. He had been writing seriously for twenty-five years and the frustrations and all the futile battles, from the stupidity of the Civil War right up to his confrontations with the Church, State, Abbey and Censorship Board, had left their mark. The byways of Ireland and the slums of Cork had previously been the main source of his stories but now he was living in rural England and, whether he realised it or not, he was writing stories in England for an English audience.

He worked ceaselessly on his new book, *The Common Chord*. It consisted of twelve stories, starting with *News for the Church*. Some were old stories which had been meticulously rewritten and others were completely new English stories. It also included a delightfully different and fuller version of *The Holy Door*, now over seventy pages long.

Michael was restless; he could never seem to stay in one place very long, and sharing a small cottage with five others certainly didn't help. The ever-present problem with Joan must have haunted him, and so he returned to Ireland. In June *The Common Chord* was published by Macmillan. Michael was shattered when he heard the news that it had been banned. The Censorship Board and De Valera were the object of his anger and he took particular delight in the defeat of Fianna Fail in the election of February 1948, but the Censorship Board was just as severe under the Coalition Government.

As De Valera was leaving office, Michael, like a literary itinerant, was once again leaving Ireland for London. The BBC had offered him a twice-weekly series called *The Critic*. His performance on one occasion went a long way to summing up how he felt at that troubled period in his life. The programme, on the merits of Rembrandt, was half-over; it had been ambling along quietly with each of the panellists dwelling on the artist's good points and generally showering praise on the painter when the chairman finally asked 'the Irish writer, Frank O'Connor' for his opinion.

Michael replied impatiently, 'I don't understand all this talk about Rembrandt. After all, what was he – only an inspired doodler.'

There was a long pregnant pause. He really wasn't attacking

Rembrandt, but the over-polite floweriness of the panel had bored him.

All the time he was spending in England didn't help the harmony in the O'Donovan home. Evelyn was getting more concerned about her husband's visits to England and saw Joan as a very real threat to the stability of their marriage. If trouble had been brewing when he left, it definitely came to a head four months later when he returned. While he was missing, Evelyn had borrowed money to build a bungalow in County Wicklow. This drove him to distraction. He had known nothing about it and felt it was a reckless decision by his wife. What with one thing and another, money was scarce. The banning of his books and now Evelyn's financial adventure added to his anxiety. From Evelyn's point of view, the children were growing up and she wanted somewhere to escape to in the summer.

While he had been working on *The Critic* for the BBC, his book on Shakespeare, *The Road to Stratford*, was published by Methuen. For a man who had openly proclaimed his dislike of Shakespeare and of Father O'Flynn Shakespearean Compnay all those years ago in Cork, *The Road to Stratford* shows that, behind all the hullabaloo, he had a deep admiration for the Bard. Even though his opinions and conclusions on some of the classical plays ruffled a few intellectual feathers and raised eyebrows in academic circles, the book did very well. Some detractors aimed a few critical digs at him and accused him of making veiled comparisons between himself and Shakespeare. There is an inadvertent analogy in the following extract where he discusses Shakespeare's achievements at forty-five when he himself was that age.

> Shakespeare, like many other provincials, developed exceedingly late. He was close to thirty when *Richard III* was produced. Within five years he was the greatest of European writers; within ten perhaps the greatest writer who ever lived.

At the end of June the bungalow was finished and Evelyn and the children took the train to Wicklow for a holiday as Michael headed for London. In between his comings and goings he was under pressure to accumulate enough stories for another book. He appreciated his work with the BBC but his writing suffered for the lack of a more permanent home base.

While he was in England moves were under way to return Yeats's remains from France. His widow, Georgina, wrote to him and asked if he would give the oration at the burial of her husband's body in Drumcliffe Churchyard. Michael felt honoured and immediately agreed but when he sailed home in September there was a change of plan. The Irish Government made it clear that Michael should not give the oration and Jack Yeats stepped in and decided that no one should speak over his brother's grave. Michael did make the journey to Sligo and attended the ceremony on 17 September 1948, his forty-fifth birthday. It was a simple occasion. He watched quietly in the background as the soft grey rain swept in from the sea and soaked the tricolour on the plain wooden coffin.

For the remainder of that year he was as restless as ever. He did broadcasts in Belfast, a lecture in Copenhagen (to his horror, he had to fly there), and he wrote a script for a film in Manchester before returning to Belfast to give a talk and read his story, *Christmas Morning*, for the BBC. Then he finished 1948 by working on radio for Radio Eireann on Christmas Day; after five years, the black sheep was welcomed back into the fold by the national station.

The spring of 1949 saw the start of the break-up of Michael's marriage. Evelyn was now spending as much time in the bungalow in Wicklow as he was in England. He knew that his marriage was rapidly falling apart and this crisis seemed to spur him on to greater things. During this troubled time he turned out some of his best stories, including *The Adventuress, D'arcy in the Land of Youth, Man of the House, The Idealist* and *The Drunkard*. On St Patrick's Day he read *The Idealist* and on 11 May he read *The Drunkard* on BBC radio.

Minnie was an unwilling spectator in her son's marital conflict and at the end of the summer she went to Cork to stay with her cousin May O'Donovan in her little house near the Barrack Stream. May's husband Jimmy had died that July while still a young man, and Minnie went to comfort her. Minnie offered to sleep on the floor but May made up a bed for her on the landing and, although there was almost forty years of an age difference, the two women were dear friends and behaved like mother and daughter.

Shortly after Minnie's departure, Evelyn packed her bags and left for Wales with the children. It was all over. That same week Michael also left Strand Road, never to return. His mother was in Cork and his family was in Wales. Alone again, he spent long hours pondering on his uncertain future. Before his marriage to Evelyn, the divorce court proceedings between her and Speaight had been long drawn out and tedious, and now ten years later he hated having to go through that same dreadful experience again. He tried to overcome it in the only way he knew: by working at a furious pace.

Now homeless, like a modern-day vagabond, he kept on the move; as frustrated, impatient and worried as ever he returned to London to work with the BBC and to rewrite the final stages of his new book, *Leinster, Munster and Connaught.* He moved in with Joan temporarily, but at the end of the year he travelled back to Ireland to attend a court hearing in Dublin. He was nervous, but old friends O'Faoláin and Dermot Foley stood by him and gave him every encouragement. There was no divorce in Ireland; there was only the possibility of legal separation, which did not entitle either party to remarry. Nevertheless, when Michael was granted a separation from Evelyn it was a relief; he immediately headed back to Joan but he had difficulty in sustaining concentration, possibly due to the presence in the house of a lively four-year-old.

At last, *Leinster, Munster and Connaught* was published by Robert Hall Ltd. It was a similar book, almost an extension, to *Irish Miles*, covering well-known monuments in all the relevant counties. It was coloured with a variety of fine old photographs and interesting anecdotes but, again, received harsh reviews, especially from the *Irish Times*.

In an agitated and aimless mood, he travelled to France for a week's working holiday. The solitude suited him and he spent Christmas writing in peaceful isolation. That week his own situation may have been on his mind as he wrote the story, *The Pretender*, a sensitive account of an illegitimate boy's search for his natural mother.

After Christmas he went back to Joan in London and surprised her by asking if she would bring Oliver with her and live with him in Dublin. She was apprehensive but agreed. It was one thing to live in the relative anonymity of London, but she was worried about being pointed out as the woman living 'in sin' with the 'shameless' Frank O'Connor.

For a while there was some semblance of stability in his life. His mother returned from Cork and stayed with them, and he finished his collection of stories for *Traveller's Samples*. The book, his fifth collection of short stories, was published by Macmillan in February 1951 and was dedicated to his American friend, John V. Kelleher. It consisted of thirteen of his best stories, some old and rewritten and others completely new. Starting with a fresh *First Confession*, it includes *The Idealist, The Thief, My First Protestant, The Drunkard* and that lovely tale, *Man of the House*. This is an extension of *The Drunkard*, in which an innocent little boy is determined to look after his sick mother but is led astray by an older and wiser little girl who inveigles him into drinking his mother's medicine, a cough bottle, and the child eventually arrives home, staggering and repentant. *D'arcy in the Land of Youth*, one of the newer stories, finishes off the book. The reviews were mixed; the main criticism was that the blend was wrong.

Two months later, to his utter frustration, *Traveller's Samples* joined *Dutch Interior, The Midnight Court* and *The Common Chord* on the banned list. He kept going as best he could and was highly acclaimed for his radio readings of *Man of the House* and *My Oedipus Complex* for the BBC. When asked if he would appeal against the ban on *Traveller's Samples*, he said, 'Censorship is not law. It is outlawry. What is the use of appealing to a pickpocket to be a gentleman and put the wallet back.'

He felt he was being singled out and victimised by the Censorship Board and the 'bloody country'. A sensitive and proud man, the banning of *Traveller's Samples* was the last straw. His domestic problems were also taking their toll, and even though in this period of his life he was extremely prolific, it was essentially a time of great restlessness and uncertainty; he didn't know in which direction his life was moving. His books were not selling well in Britain and, thanks to the Censorship Board, weren't even on sale in Ireland. Money for maintenance and child support was a further financial drain. It must also be remembered that he had the constant fear of the cancer diagnosis hanging over his head. The dreaded five-year time limit had long passed and the crippling illnesses which never seemed to be very far away must have been a mental millstone around his neck and a nagging reminder of impending death.

On his mother's eighty-sixth birthday, 18 July 1951, the Abbey caught fire and was badly burned. He had mixed feelings as he stood there looking at the smouldering shell of the famous old theatre. It brought back memories of the bickering and bitterness and reminded him of the same sense of loss he felt all those years ago in Cork when he had gazed helplessly at the crumbling skeleton of the Carnegie Library.

For quite some time now, especially when they were alone, Minnie, conscious of her age, had begun to open up her soul to her son and quietly reminisce about memories of her parents, being orphaned, saying goodbye to her mother, her years in the convent and her traumatic teenage life. With his encouragement and gentle prompting, she struggled through these painful episodes in her distant past, while he meticulously recorded every detail. She frowned on his general dislike of nuns because she always retained a great love for the Sisters of the Good Shepherd Convent who took her in and fed and educated her for sixteen years. Just a few short years later, these poignant memories of his ageing mother appeared in *The Bell* and nearly twenty years later formed the backbone of his autobiography, *An Only Child*.

Although legally separated, Michael was finding it increasingly difficult to get access to his children, and the prolonged court hearings seemed to be never-ending. Then Evelyn, who had opposed his visits, suddenly changed her mind and dropped her objections to his seeing them. He and Minnie, who really missed the children, could now see them when they wished. And yet, although he now had access, he took the surprising decision to emigrate and live in England with Joan and Oliver. Joan, who had given up everything to travel to Dublin with him, felt confused, but he was adamant. He had had enough of Ireland, the country that he hated and loved with equal passion. So for the umpteenth time, he packed his bags and left for England. They settled in Lyme Regis. For some months there was a regular pattern to his life as he wrote every day, completed several new stories, and indulged in his obsession of rewriting some of the old ones. He was forever chasing the 'perfect' story.

7. THE NEW WORLD

THE YOUNG AMERICAN ACADEMICS, RICHARD ELLMANN AND JOHN Kelleher, had remained firm friends with Michael, and over the years had been in constant touch by post. They had always felt that he would do very well in the United States. With his vast knowledge of books, they both thought that he was the ideal man to lecture on Irish literature to the eager college students in America. Early in 1952 Ellmann succeeded in arranging for Michael to teach for three months during the spring at Northwestern University in Evanston, and Kelleher did likewise for the summer at Harvard. Although nervous about this big step into the new world, Michael gratefully accepted the exciting offer from his two young friends. When an *Irish Times* reporter enquired how he felt about the invitation, his apprehension showed: 'Frankly, the prospect of teaching anybody anything terrifies me,' he replied. 'I've never even been to school.'

Joan chose to stay in England with Oliver and Michael travelled to Cork where he set sail from Cobh to New York aboard the SS *Samaria* on Sunday, 16 March. It was to be the beginning of a love affair with America. During the journey he kept himself busy by writing that fine story, *Unapproved Route*.

Even though he had some experience as a teacher of Irish, there was nothing to compare with the magnitude of his task at Northwestern. He was responsible for two courses, one an Irish literature class and the other a creative-writing class. He soon found this schedule much more taxing than he expected. He suffered from his old failing of trying to achieve too much too soon. Not content to reel off an hour-long lecture on a set subject, he put himself under unnecessary pressure by wanting to give two hundred per cent every time – an Oscar-winning performance at every class. He sometimes felt that he was a small boy from nowhere trying to climb an academic mountain; a writer rather than a scholar.

THE NEW WORLD

He had strong opinions on Joyce, O'Casey and Yeats and was never slow in voicing them, whether his students agreed with them or not. They, in turn, were hypnotised by this strange, gregarious enigma of an Irishman with his eccentric clothes and booming voice. His classes, always packed, were magical and it wasn't long before he became something of a hero.

One of the drawbacks of his popularity was that socially he was in constant demand. The time and effort he put into preparing his lectures also meant that for three months he hardly wrote at all. When his stint at Northwestern ended, he did write the story, *The Little Mother*, before moving on to Cambridge to begin his term at Harvard.

The format there was the same and he found lecturing every day, particularly in the summer heat, very difficult. His ideas and conclusions on the merits of the great Irish writers were often the cause of contentious debate amongst the students. These classes were very different to what they normally expected, and some of the mature students took a long time to come round to his way of thinking. Again, so popular were his lectures that it was practically impossible to gain admission to his classes, and even college professors were often locked out.

One day, on entering the library where he gave his lectures, he couldn't help overhearing a pretty young student heatedly stating to some of her classmates: 'I don't care what Mr O'Connor says about Deirdre.* I still say she was a bitch.' She was embarrassed when she noticed him standing there. He smiled and said, 'Come for coffee and tell us why you think that.' He made discreet enquiries about who she was and later at a party he made it his business to meet her again. As he couldn't drive he plucked up the courage to ask her if she would drive him home.

Harriet Rich was the only daughter of a Baltimore businessman. At that particular time in her life she was at a loose end, and after reading one of Michael's stories, and then discovering that he was doing a summer school in Harvard, she decided to enrol in his class. She was a bright, lively young American twenty years his junior and she found his old-world charm totally different from that of anyone she had ever met. From the start she felt comfortable and completely at ease in his company. All through that summer term, whenever he could get away

---

* Character in Synge's play, *Deirdre of the Sorrows*

from his heavy schedule, they met frequently. With typical honesty, he hid nothing from her. She was well aware of Evelyn and the situation with Joan. Every chance they got, especially on weekends, they managed to escape from the heat of the city. Harriet made good use of her car and she sometimes drove him to the cool quietness of the seaside where they could be alone.

His term in Harvard was extremely happy but he was tired from his heavy workload. Every lecture was like running a marathon and he was often left mentally and physically drained. In between, he worked on radio. One broadcast appealed to his sense of humour and gave him great pleasure because it was sponsored by the Jesuits. In August his new book, *The Stories of Frank O'Connor*, was published by Knopf in the US and by Hamish Hamilton in Britain, and he was delighted by the excellent reviews. His six months as an American professor flew and he was invited to return in the spring.

Harriet, with mixed feelings, saw him off from New York on Thursday, 4 September 1952. She knew that he was sailing back to Joan. He had blown into her life like a whirlwind and she wondered what the future held for her. True to form, Joan also knew all about Harriet. She hired a car and met him at Cobh and they returned to Lyme Regis.

While he was in America, he had been aware that Minnie wasn't well, but he hadn't realised how ill she really was. She was now eighty-seven and her health had deteriorated alarmingly in his absence. Joan looked after her but she was in terrible pain. The doctor advised her to take morphine to ease the suffering. Before going to sleep on Monday, 10 November, she quietly told Joan that she loved her. A few hours later she died peacefully in her sleep.

The dreaded moment had arrived and it hit Michael harder than he had expected. Since the day he was born she had always been there in the background, supportive to the end. When he was sick as a child she was there. When he was bullied or rejected or lost his job she was the one steady influence, and when he returned ashamed after being interned it was she who unreservedly welcomed him home with open arms. She watched him grow with pride, from boy to man, and she was behind him all the way. It must have been a shock when he went to live with Evelyn, yet she never once passed judgement, and when she, Joan and Evelyn lived under the one roof she just carried on and quietly did what she could to help. Now the one, ever-present rock in his life was no more.

It took him a long time to get over his mother's death. Her body was brought home by boat to Dún Laoghaire. In Dublin he was inconsolable with grief and Seán O'Faoláin stepped in and took control of the arrangements. The funeral was held after Mass in St Mary's church on Pope's Quay, Cork, where Big Mick had attended Mass every Sunday morning. She was buried and reunited with her husband in the family grave in Caherlag. Very few O'Donovans turned up. They felt that she 'really wasn't an O'Donovan'. The big old headstone still towers over the grave today. Neither of their names is on it.

Evelyn allowed her eldest boy, Myles, to live in England with his father; so Joan, Michael and his two sons returned to what was now their home. Myles had fallen behind in his studies, especially his reading, and Joan, who was a teacher, gave him special attention and worked very hard with her new 'son' until he was up to scratch. As usual when his life was in turmoil, Michael reverted back to his tried and tested formula and buried himself in his work; he wrote a story, *Masculine Principle*, and tore into another book for Knopf.

The trauma of his mother's death haunted him for quite some time. The one consolation was that she had lived to see and enjoy his success. He knew well how she felt about him; once, when visiting Cork, he found her in a fever of sickness at home with her worried husband by her bedside, big and useless and unable to do anything. She kept calling out to her son – in her semi-conscious state she didn't know he was present. She repeated over and over again that he took her from the gutter where life had thrown her. Her passing had left him disturbed, confused and uncertain.

He was separated from Evelyn but the ever-messy divorce proceedings still dragged on. O'Faoláin acted as a mediator in the whole nasty ordeal. Michael's relationship with Joan was stuttering and he didn't know whether he would marry her or not. The constant flow of letters to and from Harriet was an added strain on their relationship.

At long last, on Thursday, 12 March 1953, Michael was finally divorced. The following Saturday he set off from Southampton to the United States for another six months of teaching. It had been a distressing time for him: his mother's death and funeral, the court hearings, and then the relief of the divorce. It was a weight off his mind. In effect, he landed in America a single man. He was excited but apprehensive about what lay ahead. He knew that he would have very little time off in the following six months. When he got the opportunity he loved to socialise with the cream of America's critics, writers and scholars.

As in the previous year, the combination of teaching and lecturing was extremely difficult and time consuming. His students, many of them adult writers, were more demanding and inquisitive than the youngsters he had lectured to before. He sometimes struggled just to keep up with them. They had to be of a certain standard to get into the class. Much to his frustration, he had practically no time to write.

Yet with all his activity he was still very lonely. He met Harriet briefly in March but hardly saw her at all during the summer. Their relationship had cooled a little. She went off on a summer holiday but they did keep in contact by post. At the end of August she drove to Cambridge where he was staying and they crammed as much as they could into his last few days in America.

A tired Michael arrived in Southampton on 8 September. Joan was there to meet him but there was a noticeable tension between them. They headed for Dublin to try to settle a legal problem over a child the newly married Evelyn had given birth to just before her divorce was finalised. To compound the predicament, her solicitors were hounding Michael for maintenance. The second reason for his visit to Ireland was that on Friday, 17 September, a huge dinner party was given at the Wicklow Hotel to honour his fiftieth birthday. All his old friends were there including Joan, Dan Binchy, Honor Tracey, Denis Johnston, Stan Stewart and Seán O'Faoláin, and Doreen and Dermot Foley who had made the journey from Ennis to be there. They had a wonderful evening but it was obvious to everyone present that all was not well between Michael and Joan.

The feuding couple returned to England but their domestic situation grew steadily worse. Harriet's name cropped up frequently in their arguments. Eventually Joan left. On 9 October he wrote to Harriet. The letter was short, to the point, and is surely one of the most unromantic proposals any woman ever received.

H,
At last I feel morally and legally free to ask you to marry me. If you want to I'd be delighted. I don't know what I can promise you.
Love
M

Although cautious friends were genuinely worried about her and tried to warn her about the potential problems of marrying this notorious Irishman, who was a relative stranger, much older than she, and often in poor health, Harriet totally ignored them. She was never more certain of anything in her life and felt that five years with him would be better than fifty years with any other man. She immediately sent him a telegram saying yes to his proposal. He was overjoyed. His mother had been dead a year and Joan was irrevocably gone. He knew that Minnie had been very fond of Joan and had always treated her like a daughter.

For several weeks his life was a vacuum; unable to concentrate on his writing and impatient and anxiously awaiting Harriet's arrival. Myles, now a handsome young man, was staying with him; father and son became closer than ever, thrown together in this unlikely situation. Michael was in many ways as useless and impractical as his own father, and could hardly boil an egg or make a cup of coffee for himself. Myles stepped into the breach and between them they just about managed to survive.

When Nancy McCarthy had refused to marry him all those years ago, he had jokingly remarked that one day he'd marry a rich American. How prophetic that was. On Saturday, 5 December 1953, Michael O'Donovan and Harriet Rich were married in England at Bletchley Registry Office. There were only three guests: fourteen year-old Myles, and old friends Bill and Erna Naughton. The groom was fifty and the bride was thirty.

Two days after the wedding, he had to appear in a London court. The wrangling over custody of the children had grown nastier by the day. There was still no outcome, but it failed to spoil the festive season for the newly-weds.

From the very start Harriet got on famously with her stepson and a visit from Michael's old friend Stan Stewart was the icing on their

Christmas cake. At this difficult period in Michael's life, Harriet was like a breath of fresh air. Her positive attitude and youthful enthusiasm lit up their home. She coped admirably with her new husband's fickle eating habits and unselfishly rearranged her life to accommodate his working schedule. The bitter cold rain and snow was a huge change from the balmy warmth of her native Baltimore, and living with Michael was a far cry from her comfortable and relatively sheltered upbringing, but she worked hard at being the wife of a demanding writer and helped to shake him out of this brief lethargic mood.

She knew that his last collection, *Stories*, had done extremely well especially in America, and the publisher, Knopf, was delighted and very keen for him to do a follow-up. He agreed and again threw all his energy into writing several new stories and extensively revising some old favourites like *Guests of the Nation* which was now completely different to the story which had made such an impact in 1931. Sixteen of the stories had not previously appeared in book form. His new book, *More Stories*, was a massive collection containing twenty-nine stories and again did very well in the States.

Michael had developed a fondness for the American way of life; he liked the friendliness and hospitality of the people and he admired their open-minded attitude to life. He was growing more and more disenchanted with his situation in Britain regarding Evelyn. Her solicitors were demanding maintenance payments, and the constant stream of threatening letters made it difficult for him to write. He had been invited to teach at Harvard once again during the summer of 1954 and for some time had been toying with the idea of taking up permanent residence in the USA. Eventually he took the plunge. He wanted to take Myles with him, which created another problem, and he had to sign an agreement to return him to Britain, if required to do so by Evelyn.

On 26 June, Michael, accompanied by his young American wife and his son, set sail aboard the *New Amsterdam* hoping to start a new life in New York. Myles went to stay with friends while Michael and Harriet made their way to Cambridge where he began preparing for his third spell as a professor in Harvard. His lectures were as popular as ever and his short-story classes were equally exciting, controversial and physically draining.

The one sad note was his falling out with John Kelleher. The

Kellehers had taken a liking to Joan and expected Michael to marry her. The break-up of that relationship and his marriage to Harriet did not go down too well with them.

When the summer school at Harvard ended, Michael, Harriet and Myles moved to a flat in Brooklyn and he got down to some serious writing. He began working on a new book partly based on the lectures he had given at Harvard in 1954 but which had been in his head for years: a comprehensive study of the novel and an analysis of the great writers from Jane Austen to James Joyce and Gogol to Turgenev. It was another labour of love. He called it *The Mirror in the Roadway*. He also did two fine recordings of two of his best stories, *The Drunkard* and *My Oedipus Complex*, and wrote regular book reviews and articles for magazines and newspapers. This was one of the most prolific periods in his life; he churned out a conveyor belt of short stories including *A Bachelor's Story*, another Larry Delaney tale.

But he was overdoing it and in February he collapsed with a serious bout of bronchitis brought on by overwork, and was confined to bed. His blood pressure was ominously high. A month later he suffered an attack of angina. Harriet had her hands full looking after him and trying to persuade him to slow down. It didn't help when he received the sad news from Ireland that one of his closest friends, Father Tim Traynor, had died suddenly. Although he knew it might cause legal repercussions, he left Myles in America while he and Harriet travelled to Ireland. He wanted to visit his beloved Gougane Barra and pay his respects at the graveside of Father Tim who was buried practically alongside the Tailor and Ansty. He returned to America angry, frustrated and weary of the still-unresolved maintenance situation.

At the end of the autumn, the O'Donovan family decided to leave Brooklyn and set up home in Annapolis where Harriet's parents lived. Michael never really got on well with his father-in-law. Both men were equally stubborn, and Jack Rich found it hard to accept that his only daughter had married a man almost his own age.

Still, Michael drove himself; he finished *The Mirror in the Roadway* and continued to consult his dream book and his old theme notebook in a relentless search for ideas for new stories. He was also in constant demand for television and as a lecturer and critic, and editors were queuing up for his services. Not satisfied, he embarked on an exhausting lecture tour of six universities. Due to his fear of flying, he criss-crossed the length and breadth of the US by train.

Harriet was forever by his side helping him, advising him, making sure he took his medicine, but worried about his health and the furious pace he was setting himself. She had been married only two years but the thought of early widowhood must have occasionally crossed her mind. Yet it was her hyperactive husband who seemed to thrive on the hectic shedule. He loved being in the limelight.

They duly arrived back home in Annapolis but Michael found it as provincial as Cork and couldn't settle down there. In September 1956, after just one year, they moved back to Brooklyn Heights in New York where he spent three months polishing up his stories for his new collection, *Domestic Relations*. He finally settled on fifteen but it was to be another eight months before the book was published in New York by Knopf and in London by Hamish Hamilton. It contained six Larry Delaney stories and received excellent reviews. Frank O'Connor was now hugely popular in America. A group of eminent psychiatrists even carried out an in-depth series of tests on his genius. He thought the whole thing was hilarious but, in true American fashion, they gave him a free trip to California for his trouble. They said the tests indicated that he was the most honest man they had ever met.

In April he was invited to Copenhagen to attend a literary conference and Harriet, who had never been to Scandinavia, pressed him to accept. On the way to Denmark they broke their journey with a brief stay in Cork where he gave her a guided tour of the playground of his youth: the Mardyke, the Good Shepherd Convent, Sunday's Well, the Women's Jail and the Barrack Stream. They met all his old friends including Seán Hendrick, Séamus Murphy and Dermot Foley who was now head librarian in the city. The highlight of the visit was a meeting with Nancy McCarthy. Michael and Harriet were staying in the Imperial Hotel one day when a waiter came to the table and said, 'Excuse me, sir, but there's a lady on the phone who says she'd like to speak to you, if you'd like to speak to her. She's a Miss McCarthy.'

'Good Lord,' Michael replied, 'My long-lost love.' He turned to Harriet: 'Would you like to meet her?'

Half amused and half curious, Harriet said she would, so after lunch they took the bus to Douglas and walked up to Nancy's bungalow. He was apprehensive especially after the frosty reception Nancy had received from Evelyn. He needn't have worried: the two women struck

THE NEW WORLD

up an immediate rapport and remained the closest of friends for the rest of their lives. Nancy later came to stay with them in Dublin and they visited her in Cork. They gave her the beloved poodle, Mike, driving to Cork with him when he was a tiny puppy. They phoned regularly when they were in America and at least once a week when they were in Ireland.

On one visit to Cork, Michael told Nancy that he was thinking of writing his autobiography and was worried that he might get the timing of various incidents in his early life wrong. Nancy listened with a smile and then said, 'Do you think the letters you wrote me would be a help?'

'My God! You don't still have them?'

'Of course. They're in the attic.'

Nancy duly gave Harriet six bundles of letters, arranged chronologically and tied in blue ribbon. At his urging, she read them first and they were a great help to him. He thought it was an amazing act of magnanimity for an early love to give her love letters to the wife of the man from whom she had received them.

Years later, Nancy had a brief, unhappy marriage. Michael and Harriet were living in California when they got word of Nancy's husband's death. Michael insisted that they call her immediately, even though it was 3.30 a.m. in Cork. Harriet phoned and they talked and talked for hours. That night Nancy slept for the first time since her husband had died.

Nancy McCarthy had a razor-sharp intelligence and was incredibly active. She was involved in theatre, music, the Cork International Film Festival and the Cork Ballet Company all her life. Although she took up mountaineering very late in life, she became a more than capable climber. The night before she died she visited an art gallery.

In October 1988 I called at her bungalow to see her. We had a cup of tea, a slice of brown bread and a long cosy chat. Her front room was like a shrine to Frank O'Connor – or as she called him, 'My darling Michael'. As we talked about him for hours, her face glowed with affection and she kindly showed me dozens of old poems and love letters he had written to her and she played tapes and records of his wonderful voice. She was clearly in love with him all her life and before I left I got up the courage to ask her one last question.

'Nancy, will you tell me one thing? Why didn't you marry him?'

She was quiet for a moment. 'There was sickness in the family at the time.'

She was looking out the window as she spoke almost to herself. What she said was quite true. Her mother had been very ill for long periods and Nancy had a genuine fear that there might be a touch of insanity in the family. Michael, who was aware of this, cheered her up one day when he put his arm around her and said, 'You know, Mac, you were always afraid of insanity but, by God, you're the sanest damn person I know.'

But this may not have been the only reason for her refusal to marry him. His anti-clericism may have been another stumbling block. There was no way Michael would have married in a church and, equally, there was no way Nancy, who came from a very religious family, would have married outside the Church. Their personalities were similar in many ways: both were singleminded and stubborn and, although she loved him dearly, she may have been wise enough to realise that their marriage would not have survived on a long-term basis.

Nancy died the following week and surprised many by having her remains cremated. She told a friend, 'I don't want the pigeons to be talking about me.' She had asked Harriet to arrange to have her ashes scattered in her beloved Dunquin on the rugged County Kerry coast. Friends turned up from all over the world to pray and watch as her ashes dissolved in the wild Atlantic Ocean in a simple but moving ceremony. It was typical of her that she left strict instructions that the 'scattering' was to take place only when the wind was blowing out to sea. She didn't want the ashes to blow into the faces of anyone in Cork.

Afterwards, everyone retired to Kruger's hostelry in Dunquin where, naturally, the conversation turned to Nancy. One story followed another. One friend told of the time Nancy came across a man halfway up a steep mountain. Undaunted, she climbed over him and carried on regardless. Another recalled the day Nancy was caught in a hail of bullets during the Civil War and dived for cover behind a wall. When a Free Stater asked her if she was afraid of being shot, she said indignantly, 'No, 'tis playing marbles, I was.' It was common knowledge that she got great pleasure from the fact that the Civil War was put on hold for ten minutes every morning while the milkman delivered milk to her house near Monkstown. The evening ended with one final toast to 'Herself'. It was only right that Nancy had become part of the elements, as befitted such a free spirit.

The topic of the conference in Copenhagen was 'The Writer and the Welfare State'. Michael was his old self as he gave a fine lecture on what it had been like to grow up in a country where there was little or no government help for the poor. To his amazement, he found that the Scandinavians were jealous of his deprived childhood because it gave him so much to write about. But it wasn't all work in Copenhagen. He and Harriet had great fun. The writer Kingsley Amis was also present and Michael was delighted to meet him as *Lucky Jim* was one of his favourite books.

When the conference finished the O'Donovans got the train back to Paris where they met up with Donal Brennan, a poetry-mad friend who worked for Aer Lingus. Harriet and her husband were to return to the US by plane and she knew how nervous he was about flying. She reassured him and cajoled him but to no avail. Then they had a stroke of good fortune when the head of police recognised the famous Irish writer and personally supervised his departure from the airport. Michael was delighted with the special attention and forgot all about his worries.

Evelyn and her new husband were now living in Canada and the following month Michael's children, Liadain and Owen, came to Annapolis to visit their father. After many years he was at last reunited with his three children. Owen stayed for the summer before returning to his mother but Liadain was overjoyed to be back permanently with her father and she was to discover, as Myles had, that Harriet was as loving a stepmother as any child could wish to have. Harriet had another surprise for her husband: she was pregnant. He was delighted but worried about his age. Harriet, too, was a little apprehensive; she was having her first baby at the age of almost thirty-five. There were more problems: Harriet got the measles. They immediately called the doctor who took one look, confirmed that they were the 'safe' type of measles and demanded twenty-five dollars. When Michael asked him how he knew without seeing the patient, he said, 'By smell,' and left quickly with his fee.

Michael didn't like living in his father-in-law's shadow. Like two stubborn elks they had locked horns a few times, but common sense prevailed. Both men had Harriet's well-being uppermost in their minds and two months before the baby was due she wisely went to live with her parents – her father was chairman of the board at the local hospital. The move was a practical one and it took the pressure off the expectant couple although Michael was never relaxed in Jack Rich's patch.

While awaiting the baby's arrival, he became deeply interested in the notes on Minnie's reminiscences. Recalling both his own and his mother's distant childhood must have been painful but all his old passion and urgency returned as he became engrossed in getting all their early memories down on paper. He called this first portion of his autobiography, 'Child, I Know You're Going to Miss Me,' after the title of a negro spiritual Oliver used to sing to him just after Minnie had died. The song haunted him and brought back memories of his mother's death.

At 4.52 a.m., on a steaming hot Wednesday morning, 25 June 1958, Harriet gave birth to a gorgeous little girl, destined to be the only child of parents who were themselves only children. She weighed 6lbs 15 oz. Harriet's nickname was Hallie so the baby was called Hallie-Óg (young Hallie) after her mother. When Michael heard the news he rushed to the hospital to see them. In his excitement he picked out the wrong baby, saying, 'This one must be mine because it has the face of an Irish priest,' but the nurse pointed out the correct baby, who was to become the apple of his eye. Both mother and child were well but Harriet had to have a long period of recuperation after the Caesarean birth.

While Harriet recovered, her husband travelled to New York to show the manuscript of *Child, I Know You're Going to Miss Me* to Bill Maxwell, the editor of *The New Yorker*. Over the years Bill had become a trusted friend (the magazine would eventually publish over fifty of his short stories) and Michael valued his opinion like that of no other, readily agreeing to practically any of his editorial suggestions. Bill Maxwell was also a fine writer and when he was having problems with his new novel, *The Chateau*, Michael took the manuscript, read it meticulously, and kindly offered to help in every possible way. *The Chateau* was successfully published two years later. The O'Donovan and Maxwell families became close friends.

Two months after the birth of Hallie-Óg, Michael suffered severe pains in the chest. The doctor strongly advised him to slow down. It is difficult to understand why he refused to take it easier. He was now relatively well off and there was no need to push himself so hard. His constant, relentless, punishing schedule was taking its toll. At times he felt he was still the poor boy reared in the slums of Cork. That hopeless, poverty-stricken period in his young life sometimes haunted him and he was determined never to stop writing. He genuinely felt that he was being paid too much for his work and he feared that it could all suddenly end. Harriet teased him and begged him to ease off. She tried to frighten him by insisting that he carry an identity card in his pocket so that she could be immediately notified if he collapsed.

Writing about his early life stoked up nostalgic feelings for the old country. He was always afraid of becoming sentimental about Ireland, though, and felt the only antidote to that was to return there. He decided to leave the USA and on 27 September moved back to Ireland with his two young ladies. He continued to work steadily in his old stamping ground. They rented an apartment at Mespil Flats in Dublin and in no time there was a regular flow of friends to wish them well. Through Dan Binchy he developed a renewed interest in ancient Irish and started working on a book of translations. Radio Eireann had long since buried the hatchet and invited him to do broadcasts of *In the Train*, *The Luceys* and *The Long Road to Umera*. He also worked regularly with the Radio Eireann players, directing performances of his own stories. He took great pleasure in once again wearing his director's hat but he sometimes became too involved with the script and drove the actors to distraction by rewriting their lines. His story, *Mass Island*, was published in *The New Yorker*. This was to be the last of a number of stories featuring Father Fogarty, a figure loosely based on Michael's close friend, Father Tim Traynor.

That Christmas in Dublin was spent in quiet contentment. Michael was at peace with himself. The precocious Hallie-Óg was a source of immense pleasure to him and a visit by Stan Stewart made the festive occasion even more special. A great deal of the credit for Michael's happiness has to go to Harriet; a young wife thrown in at the deep end, she moved to Dublin with him without question and adjusted to what must have been a completely different way of life in Ireland with admirable ease. She was always there, quietly in the background, ready to help her husband. In many ways she got the best of him. In recent years he had mellowed a little and had put away his self-righteous sword. Yet, when he was aroused, it was a bad place to be a dragon. His old reputation still lingered on in Dublin and it sometimes hurt his pride when he was unfairly and deliberately snubbed by people in high places. Undoubtedly, the happiest period in his life was when he was with Harriet. They shared a deep love. He always treated her as an equal and constantly asked for her advice or opinion on a story or first draft. He doted on Hallie-Óg and any chance he got he proudly pushed the pram up and down O'Connell Street – a rare sight for an Irishman in those times. Sometimes, inquisitive women dented his ego when they thought he was the grandfather.

Spring was livened up when Harriet's parents paid them a flying visit. Jack Rich still resented the fact that Michael had married his daughter much too quickly and in faraway England. He would have preferred them to wait and have a big ceremony in America. The arrival of Hallie-Óg had defused the situation; the grandparents also loved the child, and the two men in Harriet's life declared a lukewarm peace and got on reasonably well for the duration of the stay.

Michael kept busy by continuing to work on his autobiography and he did several broadcasts for the BBC in Belfast. In June his book of translations, *Kings, Lords and Commons*, appeared; it received magnificent reviews but was immediately banned. One critic hit the nail on the head when he pointed out that, although the translations were from centuries-old medieval Irish, they had a unique freshness and were like original poems in their own right.

In September the O'Donovan family decided to move back to the USA and settled down in a beautiful new flat in Brooklyn Heights, overlooking the city. For the next two months Michael was embroiled in finishing his autobiography. Then he sent copies of the manuscript to Seán Hendrick, Séamus Murphy and Nancy McCarthy to make sure he hadn't written anything that would upset anybody unduly. *An Only Child* was a magnificent tribute to Daniel Corkery. The fact that Corkery failed to acknowledge this in any way hurt Michael deeply. They gave it the thumbs up; Nancy, in particular, loved it. He brought the manuscript to Bill Maxwell at the offices of *The New Yorker* where the two friends, the passionate writer and the dedicated editor, spent weeks polishing it.

Just before Christmas he got a surprise visit from Liam Clancy (the Clancy brothers, Liam, Tommy, Paddy and Tommy Makem were a highly successful ballad group); the enthusiastic Liam, then only twenty-one, wanted to stage a tribute to Yeats and wondered if Michael would help or advise him in any way. Michael would have done anything to keep the memory alive of his old friend and readily threw himself into the project. The end product was that four of Yeats's plays under the title *Yeats and Cuchulain* were performed at the Kaufman Auditorium in New York on St Patrick's night. Michael didn't want to give a speech at the event, but in the end he delivered a masterful analysis of the way Yeats had used the Cuchulain sagas to write about his own life.

By April he felt that his autobiography was ready so he took it to Knopf with a view to publication. He had a gut feeling that it was something special and he was very conscious of the debt he owed to the editorial skill of Bill Maxwell. He wanted to call the book *Invisible Presence* but it was pointed out that this almost religious title might put people off. He then chose *Mother's Boy* but when reminded that this had effeminate undertones he decided to settle for *An Only Child*. This title was immediately accepted.

The problems one encounters in writing an autobiography are numerous. While, on one hand, you have to bare your soul openly and honestly about the intimacies of your life, on the other hand you have to stand back objectively outside of yourself as if you were writing as another person. Michael achieved this balancing act to perfection. He puts a comforting arm around the reader's shoulder and draws him into his confidence and quietly tells him of the sad early days, the grinding poverty and uncertainty, the sacrifices of a loving mother, the terrible fear of a child whose father was drunk (some of the O'Donovans still haven't forgiven him for that), his involvement in the fight for Irish freedom which led to his internment as a frightened teenager, the tragic Civil War and his never-ending quest for education. *An Only Child* turned out to be a sensitive, poignant masterpiece.

He was at peace with the world in his new flat in Brooklyn Heights; the view of New York was glorious. He felt refreshed and the creative juices started to flow with a renewed enthusiasm. He wrote two stories, *Weeping Children* and *The American Wife*, which appeared in *The New Yorker*. Shortly after, he was invited to Stanford University in California for five months as a visiting professor. The format was similar to that at Northwestern and Harvard: lectures on the modern novel, which he loved, and running short-story classes, which he hated. He was to give forty lectures (four times a week for ten weeks) on the novels of the nineteenth century; each one to a rapt audience; each one a marathon, virtuoso performance. For the second ten-week period it was a different situation; twice a week he held the writing classes. These were a tough grind because the specially selected students were accomplished writers in their own right. He had been writing short stories for over forty years but he found it difficult to persuade the students to accept his method of constructing a short story. They were very talented but also stubborn and set in their ways.

Halfway through his term in Stanford, *An Only Child* was published by Knopf. It was so popular that it was practically sold out in eight weeks. A revised edition of *The Road to Stratford* under the new title of *Shakespeare's Progress* also appeared. He had been under enough pressure preparing and teaching his seminars but now he was inundated with requests for newspaper, radio and television interviews and he was featured in numerous magazines including *Newsweek*. Although very tired, he was in sparkling form. The reviews were unanimous in their unstinting praise; one even compared him to Turgenev.

Wallace Stegner, who was responsible for bringing him to Stanford, had been asking Michael for years to write a book on the art of the short story. Unknown to Stegner that book, which was to be called *The Lonely Voice*, had been in Michael's head for years.

Although Harriet had settled in comfortably in California, she liked the constant good weather, her husband was getting more and more homesick and frequently brought up his native city in their conversation. A sometimes tongue-in-cheek letter to Seán Hendrick in Cork sums up his feeling at that time:

> 4102 Amaranta Way,
> Palo Alto, Calif.
> My dear Jack,
>
> I owe you two letters, and I have no excuse except one that is rare with me – pressure of work. This whole notion of escaping the New York winter was misconceived from the start because as you once said to me, 'You'd make an impossible editor because you'd want to edit the

advertisements as well.' I cannot *not* get involved, and in a university the size of this, there are a hell of a lot of interesting young people to become involved with.

The reviews of the book are pouring in, and the one thing that would interest you, as it interests me, is the massive attention to Childers. Wouldn't it be ironic if Childers' reputation were to be restored by yourself and myself, who went through it all in a sort of haze? And, though Corkery may be mad, he's got his share of the attention and praise.*

As you've gathered, I hate professoring, but our friend, O'Faoláin, has taken to it in wonderful style. He is Phi Beta Kappa lecturer for next year – he told Ita** he was going back to Ireland this year to die, but he's obviously postponed his demise and intends to die in style. I wish to God he'd get back to being Shelley, which is how I remember and like him best. Further, I suspect it's the real Seán and the others are all just phonies. However! I lost my temper with Brendan Behan during his most recent incarnation, and described him as the Brigitte Bardot of Ireland, which wasn't malicious but a protest at the resurrection of the Stage Irishman whom we innocently thought we'd killed. (As Martin Corry‡ once said, 'We didn't shoot enough of them.')

The parents have been here to see their darling granddaughter, and we had drinks last night in a place called 'Top of the Mark' from which one can see the whole city of San Francisco, as we used to see Cork from Dermod Nagles' house in Montenotte. After I'd been there two minutes I realised Hallie had brought me there only to show me what she calls 'Seumas' Church'. Women are always subjective.

We finish here in June, and as soon as we get a passage, we'll get over. I wish you could find us the ideal flat in Cork. This house we're living in is a wooden structure of which sixty per cent is glass – glass being cheaper than

---
* He and Corkery had drifted apart. Corkery was angry because he had remained a staunch Nationalist and Catholic and disliked the direction Michael's career had taken
** A mutual woman friend from Cork
‡ A prominent Republican Member of Parliament in Ireland

timber - and in the garden are lemon and orange trees. It's still like Cork, in the rain and in the feeling that one is at least three thousand miles from culture.

But before I close I must tell you. We have a letter from an old lady called Margaret Donovan, who gives her age coyly as 'over 85' addressed to 'FOC. Writer and Orator' beginning by saying that God has sent me to be the leader of the Irish race in America, assuring me that I'm right in saying the Irish here could finance the whole economy of Ireland but that they prefer to make demonstrations. Apparently, I've been saying the wrong things because an article in the Baltimore *Sun*, the best informed paper I know, says that Lemass has practically fixed Partition. I've been saying we should bring our troops back from the Congo and turn them on Northern Ireland. However, in politics I never seem to get anything right.

Love to Kitty, Mairgread and Seumas
Michael

His heavy workload began to tell and he became very ill; he was worried about the nagging pains in his chest. Then on 1 June, while walking to college, he felt dizzy and collapsed. The doctor diagnosed a slight stroke and ordered him to bed and complete rest. His blood pressure was dangerously high and the remainder of his term had to be cancelled. He was advised by the doctor to travel back to the east by train and to make sure he religiously took his high blood-pressure and tranquillising medication. Harriet, nervous about his condition, asked for one of his tranquillisers and, by mistake, he gave her the wrong tablet. By the time the train reached Chicago, he felt fine but her blood pressure was so low she could hardly move. She was exhausted. Despite her protests he went off to visit the Chicago Art Institute while she slept off the effects of the medication. Still, he was growing more anxious about the state of his health and his future. The following month he said goodbye to all his American friends and set sail for Ireland. He was coming home to stay.

They moved into a flat in Wilton Place in Dublin. Old friends were delighted that he was back again but they couldn't help but notice the change in him. The shadow of death and the years of pain had quietened him; the voice and the twinkle in the eye were still there but the cigarettes had been replaced by a pipe. Harriet hovered in the background in case he needed anything.

When word got out in Dublin that Michael was home and recuperating from serious illness there was a steady stream of journalists to Wilton Place. He had put on weight and they found him surprisingly relaxed and not at all the fearsome tiger they had come to expect. He spoke to everyone; no one was refused. Radio Telefis Eireann wanted to shoot a film of *In the Train* and interview him for Irish television which was just about to commence broadcasting. The BBC did a film on his early days in the Barrack Stream. These were exciting times in Ireland; television was just coming in and most houses in Harrington Square had aerials attached to their chimneys. As the film was set before the 1920s most of the neighbours, when asked by the film crew, kindly removed the aerials for authenticity while filming was in progress; but some O'Donovans with long memories refused point blank to co-operate with anything involving Michael, and several scenes had to be relocated.

Meanwhile, he was kept busy trying to finish *The Lonely Voice* and had commenced a second volume autobiography based on his adult life, as well as working for Radio Eireann. But his abiding passion remained translations from the old Irish. Gaelic had always been on his mind and now that he was back in Ireland it once more came to the surface. He eagerly set to work on mediaeval Gaelic poetry with Professor Greene of Trinity College. He seemed to derive immense pleasure from this tediously difficult process and, usually to much academic surprise, always came up trumps with the end product. He started working for the *Sunday Independent*, this time dropping the disguise which, for him, took a little bit of the fun out of it. Every Sunday he came out fighting, a pen blazing in each hand. He wrote about everything from weeds in the national monuments to pompous politicians. Although worried by the stroke he kept turning out articles by the dozen, some of which he used to attack bad theatre, censorship and the neglect of Ireland's monuments. Also, he never let up on the controversial Casement diaries; for years he was absolutely convinced that they were forgeries, especially the allegations of homosexuality. Another pet hate was Britain's part in the famine. He wrote a scathing review of Cecil Woodham-Smith's *The Great Hunger: Ireland 1845–49*.

He wasn't critical of the author but of the apathy of the British Government in allowing millions of Irish people to starve to death.

He was born with a book in his hand and fire in his veins and was a walking encyclopedia with a phenomenal memory – and yet, except for his winning essay on Turgenev as a teenager for which he got nothing, Michael had never received an honour of any kind. On 5 July 1962, at long last, Trinity College bestowed on him an honorary doctorate, Doctor of Literature. Complete with academic gown, he looked nervous as he spoke at the dinner. But behind his nervousness he was proud. The small boy who had never gone to school had finally arrived. Even Big Mick surely would have been impressed by his 'good-for-nothing' son. He would probably have asked if there was a pension going with it. It is interesting to note that Michael was never honoured by University College Cork; he never lectured there and was generally neglected and swept under Cork's literary carpet.

That summer he made his Irish television début in a talk called 'Interior Voices'. It was directed by Michael Johnston, son of Denis. Before the show, Michael was a bag of nerves as usual, but once he got into his stride he was magnificent.

He was now a regular visitor to Belfast where he was to do twelve broadcasts over the next few years ranging from talk shows on art to interviews and readings of his stories. Early in 1963 he completed a highly successful series called *Ulster Miles*. In between all this radio activity he prepared another collection of short stories and struggled on with the autobiography; one of the problems was that *An Only Child* was so good that it was a hard act to follow. The first instalment of his translations with Professor Greene, *A Golden Treasury of Irish Verse*, appeared in the *Sunday Independent* but Myles Na gCopaleen gave Michael a slating in his column in the *Irish Times*. (He once called him 'the Dean of the Celtic Faculty'.)

In August he was invited to Sligo as the principal speaker at the Yeats International Summer School. The trip brought back a lot of old memories. He went to the humble little graveyard at Drumcliffe in the shadow of bare Benbulben to pay his respects to his dear friend, and later spoke with great dignity to Yeats enthusiasts from all over the world.

On returning to Dublin he finally finished twenty translations from the old Irish. He had been working on them and revising them for years and he now felt they were as near to perfection as possible, and was delighted when Dolmen Press agreed to publish them under the title *The Little Monasteries*. A limited edition of 1,050 copies appeared. It was a gem of a little book, forty-one pages of twenty translations. One poem, 'Eve', demonstrates its delightful simplicity:

I am the wife of Adam, Eve;
For my transgression Jesus died;
I stole heaven from those I leave;
'Tis me they should have crucified.

Dreadful was the choice I made,
I who was once a mighty queen;
Dreadful, too, the price I paid –
Woe, my hand is still unclean!

I plucked the apple from the spray
Because of greed I could not rule;
Even until their final day
Women still will play the fool.

Ice would not be anywhere,
Wild white winter would not be;
There would be no hell, no fear
And no sorrow but for me.

Several American universities invited him over to the States but his health posed a problem and he didn't feel up to travelling. Instead, he accepted an offer from Trinity to do a series of lectures on Irish literature. Each week he was extremely fidgety immediately before but once he began he stood there at the lectern, his impressive black gown covering his Donegal tweed, he had the packed hall in the palm of his hand. His lectures were so popular that eventually they were published as a book, *The Backward Look*.

The winter of 1963 was particularly bad and to escape the poor weather Michael took Harriet and Hallie-Óg to the South of France in January. They chose to stay in one of Yeats's favourite hotels, the Hôtel des Anglais in Menton. The relaxed atmosphere and the warm sun worked wonders and he returned to Dublin a new man. A visit by the poet John Betjeman, who had been a good friend for years, cheered him up no end. He continued his lectures in Trinity until the end of term but was gradually growing tired of them. They took up the bulk of his time and he felt that his course should be broadened in scope by bringing in subjects like languages, art and history under the umbrella of a school specifically for Irish studies.

He resumed working for RTE, doing a documentary series with the young writer James Plunkett. The film crew visited decaying monuments all over the country with Michael commenting on them as they went. These were the same monuments he had pinpointed for preservation all those years ago on his trusty bike, and yet to his frustration nothing had been done about thir upkeep. Then with no lecturing, broadcasting or teaching to disturb him he started to write stories with a renewed vigour. He finished *School for Wives*, *A Life of Your Own* and *The Corkerys* in quick succession and followed with those fine stories, *The Cheat* and *An Act of Charity*.

For most of his life Michael had fought with the institutional Church, yet the priesthood held a magnetic fascination for him. He often stated when he was younger, that he had always wanted to be a priest, even though close friends laughed at this suggestion. He had recently developed a friendship with a young priest in Dublin, Father Maurice Sheehy. A highly intelligent man, Sheehy was a lecturer at University College Dublin and several things about him impressed Michael: he had studied in Paris and Rome and had a great interest in Latin manuscripts of monastic Ireland. Harriet, herself a religious woman, derived great fun from the two men's heatedly discussing some minute theological point. They disagreed fiercely about Dr John Charles McQuaid, Michael disliking the archbishop and Father Sheehy defending him vigorously.

On the last day of 1964, he received the sad news from Cork that Daniel Corkery had died. It affected him deeply and was a grim reminder of his own mortality. The memories came flooding back: Corkery had introduced him to the Irish language, classical music, European literature, the arts and theatre and had influenced and immeasurably shaped his early days.

Throughout that winter he was very ill. He should have been resting but he stubbornly kept active on a variety of different projects: his poem translations ran for twelve weeks in the *Sunday Independent*; he was involved in revising the biography on Michael Collins while at the same time working on another collection of short stories, and his second volume of autobiography was proving difficult to complete. Yeats, Richard Hayes, Geoffrey Phibbs, Tim Traynor, AE, the Abbey, and his mother were haunting him. The text was painful and patchy and it irritated him that he hadn't enough time to devote to it because he was also working on scripts for RTE with James Plunkett. That spring of 1965 was an exciting time for him. It was the hundredth anniversary of Yeats's birth and the BBC had asked him to do a documentary on the great man's life and poetry. He was to work with Brendan Kennelly on this. Kennelly, from Kerry, was a rare individual, an effusive young lecturer at Trinity who loved poetry even more than Michael did. He had a silver-tongued, bouncing brilliance and a voice like honey to go with it.

In the middle of February Michael suffered from dreadful pains in his stomach. His doctor was worried and insisted on an immediate operation at Portobello Hospital. Myles, now twenty-five, flew in from New York to be by his side. Father and son had become very close and for the following ten days Myles and Harriet waited, watched and worried. For the next month Michael was unable to leave his flat. He had a constant flow of visitors: Dan Binchy, Hector Legge of the *Sunday Independent*, Dermot Foley and the writer Mary Lavin brought him books and tried to cheer him up. Even Joan, who by now had written several novels, sent him a book which he enjoyed very much. But the incessant pain was crippling him and not being able to go out for a walk was frustrating.

After five weeks' detention Harriet drove him to Sligo, where he worked on the Yeats documentary for the BBC, but he wasn't well and when he finished filming and returned home he suffered a similar vicious attack of pain, which necessitated another stay in hospital and a series of tests and examinations which revealed nothing. This didn't surprise him. All his life he was never a great lover of doctors and nuns.

There was a ceremony coming up in Sligo commemorating Yeats's centenary and, sick or not, he was determined to attend. His dear friend, Mrs Yeats, who was herself ill, insisted that he give the graveside oration this time. Nothing was going to stop him, so he and Harriet again drove to Sligo. On the morning of the service he suffered another violent attack but he struggled on and at the tiny graveyard spoke with great warmth and feeling in a poignant tribute to William Butler Yeats. Thankfully, when he arrived back in Dublin, his health improved and he continued to write every day. At the end of June, as part of the BBC documentary, he gave a lecture at Trinity. His young friend, Brendan Kennelly, read poems and gave a beautiful narration to the film.

Joan and Oliver came to Dublin in July. Oliver stayed with the O'Donovans and got on very well with his father. They chatted for hours on end and he was delighted with his son's academic achievements. Now in his twenties, he was a brilliant student and was to become a professor of moral theology at Oxford.

At last Michael was getting to grips with *My Father's Son*, his second volume of autobiography, and he finally finished revising his collection of stories. Health permitting, he hoped to go to the US himself to see Bill Maxwell and his other American friends and to talk to Knopf about publishing the book.

Liadain had spent the summer in Dublin and she met her father frequently. They walked and talked endlessly and she was thrilled when he told her how proud he was with the way she had overcome the difficulties of her troubled teenage life. She had had a lonely existence. The uncertainty of her parents' relationship and the prolonged divorce proceedings had left their mark. But now she had grown into a lovely and assured young woman.

As he was often liable to do, Michael got an impetuous urge to go to France for a short holiday with Harriet. They flew to a little town near Lourdes where Father Sheehy met them with a car, and they made a quick tour of the country mainly visiting Romanesque churches. Father Sheehy wore a sweater and the three of them were the centre of attraction every day in their hotel: one old man, one young man and a woman. Then, on Sunday, Father Sheehy turned up for breakfast wearing his collar and the mystery was solved: husband, wife and chaplain. They stayed in Auch where Father Sheehy said Mass one morning. He had no one to assist him so Michael stepped in and had the unusual experience of serving at Mass. But he suffered a savage attack of pain which ruined the holiday and they had to return to Dublin.

He was now constantly on painkillers though they did little to relieve the terrible suffering. After they had to call out the doctor one morning at two o'clock, he left some morphine with Harriet and showed her how to give an injection. She often spoke afterwards about how good a patient her husband was. When she mentioned this, he replied, 'Don't you know the old Irish saying? When you're in the hands of your enemies you had better be good.' In September he was back in hospital. After a month of intense tests the doctors still couldn't identify the cause of the pain and he was reluctantly allowed home.

At the beginning of 1966 Michael was feeling tentatively optimistic. There was a great revival of the arts in Kilkenny and he travelled down to see the Kilkenny Design Centre and was highly impressed with it. When he got home there was a surprise for him: Oliver came to Dublin for another brief visit and proudly told his father that he was about to become an Anglican priest. The announcement was received with pride and some amusement. It would be interesting to speculate on how Minnie would have felt about her grandson's choice of career. No doubt she would have loved him.

At the end of March old friends from America, Dick and Betty Gill, called to see Michael. Harriet threw a party to honour them and a great night of talk and singing was had by all. But the following morning Michael's searing pain returned with a vengeance. It kept coming and going and he did his best to work in between. His new edition of *The Big Fellow* had recently appeared and it received fine reviews – a big change from the apathetic response for the first edition twenty-nine years previously. One critic praised the book and said that the author told the truth that nobody wanted to hear, which is exactly what Michael had tried to do.

The film about Yeats, *Horseman, Pass By*, was finished and the O'Donovans, accompanied by Brendan Kennelly and several friends, were invited to the RTE Studios for a private viewing; but halfway through the film Michael got yet another savage attack and had to be driven home. His doctor strongly advised him to cancel two lectures he was to give that week at Trinity. The lectures were on early Irish storytelling and, unusually, he was all fired up and looking forward to them. The doctor reluctantly agreed to let him go ahead but warned his friends of the seriousness of the situation. Most of the audience were unaware of anything being amiss as he gave two rousing performances on Tuesday and Friday. The following week the BBC showed an adaptation of his story, *Song Without Words*. To his amazement, they called it *Silent Song*. It got rave reviews and received the Prix Italia.

At the end of February he was reading in his flat when the phone rang. Harriet answered it but couldn't understand a word as the caller spoke in Irish. She called her husband and listened in wonder to his half of an animated conversation. After five minutes he slammed down the phone and the room almost shook as he burst into loud laughter. When his surprised wife asked him what was wrong, he told her that he had been talking to a priest who had invited him to give a talk in Maynooth College, Ireland's famous seminary. Behind all the laughter there was a mischievous delight. 'I can't blame the whores for being ignorant if I don't go and enlighten them,' he said.

The following day Father Sheehy drove him to the college where, ironically, Michael gave his last public lecture to a standing ovation.

Determined to keep busy he finished the final chapter of *My Father's Son* and it appeared in the *Saturday Evening Post* on 26 February. He also completed an article on Yeats called *A Gambler's Throw*. On Friday, 4 March, he attended Professor Edward's seminar in Trinity and thoroughly enjoyed answering questions on his own work. The students were grateful for his co-operation and his typical honesty. On the following Tuesday, although he could hardly walk, he made it to Trinity again to hear a lecture by Dan Binchy, a dear friend and a man he admired very much.

Two days later, on Thursday, 10 March, he was sitting at home reading when he told Harriet that he wasn't feeling well and went to lie down in the bedroom. A few moments later she went in to see how he was doing. As she lay on the bed with him he took her hand in his, smiled, and said, 'I hope you don't expect me to entertain you.' His breathing changed and he quietly passed away. At last he was at peace. He was just sixty-two.

Harriet immediately phoned Father Sheehy who was there in fifteen minutes and gave him the last rites. The doctor arrived soon after and tried to revive him but he was gone.

Harriet later phoned Nancy and asked her where she thought they should bury him. She knew that there could be trouble in having the funeral in Cork because the conservative Bishop Lucey was in charge of the diocese there. She also knew that the O'Donovans had already said that the grave in Caherlag was full. 'Give me half an hour,' Nancy said, and consulted several friends in Cork who gave her conflicting advice. She felt sure that Michael would want whatever was easiest for

Harriet, so she advised her to let Father Sheehy arrange everything in Dublin. She got the first train up from Cork and spent the next three days at Harriet's side. She was a rock of strength.

It was a subdued gathering at the O'Donovan home that evening: Nancy, Dan Binchy, Brendan Kennelly, Hector Legge, Mary Lavin and a tearful Dermot Foley all found it hard to comprehend that they would never hear that sonorous voice again.

Father Sheehy organised everything. The funeral was to be from Westland Row church after Mass and then on to Deansgrange Cemetery. For the next few days tributes poured in from all over the world and newspapers, radio and television were glowing in their praise of the man now that he was dead. One observer said that Michael had a curious love-hate relationship with his native city. He loved the place because it was his cradle and because of its lost opportunities but he hated its occasional tyranny and smugness. He added that, although Michael had had only a few years of formal education, he was the most widely educated man he had ever met. Séamus Murphy said, 'Michael's enthusiasm for the things he liked was infectious and you found yourself being won over completely. He was utterly convincing; he not alone set fire to himself but he set fire to everyone.' Harold Macmillan, his publisher, wrote: 'Michael had two names and lived a life with many facets. Yet everything he did, however unexpected or contradictory it might seem, was informed by the same singleminded and passionate integrity. The young Irish rebel and the mature wartime friend of Britain, the eccentric librarian, the enthusiastic man of the theatre and the meticulous self-taught scholar, the sonorous translator of Irish poetry and the superlative short-story writer, the inspiring public lecturer and the dogged master of the seminar – all were unquestionably the same unique and original man.'

Loyal to the end, May O'Donovan and her cousin Christy travelled up from Cork to join Liadain, Myles, Oliver and Joan in grief. There was a great variety of mourners present as Father Sheehy celebrated the Mass: academics, writers, theatre critics and journalists, and television cameras covered the event. It was sad to note that De Valera failed to turn up; he was otherwise engaged in opening an extension to a school in Dublin. Michael, who had done more to put Ireland on the world map than a succession of Irish governments over the previous forty years, was ignored by that same government.

At Deansgrange Cemetery Father Sheehy said a quick prayer over the coffin before Brendan Kennelly, in an emotional oration, praised the passing of a true friend: 'When Michael was around, the air was alive with possibilities. His very presence held a promise of wonderful things. To me, he looked like a king, felt like a poet, spoke like a god. Negative things formed no part of his life or outlook: his emphasis was always on the positive and possible, especially in his relationship with the young. That is what I meant when I said that he was an inspiration.' Brendan then spoke the lines Michael chose for Yeats's epitaph.

> And so I chose the laughing lip
> That shall not turn from laughing
> Whatever rise or fall;
> The heart that grows no bitterer
> Although betrayed by all;
> The hand that loves to scatter; the life
> Like a gambler's throw.

Harriet dropped a bunch of flowers into the grave and left in tears. Ten days later she went to live with her parents in the United States. She was tired and uncertain about what the future held for her. Looking after Hallie-Óg, who was nearly eight, helped her to cope. Father Sheehy kindly looked after things in Ireland for her. He went through all her husband's writing and helped her to piece together *My Father's Son* which was published by Macmillan. They continued to see a lot of each other and he stayed in Harriet's parents' home while on an American lecture tour. Although they had been sparring partners, Michael loved and treated Maurice Sheehy like a son. He asked him to celebrate Mass every year on the anniversary of his mother's death and was always present at the service. Father Sheehy was twenty-five years his junior. Michael told him once, when he was particularly ill, that if anything ever happened to him he wanted Sheehy to look after his wife. Maurice Sheehy had grown very fond of Harriet and one day, in a roundabout way, he proposed to her.

'I wonder did Michael mean I should marry you?' he asked.

Harriet was surprised and flattered. The one big stumbling-block, obviously, was that he was an Irish priest. She agonised over it for a long time until finally they agreed that if Maurice got a dispensation from the Pope they would go ahead. After a year he got permission from Rome and they married in 1969. Michael would have been amused.

When Michael's name is mentioned, the words obstinate, self-educated, brave, formidable, generous and humane spring to mind. His greatest fault was also his greatest gift: he told it as he saw it. His clear and brilliant understanding of the nature of the short story is best summed up in his own words: 'It doesn't deal with problems; it doesn't have any solutions to offer; it just states the human condition.' Perhaps this is why the story-telling of Frank O'Connor has and always will have such a universal appeal.

THE WORKS OF FRANK O'CONNOR

SHORT STORIES
'Achilles' Heel': *New Yorker*, November 1958; trans. to German.
'Act of Charity, An': *New Yorker*, May 1967.
'Adventure': *Atlantic Monthly*, January 1953.
'Adventuress, The': *Far and Wide*, December 1948 ('Lady Brenda').
'After Fourteen Years': *Dublin Magazine*, April 1929; read by author BBC Radio, 14 March 1938.
'Alec': *Guests of the Nation*, 1931.
'American Wife, The': *New Yorker*, March 1961; trans. to French.
'Anchors': *Harper's Bazaar*, October 1952.
'And we in herds thy Game': *Crab Apple Jelly*, 1944, ('Star that bids the Shepherd Fold'), ('The Shepherds'); trans. to French.
'Androcles and the Army': *Atlantic Monthly*, May 1958; trans. to German and Flemish.
'Attack': *Guests of the Nation*, 1931.
'Awakening, The': *Dublin Magazine*, July 1928.
'Babes in the Wood, The': *New Yorker*, March 1947; trans. to German.
'Batchelor's Story, A': *New Yorker*, July 1955; trans. to German and Dutch.
'Baptismal': *American Mercury*, March 1951 ('A Spring Day').
'Black Drop, The': *Lovat Dickson's Magazine*.
'Book of Kings, The': read on Radio Eireann, November 1940.
'Bones of Contention': *Yale Review*, June 1932; trans. to German.
'Bridal Night, The': *Harper's Bazaar*, July 1939; trans. to German, Flemish, Danish and Swedish.
'Brief for Oedipus': *The World of Law* ('Counsel for Oedipus').
'Call, The': 1971, The Cornet player who betrayed Ireland, 1981.
'Cheapjack, The': BBC Radio, 1942, ('The New Teacher').
'Cheat, The': *Saturday Evening Post*, May 1965.

'Christmas Morning': *New Yorker*, December 1946 ('The Thief'); trans. to German.
'Climber, The': *Harper's Bazaar*, April 1940; read by author BBC Radio, March 1938.
'Conversion, The': *Harper's Bazaar*, March 1951.
'Corkerys, The': *New Yorker*, April 1966; trans. to Dutch.
'Cornet Player who betrayed Ireland, The': *Harper's Bazaar*, November 1947, ('Solo on Gabriel's Trumpet').
'Crossroads': *New Yorker*, February 1952; ('First Love').
'Custom of the Country, The': *The Common Chord*, 1947.
'Darcy i dTir na nOg': *Nuascealaiocht*, 1952.
'Darcy in the Land of Youth': *New Yorker*, January 1949.
'Day at the Seaside, A': *The Bell*, January 1941 ('*Old Fellows*'); trans. to German and Flemish.
'Day Dreams': *New Yorker*, March 1957; trans. to German.
'Don Juan's Apprentice': *Harper's Bazaar*, August 1954; ('The Sorcerer's Apprentice'); trans. to German.
'Don Juan Retired': *The Common Chord*, 1947.
'Don Juan's Temptation': *The Common Chord*, 1947; trans. to Danish, German and Italian.
'Drunkard, The': *New Yorker*, July 1948; read by author BBC Radio, May 1949; BBC TV, January 1953; trans. to Danish, Flemish and German.
'Duke's Children, The': *New Yorker*, June 1956; trans. to Danish and Swedish.
'English Soldier, The': *Yale Review*, December 1934.
'Eternal Triangle': *Cornhill Magazine*, 1951; ('The Rising'), ('The Tram'); trans. to German and French.
'Expectation of Life': *New Yorker*, August 1955; trans. to German and Danish.
'Face of Evil, The': *New Yorker*, April 1954.

180

'Faith moved his Dictionaries': *Everyman*, May 1935.

'Father and Son': *More Stories*, 1954; trans. to German. 'Father Fogarty's Ireland': *John Bull*, August 1959; ('The Mass Island').

'First Confession': *Lovat Dickson's Magazine*, January 1935; ('Repentance'); read by author BBC Radio, February 1944; BBC TV, November 1952; trans. to Danish, Italian, German and Swedish.

'Fish for Friday': *New Yorker*, June 1955; trans. to German.

'Flowering Trees, The': *Ireland Today*, December 1936.

'Francis': *New Yorker*, November 1954; ('Pity'); trans. to German.

'Freedom': *The Stories of Frank O'Connor*, 1952.

'Friends of the Family': Reginald Moore's *Modern Reading*, November 1946.

'Frying Pan': *The Common Chord*, 1947; trans. to German.

'Genius, The': *Winter's Tales*, 1955; ('The Sissy').

'Ghosts': 1972, *The Cornet player who betrayed Ireland*, 1981.

'Goldfish': *Harper's Bazaar*, February 1938

'Grand Vizier's Daughters, The': *Three Tales*, 1941; trans. to German.

'Grandeur': *Ireland Today*, August 1936.

'Great Man, A': *New Yorker*, May 1958.

'Guests of the Nation': *Atlantic Monthly*, January 1931; trans. to French, German, Slovak and Flemish.

'Holy Door, The': *The Common Chord*, 1947; trans. to German and Danish.

'House that Johnny Built, The': *The Bell*, March 1944; read by author BBC Radio, February 1943; trans. to German.

'Hughie': *The Bell*, October 1941.

'Idealist, The': *New Yorker*, February 1950; read by author BBC Radio, March 1949 and March 1964; trans. to Italian, German and Danish.

'Impossible Marriage, The': *Woman's Day*, March 1957.

'In the Train': *Lovat Dickson's Magazine*, June 1935; trans. to German.

'Jerome': *Traveller's Samples*, 1951; read by author BBC Radio, May 1951; trans. to German.

'Judas': *The Common Chord*, 1947; BBC Radio, March 1947; ('The Rivals'), ('Night of Stars'); trans. to French, Italian and German.

'Jumbo's Wife': *Guests of the Nation*, 1931; trans. to German.

'Ladies of the House': *Harper's Magazine*, October 1954; ('Lonely Rock').

'Lady in Dublin': *Today's Woman*, October 1946; ('Lady of the Sagas').

'Landlady, The': *Penguin New Writing*, 1949; ('The Lodgers').

'Last Post, The': *Irish Times*, November 1941.

'Late Henry Conran, The': *Guests of the Nation*, 1931.

'Laughter': *Guests of the Nation*, 1931.

'Legal Aid': *Harper's Bazaar*, December 1946; ('A case for the Roarer'); trans. to Danish.

'Life of Your Own, A': *Saturday Evening Post*, February 1965.

'Little Mother, The': *Harper's Bazaar*, July 1953.

'Lofty': *Bones of Contention*, 1936.

'Long Road to Umera, The': *The Bell*, October 1940; trans. to German and Flemish.

'Lost Fatherlands': *New Yorker*, May 1954.

'Luceys, The': *Crab Apple Jelly*, 1944; trans. to French.

'Mac's Masterpiece': *London Mercury*, May 1938

'Machine Gun Corps in Action': *Guests of the Nation*, 1931; trans. to Danish.

'Mad Lomasneys, The': *Crab Apple Jelly*, 1944; ('The Wild Lomasneys').

'Majesty of the Law, The': *Fortnightly Review*, August 1935; read by author BBC Radio, January 1948, January 1964 and Radio Eireann, January 1956; trans. to Swedish, French and German.

'Man of the House, The': *New Yorker*, December 1949; read by author BBC Radio, November 1949, November 1950 and January 1966; Radio Eireann, January 1956; NBC, November 1955; trans. to German, Slovak and Danish.

'Man of the World': *New Yorker*, July 1956; trans. to German.

'Man that stopped, The': *Bookman*, August 1934.

'Martyr, The': *John Bull Magazine*, December 1951.

'Masculine Principle': *New Yorker*, June 1950.

'Masculine Protest': *New Yorker*, June 1952; read by author BBC Radio, June 1954; trans. to Swedish and German.

'May Night': *Life and Letters*, April 1935.

'Michael's Wife': *Lovat Dickson's Magazine*, February 1935; trans. to German.

'Minority, A': *New Yorker*, September 1957.

'Miracle, The': *Life and Letters*, May 1934.
'Miracle, The': (different from above) *The Common Chord*, 1947; trans. to German.
'Miser, The': *Crab Apple Jelly*, 1944; trans. to Danish.
'Mortal Coil, This': *New American Mercury*, December 1950.
'Mother's Warning, A': *Saturday Evening Post*, October 1967.
'Murderer, The'; BBC Radio based on 'First Confession', March 1948 and February 1966.
'Music When Soft Voices Die': *New Yorker*, January 1958.
'My Da': *New Yorker*, October 1947; read by author BBC Radio, July 1951.
'My First Protestant': *Traveller's Samples*, 1951; trans. to French.
'My Oedipus Complex': *Today's Woman*, December 1950; read by author BBC Radio, November 1950 and October 1963; trans. to Danish, German, Swedish, Dutch, Finnish, Hungarian and Italian.
'News for the Church': *New Yorker*, September 1945; trans. to French, Danish and German; ('The Sinner').
'Nightpiece with Figures': *Guests of the Nation*, 1931.
'Old Age Pensioners': *Traveller's Samples*, 1951; trans. to Danish.
'Old Faith, The': *More Stories*, 1954; trans. to German; ('Soul of the Bishop').
'Orphans': *Mademoiselle*, July 1956; trans. to German.
'Orpheus and his Lute': *Esquire*, January 1936; BBC Radio, August 1963; trans. to Danish.
'Out-and-out Free Gift, An': *New Yorker*, October 1957.
'Paragon, The': *Esquire*, October 1957; trans. to German.
'Pariah, The': *New Yorker*, September 1956.
'Party, The': *New Yorker*, December 1957; Radio Eireann, January 1959.
'Patriach, The': *Guests of the Nation*, 1931.
'Peasants': *An Long*, 1922; BBC Radio, February 1947 and January 1949; trans. to German and Danish.
'Peddler, The': *Irish Tribune*, November 1926.
'Picture, The': *Irish Statesman*, April 1929.
'Pretender, The': *New Yorker*, December 1950; trans. to Flemish.
'Private Property': *Evening News*, June 1950.
'Procession of Life': *Guests of the Nation*, 1931; trans. to German.
'Public Opinion': *Mademoiselle*, September 1957; BBC Radio, January 1959.
'Rainy Day, A': *John O'London's Weekly*, August 1938.
'Requiem': *New Yorker*, June 1957; read by author BBC Radio, March 1965.
'Ring, The': *Irish Statesman*, July 1928.
'Romantic, A': *Evening News*, August 1951.
'Ryan Woman, That': *Saturday Evening Post*, January 1957; ('Ugly Duckling'); trans. to German.
'Saint, The': *Mademoiselle*, June 1952.
'Salesman's Romance, A': *New Yorker*, March 1956; Radio Eireann, May 1959; CBC, May 1966; trans. to Dutch, German, French and Danish.
'School for Wives, The': *New Yorker*, November 1966.
'Seagulls': *The Quarryman*, Volume 3, Number 2.
'Sense of Responsibility, A': *New Yorker*, August 1952.
'Sentry, The': *Harper's Bazaar*, January 1950; read by author BBC Radio, May 1951; trans. to German.
'September Dawn': *Dublin Magazine*, July 1929.
'Set of Variations on a Borrowed Theme, A': *New Yorker*, April 1960; ('Variations on a Theme').
'Shepherds, The': *More Stories*, 1954; ('The Star that bids the shepherds fold'); ('And we in herds Thy game'); trans. to German and French.
'Sion': *Irish Tribune*, August 1926.
'Sister Agatha and the Milkman': *Redbook*, May 1970.
'Sisters, The': *Guests of the Nation*, 1931.
'Soirée chez une jeune belle fille': *Guests of the Nation*, 1931.
'Soldiers are we': *Irish Statesman*, 1930.
'Solo on Gabriel's Trumpet': *Irish Times*, March 1942.
'Song without Words': *Harper's Bazaar*, February 1944; read by author BBC Radio, October 1942 and September 1943; trans. to Italian and Danish.
'Stepmother, The': *Irish Writing*, 1946; trans. to German.
'Story by Maupassant, A': *Penguin New Writing*, 1945.
'Storyteller, The': *Harper's Bazaar*, 1937; trans. to German.
'Study of History, The': *New Yorker*, March 1957; trans. to German.
'Sue': *New Yorker*, September 1958.
'Teacher's Mass, The': *New Yorker*, April 1955.

'Tears, Idle Tears': *Bones of Contention*, 1936.
'There is a Lone House': *Golden Book*, January 1933.
'Thing of Nothing, A': *Cornhill Magazine*, April 1946; trans. to German.
'Tinker, The': BBC Radio, March 1943.
'Torrent Dammed, A': *New Yorker*, September 1952.
'Twilight': (*Lovat Dickson's Magazine*).
'Ugly Duckling': *Saturday Evening Post*, 1957; trans. to German.
'Unapproved Route': *New Yorker*, September 1952.
'Uprooted': *Criterion*, January 1937; trans. to German and French.
'Vanity': *New Yorker*, July 1953.
'War': *Irish Statesman*, August 1926.
'Weeping Children, The': *New Yorker*, January 1961; trans. to German and French.
'What girls are for': *Colliers*, March 1951.
'What's wrong with the country': *Bones of Contention*, 1936.
'World of Art and Reilly': *Vogue*, July 1948; read by author BBC Radio, August 1951.
'Wreath, The': *Atlantic Monthly*, November 1955; trans. to German.

AUTOBIOGRAPHY

An Only Child (Knopf, New York 1961; Macmillan, London 1962; G. K. Hall, Boston 1985; Blackstaff 1993; Syracuse University Press 1997).
My Father's Son (Macmillan, London 1968; Knopf, New York 1969; G.K. Hall, Boston 1985: Blackstaff 1994).

BIOGRAPHY

The Big Fellow. A Life of Michael Collins (Nelson, London 1937; Revised edition, Clonmore and Reynolds, Dublin 1965; Templegate, Illinois 1966; Corgi 1969; Poolbeg 1979, 1986, 1991, 1994, 1996; St Martin's Press).

INTRODUCTIONS BY FRANK O'CONNOR

Irish Street Ballads, by C. O Lochlainn (Corinth Books, New York 1960).
Dead Souls, by Nikolai Gogol (Mentor, New American Library, New York 1961).
The Tailor and Ansty, by Eric Cross (Chapman & Hall, London 1964).
A Portrait of the Artist as a Young Man, by James Joyce (Time Reading Programme, New York 1964).

Modern Irish Short Stories (Oxford University Press 1957; Classic Irish Short Stories 1985).
A Book of Ireland (Collins National Anthologies, London, Glasgow 1959; Blackstaff 1991).

TRANSLATIONS FROM IRISH

The Wild Bird's Nest (Cuala Press, Dublin 1932).
Lords and Commons (Cuala Press, Dublin 1938).
The Fountain of Magic (Macmillan, London 1939).
Lament for Art O'Leary (Cuala Press, Dublin 1940).
The Midnight Court, by Bryan Merriman (Fridberg, London and Dublin 1945; O'Brien Press 1989).
Kings, Lords and Commons (Knopf, New York 1959; Macmillan, London 1961).
The Little Monasteries (Dolmen Press, Dublin 1963).
A Golden Treasury of Irish Poetry, A.D. 600-1200 (Macmillan, London 1967).

NOVELS

The Saint and Mary Kate (Macmillan, London 1932; New York 1932; Blackstaff 1990).
Dutch Interior (Macmillan, London 1940; Knopf, New York 1940; Blackstaff 1990).

SHORT-STORY COLLECTIONS

Guests of the Nation (Macmillan, London 1931; New York 1931).
Bones of Contention (MacMillan, New York 1936; London 1938).
Three Tales (Cuala Press, Dublin 1941).
Crab Apple Jelly (Macmillan, London 1944; Knopf, New York 1944).
Selected Stories (Fridberg, Dublin 1946).
The Common Chord (Macmillan, London 1947; Knopf, New York 1948).
Traveller's Samples (Macmillan, London 1951; Knopf, New York 1951).
The Stories of Frank O'Connor (Knopf, New York 1952; Hamish Hamilton, London 1953).
More Stories by Frank O'Connor (Knopf, New York 1954).
Stories by Frank O'Connor (Vintage, New York 1956).
Domestic Relations (Hamish Hamilton, London 1957; Knopf, New York 1957).
My Oedipus Complex and Other Stories (Penguin Books 1963).
Collection Two (Macmillan, London 1964).

Collection Three (Macmillan, London 1969).
A Set of Variations (Knopf, New York 1969).
The Mad Lomasneys and Other Stories (Pan 1970).
Day Dreams and Other Stories (Pan 1973).
The Holy Door and Other Stories (Pan 1973).
Masculine Protest and Other Stories (Pan 1977).
The Cornet player who Betrayed Ireland (Poolbeg 1981).
A Life of your Own and Other Stories (Pan 1982)
The Collar (Blackstaff 1993).
Larry Delaney: Lonesome Genius (Killeen Books 1996).

HISTORICAL AND LITERARY COMMENT
Towards an Appreciation of Literature (Metropolitan Publishing Co., Dublin 1945).
The Road to Stratford (Methuen, London 1948; *Shakespeare's Progress* in Literary Edition, World Publishing Company 1960; Collier Books 1961).
The Mirror in the Roadway: A Study of the Modern Novel (Knopf, New York 1956; Hamish Hamilton, London 1957).
The Lonely Voice: A Study of the Short Story (World Publishing Co., Cleveland, Ohio 1962; Nelson, Foster and Scott, Toronto 1963; Meridian Books 1965; Macmillan, London 1963; Papermac 1965; Putnam, New York 1967).
The Backward Look: A Survey of Irish Literature (Macmillan, London, Toronto and Melbourne 1967).

DISK/TAPE RECORDINGS
Ireland's Monuments (ACT Dublin).
James Joyce (Folkways Records).
My Oedipus Complex (Caedmon Records).
The Drunkard (Caedmon Records).
The Irish Tradition (Folkways Records).
An Nodlaig i gCorcaigh (ACT Dublin).
Leabhar a theastuigh uaim (ACT Dublin).
Nodlaig as Baile (ACT Dublin).
Oiche Shamhraidh (ACT Dublin).
Leabharlanna agus mÇ fin (ACT Dublin).

TRAVEL BOOKS
A Picture Book, illustrated by Elizabeth Rivers (Cuala Press, Dublin 1943).
Irish Miles (Macmillan, 1947; Hogarth Press, London 1988).
Leinster, Munster and Connaught (The County Books, Robert Hale, London 1950).

EARLY POEMS IN MANUSCRIPT
An Chros (1921).
Ambush (1922).
On Guard (1922).
Night in the Cottage (1923).
My Last Duchess (1923).
Duet (1923).
For the End (1923).
Theocritus on Sunday (1924).
Philosophy (1924).
Priest (1925).

EARLY POETRY
The Rosary: *Catholic Bulletin*, March 1923.
Suibhne Geilt Speaks: *Irish Statesman*, March 1925.
Brightness of Brightness: *Irish Statesman*, June 1925.
Sever me not from Thy Sweetness: *Irish Statesman*, November 1925.
Alone in the big town she dreams: *Irish Statesman*, January 1926.
Celibacy: *Irish Statesman*, February 1926.
Love: *Irish Statesman*, April 1926.
Two Impressions: *Irish Statesman*, August 1926.
Return in Harvest: *Irish Statesman*, November 1926.
Lullaby of Adventuress Love: *Irish Tribune*, December 1926.
The Madman: *Irish Statesman*, January 1927.
On Moyrus: *Irish Statesman*, February 1927.
Three Old Brothers: *Irish Statesman*, May 1927.
Quest of Dead O'Donovans: *Irish Statesman*, August 1927.
An Old Song Re-Written: *Irish Statesman*, October 1927.
In Winter: *Irish Statesman*, January 1928.
Storm: *Irish Statesman*, February 1928.
From Gugan of the Saints: *Irish Statesman*, April 1928.
The Home-coming of Dinny Pa: *Irish Statesman*, June 1928.
The Hawk: *Irish Statesman*, August 1928.
The End of Egan O'Rahilly: *Irish Statesman*, October 1928.
Reverie at Dawn: *Irish Statesman*, March 1929.
Beggars: *Irish Statesman*, July 1929.
Prelude: *Irish Statesman*, January 1930.
The Stars are Astand: *Irish Statesman*, April 1930.
Prayer at Dawn: *Dublin Magazine*, April-June 1932.
A Learned Mistress: *Commonweal*, December 1932.

RADIO TALKS
Literary Portraits: Yeats and AE: Radio Eireann, 1939-40.
Davitt – A Portrait: Radio Eireann, 1940.
Across St George's Channel: BBC Radio, December 1940.
Readings from F. R. Higgins: BBC Radio, March 1941; February 1964.
An Bóthar go hEanach Dún: Radio Eireann, September 1941.
Plays and Poetry of W.B. Yeats: BBC Radio, April 1941.
James Joyce: BBC Radio, May 1944.
W.B. Yeats: Reminiscence by a friend: BBC Radio, May 1947.
The Art of the Theatre: BBC Radio, March 1948.
John Bull and His Own Island: BBC Radio, April 1948.
The Cú Chulainn Sagas: BBC Radio, September 1948; October 1948.
The Riddle of Swift: BBC Radio, October 1948.
A.E. Coppard: BBC Radio, November 1948.
Irish Writers: BBC Radio, December 1948.
Yeats and the Theatre: BBC Radio, June 1949.
W.B. Yeats – a Dublin Portrait: BBC Radio, June 1949.
Portrait of James Joyce: BBC Radio, February 1950.
My Art and Craft – the Short Story: BBC Radio, October 1951.
George Moore: BBC Radio, February 1952.
Architect of His Own Reputation – Anthony Trollope: BBC Radio, July 1954.
George Bernard Shaw – an Irish Portrait: BBC Radio, September 1954.
One Man's Way – the Short Story: BBC Radio, June 1959.
Leabhar a theastuigh uaim: Radio Eireann, November 1959.
An Nodlaig i gCorcaigh: Radio Eireann, December 1959.
Nodlaig as Baile: Radio Eireann, December 1960.
Scrapbook for 1921 – Irish Civil War: BBC Radio, October 1961; April 1962.
Adventures in Translation: BBC Radio, January 1962.
Interior Voices: BBC Radio, January 1963.
The Art of the Short Story: Radio Eireann, January 1964.
AE – George Russell: BBC Radio, January 1965.
W.B. Yeats: BBC Radio, June 1965.
The Yeats We Knew: Radio Eireann, February 1965.
Leabharlanna agus mé féin: Radio Eireann, March 1968.

PLAYS FOR THEATRE
In the Train: in collaboration with Hugh Hunt; Abbey Theatre, May 1937.
The Invincibles: in collaboration with Hugh Hunt; Abbey Theatre, October 1937.
Moses' Rock: in collaboration with Hugh Hunt; Abbey Theatre, February 1938.
Time's Pocket: Abbey Theatre, December 1938.
The Statue's Daughter: The Gate, December 1941.

BOOKS ABOUT FRANK O'CONNOR
Michael/Frank editor Maurice Sheehy (Gill and Macmillan 1969).
Frank O'Connor – Irish Writers' Series: James Matthews (Blacknell University Press, New Jersey 1976).
Frank O'Connor – An Introduction: Morris Wohlgelernter (Columbia University Press, New York 1977).
Voices: James Matthews (Atheneum 1983).
Frank O'Connor At Work: Michael Steinman (Syracuse University Press 1990).
A Frank O'Connor Reader: Michael Steinman (Syracuse University Press 1994).
Twentieth Century Literature – Frank O'Connor Issue: Michael Steinman (Hoffstra University 1990).
The Happiness of Getting It Down Right: editor Michael Steinman (Knopf, New York 1996).
New Aspects of Frank O'Connor: editor Robert C. Evans (Locust Hill Press 1998).

ARTICLES ABOUT FRANK O'CONNOR
Mr Frank O'Connor. H. A. Bruce, Macmillan 1934.
Portrait of Frank O'Connor. Time, 1944.
The Poetry of Frank O'Connor. Geoffrey Taylor, The Bell 1945.
Coloured Balloons – a study of Frank O'Connor. Paddy Kavanagh, The Bell 1947.
Frank O'Connor's Art: F. Hackett, Day, New York 1947.
Meet Frank O'Connor. Bellman, The Bell 1951.
A Portrait of Frank O'Connor. Saturday Review of Literature, 1954.
Author of the Week: Cooney, Saturday Review of Literature, 1956.
Frank O'Connor. Breit, The Writer Observed, 1956.

Frank O'Connor: Whittier, The Paris Review Interviews, 1958.
Frank O'Connor as Paradigm: Weiss, *North West Review*, 1959.
Artist as a Boy. *Newsweek*, 1961.
The O'Connors of Cork: Mercier, *New York Times Book Review*, 1961.
A Storyteller and his Craft: MacManus, RTE Guide, 1962.
Translations of Frank O'Connor: Sealy, *Dubliner*, 1963.
O'Connor's Unflattering Picture of Bourgeois Ireland: Share, Hibernia, 1965.
A Consideration of Frank O'Connor's Short Stories: Saul, *Colby Library Quarterly*, 1963.
Also, many MA and PhD theses have been written on various aspects of Frank O'Connor's work

AS BEN MAYO IN THE *SUNDAY INDEPENDENT*

Irish ruins shocked visitors: 28 March 1943.
Why not homes as well as pensions for Ministers: 11 April 1943.
Critic waves and nonsense waves: 18 April 1943.
Pensions for great writers: Finland's plan: 25 April 1943.
Save our old mansions from the speculators: 9 May 1943.
Radio Eireann banned 'foreign' dance music: 16 May 1943.
The Clare people need books: 23 May 1943.
Should we abolish Irish history: 6 June 1943.
People rot in slums, die of tuberculosis . . . if they know Irish: 13 June 1943.
What are we doing to win the peace: 4 July 1943.
Culture in mud cabins and four-hand reels: 11 July 1943.
Our Irish towns have their attractions: 18 July 1943.
This talk about education: 25 July 1943.
Education systems that produce quarrels: 1 August 1943.
A grilled stake can overrule prejudices; 8 August 1943.
People cannot do without a purpose in their lives: 15 August 1943.
A book industry that is greatly neglected: 22 August 1943.
Should make us sit up: 29 August 1943.
Our exiles may influence our future: 5 September 1943.
The people are fallible, but they must be trusted: 12 September 1943.
Only sort of government that counts in the long run: 19 September 1943.
M.O.H.'s are the people's genuine friends': 26 September 1943.
Fianna Fail's attitude to the P.R. system: 3 October 1943.
Board of control for Irish theatres: 10 October 1943.
Eire's choice – food or money: 17 October 1943.
What kind of tourists do we want?: 24 October 1943.
Have our politicians grown too old?: 31 October 1943.
Irish – and how to revive it: 7 November 1943.
An Irish Legion of Honour: 14 November 1943.
In fond and loving memory . . .: 21 November 1943.
Levelling the community down: 28 November 1943.
Paid £1,000 for being a good citizen: 5 December 1943.
Getting a toy for Christmas: 12 December 1943.
Ben Mayo writes to Santa Claus: 19 December 1943.
That Ireland again be part of Dublin: 26 December 1943.
Pouring millions down the drain of artificial idleness: 2 January 1944.
Today Ireland needs another Brian Boru: 16 January 1944.
Making our countryside fit to live in: 23 January 1944.
Buildings that show something is wrong: 6 February 1944.
Art and 'Gas': 20 February 1944.
History is damned by Henry Ford, but . . .: 27 February 1944.
One's second thoughts are best: 5 March 1944.
Agonies of practice recipe for champions: 12 March 1944.
Before we can resume our march we must . . .: 19 March 1944.
Turf is bad and dear: why not controlled?: 26 March 1944.
Education is left at the post: 16 April 1944.
Let us give a hand to the farmers: 23 April 1944.
Is a Dublin man more English than a Clareman?: 30 April 1944.
Partition – the people are bewildered: 7 May 1944.

The next five years will be fateful or fatal: 14 May 1944.
In normal countries, with normal politicians: 21 May 1944.
One of the crucial moments in our history: 28 May 1944.
Problem in re-education of parents: 4 June 1944.
The surest way to make a profit is . . .: 11 June 1944.
Gallery of dreams that did not come true: 18 June 1944.
A children's freedom war has restored: 2 July 1944.
The Gael and start of our national movement: 16 July 1944.
Dublin of future may be menace to Ireland: 23 July 1944.
Where is planning leading us?: 30 July 1944.
The Irish empire overseas: 6 August 1944.
Tests by which Eire falls: 13 August 1944.
War has helped the growth of vocational organisation: 20 August 1944.
Planning ahead, but are we forgetting the present?: 27 August 1944.
Are Irish people lazy?: 3 September 1944.
Give the citizens a chance: 17 September 1944.
A dress reform for Irish farmers: 24 September 1944.
Danger of State control: 1 October 1944.
Same old hobby-horses go round and round: 15 October 1944.
Must the Irish railways be abandoned: 22 October 1944.
A campaign against foolish talk: 29 October 1944.
Ireland's place in a turbulent world: 12 November 1944.
Our farmers' wives are not a race of foreign beauties: 26 November 1944.
The sense of proportion is important: 3 December 1944.
Are we serious about abolishing partition?: 10 December 1944.
Drawing northern Irish youth closer to Great Britain: 17 December 1944.
And on Earth Peace . . .: 24 December 1944.
Growth of Dublin and Belfast: a Problem: 31 December 1944.
High moral standard is essential for deputies: 7 January 1945.
The newspapers of the future: 21 January 1945.
Dublin is as 'English' today as it was 30 years ago: 28 January 1945.

Limerick urged to launch out on own: 4 February 1945.
The urge for security has great dangers: 11 February 1945.
Don't forget our scientists and inventors: 18 February 1945.
Information wanted, please: 25 February 1945.
Will women of France give a world lead?: 4 March 1945.
Learning from the Ascendancy: 11 March 1945.
St Patrick's Day: some reflections: 18 March 1945.
Dublin's disgrace: 25 March 1945.
The 'export' of doctors, 'import' of scientists: 1 April 1945.
Small nations and the world's future: 6 May 1945.
Our relations with Great Britain: 13 May 1945.
Mr De Valera and Mr Churchill: 20t May 1945.
Bevin – Big man in Britain today: 27 May.
Ireland and the Commonwealth – friendly co-operation or isolation?: 22 July 1945.
We are in it, states the Taoiseach's paper: 29 July 1945.
Ruin and loss in Ireland: 23 September 1945.

LITERARY ARTICLES

Two friends – Yeats and AE: *Yale Review*, September 1939.
Synge: *The Irish Theatre*, 1939.
AE – a portrait: *The Bell*, November 1940.
The Old Age of a Poet: (W.B. Yeats) *The Bell*, February 1941.
The audience: *The Bell*, March 1945.
The writer: *The Bell*, April 1945.
The actor: *The Bell*, May 1945.
The Life and Death of a Theatre (Abbey): *Theatre Arts Magazine*, 1955.
Seán O'Casey and the Ghosts: *Holiday*, January 1956.
The Most American Playwright: (Arthur Miller) *Holiday*, February 1956.
St Joans, from Arc to Lark: *Holiday*, March 1956.
Comedy and Comediennes: *Holiday*, May 1956.
Joyce, Colum, Johnston, Meredith: *Theatre Arts Magazine*, 1958.
The Actor: *Drama Critique*, 1963.
Quarrelling with Yeats: *Esquire*, December 1964.
Willie is so silly: (W. B. Yeats) *Vogue*, March

1965.
The Scholar: (Osborn Bergin) *Kenyon Review*, 1965.
W.B. Yeats: *The Critic*, December 1966.
Bring the whiskey now, Mary: (AE) *New Yorker*, August 1967.

HISTORY

For a 200th Birthday: (Mozart) *Harper's Bazaar*, January 1956.
The Accusing Ghost of Roger Casement: *New York Times* Book Review, November 1957.
A Man of Iron: (Arthur Griffith) *New York Times* Book Review, March 1960.
John Bull's Other History: *New York Times* Book Review, March 1961.
Patrick the Ulsterman: *Irish Times*, May 1962.
Murder Unlimited (The Famine): *Irish Times*, October 1962.
The Ghost of Roger Casement: *Irish Times*, June 1964.

MISCELLANEOUS

To any would-be writer: *The Bell*, March 1941.
At the microphone: *The Bell*, March 1942.
The art of architecture: *Sunday Independent*, January 1946.
Ireland is a paradise for prigs: *Sunday Independent*, July 1946.
Is this a dagger?: *Nation Magazine*, April 1958.
Censorship: *The Dubliner*, March 1962.
Understanding your dreams: *Vogue*, November 1967.

TRIBUTES

Homage to Jim Larkin: *Irish Times*, December 1944.
John F. Kennedy: *Encyclopaedia Britannica*, Chicago, 1964.

TRAVEL AND TOPOGRAPHICAL

Three Churches: *The Bell*, May 1942.
In Galway, Kerry and Clare: *The Bell*, June 1942.
In Connemara: *Irish Times*, August 1943.
South Tipperary: *Irish Times*, September 1943.
Carlow, Poor but Proud: *Irish Times*, January 1944.
Kilkenny: *Irish Times*, February 1944.
Ireland: *Holiday*, December 1949.
In Quest of Beer: *Holiday*, January 1957.
A Walk in New York: *Holiday*, November 1958.
The Holy Places of Ireland: *Holiday*, April 1963.
Regency Colonial: *Spectator*, June 1965.

EARLY ARTICLES

Mozart: *An Long*, 1922.
Solus: *An Long*, 1922.
The poet as a professional: *Irish Statesman*, October 1925.
Egan O'Rahilly: *Irish Statesman*, January 1926.
To Spain and the World's Side: *Irish Statesman*, January 1926.
Irish Love Poetry: *Irish Statesman*, May 1926.
An Irish Anthology: *Irish Statesman*, June 1926.
The Heart has reasons: *Irish Tribune*, June 1926.
Have we a literature: *Irish Tribune*, August 1926.
Classic Verse: *Irish Statesman*, July 1927.
Munster Fine Arts Exhibition: *Irish Statesman*, November 1927.
The Traveller in the Mask: *Irish Statesman*, September 1928.
Heine: *Irish Statesman*, March 1929.
The evocation of the past – Proust: *Irish Statesman*, June 1929.
Gaelic Drama: at the Peacock: *Irish Statesman*, January 1930.
Abbey-cum-Boccaccio: *Irish Statesman*, February 1930.
Joyce – The Third Period: *Irish Statesman*, April 1930.

LATER ARTICLES IN *SUNDAY INDEPENDENT*

The disgrace of our libraries and bookshops: 25 March 1962.
The neglect of our historical monuments: May 1962.
This is provincialism: July 1962.
The Casement Diary mystery: September 1962.
The International Theatre Festival, Dublin: September 1962.
Does Kinsella lead the poets: October 1962.
That dreadful breed I call the lace curtain Irish: November 1962.
165 places still remember Lug: December 1962.
The Childhood of Jesus: December 1962.
All the way from Finn to Finnegan: February 1963.
The abuse of our heritage: Georgian Dublin and Bunratty: February 1963.

St Patrick was an outsider: March 1963.
Are we being fair to Seán O'Casey: May 1963.
Professor Binchy and the town called Charleville: July 1963.
The Abbey Theatre, Past and Present: September 1963.
Two poems by Gerald, Earl of Desmond: The last raid AD1381, The widower bed AD1392: September 1963.
Shakespeare: October 1963.
The Arts Council: November 1963.
Our Crumbling Heritage – the Restoration of our Monuments: November 1963.
Tribute to John F. Kennedy: November 1963.
The Little Man in the Big Rising (Seán T. O'Kelly): December 1963.
Our National Monuments – Clonmacnois and Clontooskert: June 1964.
A neglected monument – Glendalough: June 1964.
Our greatest monument – our greatest disgrace: Cashel: June 1964.
Jerpoint Abbey and Kilkenny: June 1964.
A Masterpiece of Irish Art – Holy Cross Abbey: July 1964.
Shame on us – Athassel Priory, Ennis Abbey, Dysert O'Dea, Quin Abbey: July 1964.
Books on Ireland: September 1964.
New Grange Tombs: September 1964.
The Book nobody knows: December 1964.
Yeats: June 1965.
Irish Monuments – mystery man takes over: September 1965.
For the conversion of Professor Stanford: November 1965.
The case for Roger Casement: January 1966.
Michael Collins, no plaster saint: January 1966.
Literature and the lashers: February 1966.

CRITICAL LITERARY ARTICLES
James Joyce – a Postmortem: *The Bell*, February 1942.
Shakespeare of the Drawing-Room: *Irish Times*, August 1945.
Stendhal: *Irish Times*, August 1945.
Charles Dickens: *Irish Times*, September 1945.
Flaubert: *Irish Times*, September 1945.
Trollope: *Irish Times*, October 1945.
The Extraordinary Story of Jonathan Swift: *Sunday Independent*, October 1945.
Tolstoy and Turgenev: *Irish Times*, October 1945.
Thomas Hardy: *Irish Times*, November 1945.
Anton Chekhov: *Irish Times*, November 1945.
Sommerville and Ross: *Irish Times*, December 1945.
And it's a lonely personal art: *New York Times Book Review*, April 1953.
The Novel Approach: *New York Times Book Review*, August 1953.
A matter-of-fact problem in the writing of the Novel: *New York Times Book Review*, December 1954.
The last of the liberals (Chekhov): *New York Times Book Review*: April 1955.
Jane Austen and the flight from fancy: *Yale Review*, September 1955.
A good Short Story must be news: *New York Times Book Review*, June 1956.
The Novelist as Politician: *New York Times Book Review*, March 1957.
Joyce and his brother: *Nation*, February 1958.
Shadows on the Artist's Portrait: *New York Times Book Review*, August 1958.
A Writer who refused to pretend: *New York Times Book Review*, January 1960.
From Jane Austen to Joseph Conrad: *Victorian Studies*, March 1960.
The Modesty of Literature: *New York Times Book Review*, January 1961.
Tell Dublin I miss her: *New York Times Book Review*, March 1962.
Country Matters: *Kenyon Review*, Autumn 1962.
The Girl at the Gaol Gate: *Kenyon Review*, Spring 1963.
The Slave's Son: *Kenyon Review*, Winter 1963.
A Master's Mixture: *New York Times Book Review*, March 1964.
The Buck (Gogarty): *Spectator*, June 1964.
Awkward but alive (Kavanagh): *Spectator*, July 1964.
But what of the author? (Gogol): *New York Times Book Review*, September 1964.
The Small Genius (James Stephens): *Spectator*, May 1965.
All the Olympians (Synge, Yeats and Gregory): *Saturday Review*, December 1966.
Why don't you write about America?: *Mademoiselle*, April 1967.
James Joyce – Thesis and Antithesis: *American Scholar*, Summer 1967.

INDEX

Abbey Theatre 94, 100, 105–9, 116–20, 127–8, 134, 148–9, 173
AE (George Russell) 58–60, 62, 69, 74, 79–80, 82–4, 85–7, 97–9, 101–3, 108–9, 173

Barry, Tom 37, 41–2
BBC 121, 127, 129–30, 131, 135, 136, 139, 143–4, 144–5, 146, 169, 175
The Bell 78, 129, 132, 136, 138, 140, 149
Bergin, Osborn 60, 80, 84, 101–2, 131
Binchy, Dan 80, 154, 163, 173, 176, 177
Black and Tans 36–8, 39–40, 41, 42
Bowen, Evelyn (1st wife) 115, 119, 141, 142, 145, 152, 156
and M's children 123, 130, 143, 149, 153, 154, 161
relationship with M 117, 120–21, 122, 127, 136–7, 146–7
Buckley, Ansty 89, 92–6, 157
Buckley, Tim 89, 92–6, 157

Censorship Board 77, 93–5, 98, 129, 136, 143, 144, 148
Clancy, Liam 164–5
Collins, Michael 29, 30, 43, 46, 81
M's biography of 97, 102, 103–4, 113–14
Connolly, James 28–9
Cork 10–11, 26, 53–4, 62, 69, 70, 80, 136, 158, 170
and Irish rebellion 34–41
Cork Drama League 64–5, 69–70
Corkery, Daniel 48, 62, 80, 98, 125, 164, 167, 172
M's mentor 24–5, 28, 33–4, 35, 46, 54
Cross, Eric 129
The Tailor and Ansty 93–5, 138
Cuala Press 85, 134

De Valera, Eamon 50, 97, 102, 104, 109, 116, 128, 130, 144, 177
Dublin Drama League 134

Easter Rising 28–30, 43, 58
Ellmann, Richard 143, 150
Evening News (London) 142, 143, 144

Foley, Dermot 109–10, 117, 121, 128, 147, 154, 158, 173, 177
librarian with M 73–4, 75–7, 78–9, 81–2
French, Seán 47

Gaelic League, The 34, 36, 79
Gate Theatre 105–7, 108, 130, 134
Gogarty, Oliver St John 81, 98, 121

Hayes, Dr Richard 100–101, 103–4, 115, 121, 131, 173
and Abbey Theatre 107, 109, 110, 119, 122
and M's health 108, 118, 120
Hendrick, Seán (Jack) 35, 64, 94, 137, 158, 164
M's letters to 46, 55, 133–4, 135, 138–9, 166–8
Higgins, Fred 83, 85, 109, 111, 116, 118, 119, 122, 131
Horizon 134–5
Hunt, Hugh 109, 111–13, 117, 118, 120

Irish Academy of Letters 97–9, 100, 104–5, 107, 121
Irish Statesman 59, 62, 77–8, 83, 84, 102, 129
Irish Times 84, 95, 127, 142, 147
Irish Tribune 63

Kavanagh, Patrick 105, 132, 134, 135, 138
Keane, Sir John 94–5
Kelleher, John 143, 150, 156–7
Kennedy, John Fitzgerald 33
Kennelly, Brendan 173, 174, 175, 177, 178
Knape, Joan 152, 155, 157, 173, 174, 177
relationship with M

190

INDEX

139–40, 142, 145, 147, 149, 153, 154
Knape, Oliver (son) 142, 147, 149, 174, 175, 177

McCarthy, Nancy 64, 65, 104, 136, 155, 158–61, 164
  M in love with 66–7, 69–70, 78, 96, 101
  as M's friend 17, 89, 93, 95, 176–7
MacCurtain, Tomás 28, 29, 35–6, 37
MacLiammoir, Michael 47, 63–4, 105, 106–7, 112, 129, 130
Macmillan, Harold 80, 97, 120, 136, 177
MacNamara, Brinsley 108, 109, 110, 129
McQuaid, John Charles (Archbishop of Dublin) 136, 172
MacSwiney, Terence 28, 36, 37, 38–9, 47, 54
Magennis, William 94–5, 107
Manning, Mary 82, 99
Maxwell, Bill 162, 164, 165, 174
Maynooth College 176
Morrow, Larry 139
Murphy, Séamus 89, 93, 95, 96, 158, 164

Neeson, Geraldine 47–8, 64
Neeson, Seán 47, 64
New Yorker 141–2, 163

O'Casey, Seán 107–8
O'Connor, Frank *see* O'Donovan, Michael
O'Donovan, Hallie-Og (daughter) 162, 163, 164, 171, 178
O'Donovan, Jimmy (cousin) 17, 21, 146
O'Donovan, Larry (uncle) 17, 21, 27
O'Donovan, Liadain (daughter) 130, 140, 161, 174, 177
O'Donovan, Mary (grandmother) 11, 21
O'Donovan, May 17, 21, 146, 177
O'Donovan, Michael (father) 11–12, 17–18, 20, 26–7, 153
  marriage 14–16, 21–3, 78, 114, 115
  relationship with M 32, 34, 53, 61, 101–2, 123–4
O'Donovan, Michael (Frank O'Connor)
LIFE
birth 9, 15
childhood 10, 14, 18, 19–20, 21, 22
relationships with family 16–17
education 19–20, 24–6, 49–50
and Irish language 21, 36, 49
reading 24, 27, 28, 30, 32
early jobs 30–32
Irish rebellion 34–5, 36, 42
Civil War 43–6
prison 48–52
excommunicated 52
teaches Irish 54, 57
librarian 54, 56–7, 60–62, 63, 69, 73, 74, 75–7, 78–9, 81, 120
pseudonym 59
translator from Irish 59, 84, 85–89, 169
and Dublin literati 60, 82–5
Cork Drama League 64–5
writing career 79–80, 104, 121, 123, 126, 143–4, 148, 157, 169
Abbey Theatre 107, 109, 110–12, 116–20, 125
radio broadcasts 109, 121, 127, 129–30, 131, 135, 144–5, 146, 148, 163, 170
in Switzerland 115
Abbey managing director 118–19, 121–3
marries 122, 155
children born 123, 130, 142, 143, 154, 162
cycling excursions 127, 128
in England 129–30, 131, 139–40, 142, 143–4, 144–5, 147, 149, 155–6
as Ben Mayo 137, 142
script-writing 139, 143–4, 173
in Copenhagen 146, 161
in USA 150–52, 153–4, 156–8, 161–3, 164–8
television 157, 169, 170, 172
honorary doctorate 170
in France 171–2
death, burial 176–8
and censorship 77, 93–5, 133–4, 144, 148
and the Church 65, 137, 172
health 24, 54, 65, 100, 104, 114, 172–5
cancer scare 81, 120, 148
and work 63, 101, 109–10, 118, 157, 162–3, 168
as lecturer 124, 150–51
and music 22, 23, 35, 47, 67
social qualities 81–2
and women 71–2, 99, 115
as writer 28, 53, 62–3, 77, 79, 144
WORKS QUOTED/DISCUSSED
books
An Only Child 15, 16, 17, 149, 162, 164, 165, 166
The Big Fellow 97, 102, 103–4, 113–14, 175
The Common Chord 144, 148

Domestic Relations 158
Guests of the Nation 79–80
Irish Miles 137, 142, 143, 147
Leinster, Munster and Connaught 147
The Lonely Voice 166, 169
More Stories 156
My Father's Son 170, 173, 174, 176, 178
The Road to Stratford 145
The Stories of Frank O'Connor 152, 156
Traveller's Samples 148
The Wild Bird's Nest 85–9
letters 58–9, 74–5, 78, 79, 94–5, 109, 127–8, 137, 166–8
to Seán Hendrick 46–7, 55, 133–4, 135, 138–9, 166–8
novels
Dutch Interior 128–9, 148
The Saint and Mary Kate 96–7, 102
plays
In the Train 112–13, 169
The Invincibles 116–18
Moses' Rock 119–20
The Statue's Daughter 129, 134
Time's Pocket 122
poems
'Ambush' 44–5
'For the End' 52–2
'The Hawk' 68
'The Rosary' 50–51
stories
The Drunkard 18–19
First Confession 21, 28
The Frying Pan 91
The Genius 27–8
Guests of the Nation 79–80, 102, 156
The Holy Door 91
In the Train 110
The Long Road to Umera 21, 129

The Luceys 28
Mass Island 96
My Oedipus Complex 18
Procession of Life 80
Song Without Words 175
translations
Kilcash 88–9
Kings, Lords and Commons 164
The Little Monasteries 170–71
The Midnight Court 140–41, 142–3, 148
The Old Woman of Beare Regrets Lost Youth 87
O'Donovan, Minnie (mother) 12–16, 17, 19, 34–5, 137, 143, 146, 147, 152–3, 178
and M's autobiography 148–9, 162, 173
and M's women 66–7, 121, 140, 142, 155
marriage 18, 20–21, 22, 114–15, 124
relationship with M 50, 53, 61, 78, 96, 140, 142
relationship with M as child 25, 26, 28, 30
O'Donovan, Myles (son) 123, 140, 153, 155, 156, 157, 173
O'Donovan, Owen (son) 143, 161
O'Faoláin, Seán 41, 62, 83, 85, 89, 93, 102, 167
as M's friend 33–4, 104, 123, 132, 137, 147, 153, 154
and Irish cultural life 70, 94, 98, 109, 119, 129, 136
O'Flynn, Fr 65–6, 69, 80

Pearse, Patrick 29, 30
Phibbs (Taylor), Geoffrey 57, 58, 59, 71–2, 130, 173

Radio Eireann 127, 137, 139, 146, 163
Radio Telefis Eireann 169, 173, 175
Rich, Harriet (2nd wife) 151–2, 154–9, 160, 161–4, 167, 168, 169, 171, 172, 173, 174–5, 176–7, 178–9
Rich, Jack 157, 161–2, 164
Robinson, Lennox 55, 56, 64, 82–3, 107, 109, 111, 117–18, 122, 129, 130
Royal Irish Constabulary (RIC) 35, 36, 37
Russell, George *see* AE

Sheehy, Fr Maurice 172, 174, 176–9
Stegner, Wallace 166
Stewart, Stan 128, 137, 154, 155, 163
Sunday Independent 137, 169, 170, 173

The Tailor and Ansty (Eric Cross) 93–5, 138
Traynor, Fr Tim 89–92, 93, 94, 95, 96, 101, 103–4, 123, 157, 163, 173
Trinity College, Dublin 170, 171, 175, 176

West Cork Brigade 41
Wilson, Robert 54–5
Women's Prison (Cork) 19, 48–9, 64

Yeats International Summer School 170
Yeats, W.B. 82–3, 84–5, 97–9, 122, 146, 165, 173–4
and Abbey Theatre 94, 107, 109, 110, 112, 117–18, 127–8